Teaching Children's Literature

Drawing on a series of recently conducted classroom workshops and live interviews with the authors, this inspiring book examines five popular children's authors – Philip Pullman, J.K. Rowling, Michael Morpurgo, Anthony Browne, Jacqueline Wilson – and the genre of comic books. Four genres are explored in detail: the picture book, written narrative, film narrative and comic books.

Teaching Children's Literature provides detailed literary knowledge about the chosen authors and genres alongside clear, structured guidelines and creative ideas to help teachers, student teachers and classroom assistants make some immensely popular children's books come alive in the classroom. This accessible and inspiring text for teachers, parents, student teachers and students of children's literature:

- includes a variety of discussion, drama, writing and drawing activities, with ideas for social and emotional aspects of learning that can be used to plan a unit of work or series of interrelated lessons for pupils aged between 7 and 14 years;
- provides detailed literary knowledge about the authors, their works, language, plot and characterisation, including exclusive transcripts of interviews with three contemporary children's book authors;
- shows teachers how pupils can be encouraged to become more critical and knowledgeable about screen, picture and comic narratives as well as written narratives;
- demonstrates how reading stories can help connect pupils and teachers to a broader pedagogy in ways that promote deeper thinking, learning and engagement.

This lively, informative and practical book will enable teachers, students and classroom assistants to plan inspiring and enjoyable lessons that will encourage them to teach children's literature in an entirely different and inventive way.

Diane Duncan, formerly a primary school headteacher and university lecturer, is now an educational researcher, writer and consultant. She is also a visiting lecturer at the University of Hertfordshire.

Teaching Children's Literature

Making stories work in the classroom

Diane Duncan

Routledge
Taylor & Francis Group

LONDON AND NEW YORK

First published 2009
by Routledge
2 Park Square, Milton Park, Abingdon, Oxon OX14 4RN

Simultaneously published in the USA and Canada
by Routledge
270 Madison Ave, New York, NY 10016

Routledge is an imprint of the Taylor & Francis Group, an informa business

Transferred to Digital Printing 2010

Typeset in Garamond 3 and Gill Sans by
Keystroke, 28 High Street, Tettenhall, Wolverhampton

British Library Cataloguing in Publication Data
A catalogue record for this book is available from the British Library

Library of Congress Cataloging in Publication Data
Duncan, Diane.
Teaching children's literature : making stories work in the classroom / Diane Duncan.
p. cm.
Includes bibliographical references and index.
1. Children's stories, English–Study and teaching. 2. Children's literature, English–Study and teaching.
I. Title.
PR830.C513D86 2008
372.64–dc22
2008008817

ISBN10: 0–415–42100–4 (hbk)
ISBN10: 0–415–42101–2 (pbk)

ISBN13: 978–0–415–42100–3 (hbk)
ISBN13: 978–0–415–42101–0 (pbk)

For Frank with love. His critical friendship and unswerving belief in this book has been more valuable and inspirational than words can ever express.

Preface

Just over ten years ago I was asked to write a course on children's literature for student teachers who were English specialists in a university education department. Just before I wrote the course, the first of Philip Pullman's *His Dark Materials* trilogy, *Northern Lights*, had attracted considerable attention in the children's book world in 1995. This dazzling book was followed in 1997 by the first of J.K. Rowling's Harry Potter series, *Harry Potter and the Philosopher's Stone*. Pullman's trilogy and the Harry Potter series are markedly different in style, content and narrative form, but both have been phenomenally successful. An adaptation of Pullman's trilogy has been staged twice at the National Theatre to packed audiences, and a film version of the first part of his trilogy, starring Nicole Kidman, has recently been released. Five of the Harry Potter series have been released as films and DVDs, and the sixth film, *Harry Potter and the Half-Blood Prince*, is scheduled for November 2008. Add to this Peter Jackson's spectacular and award-winning *Lord of the Rings* and Andrew Adamson's *The Chronicles of Narnia*, and we have probably seen one of the most exciting decades in the history of the genre of children's literature. Seldom before have children's stories taken up so much airtime, film footage and media coverage, nor have children's books reached such a wide international audience, including growing numbers of adult fans. Philip Pullman put it more vibrantly: 'children's books, for various reasons, at this time in our literary history, open out on a wideness and amplitude – a moral and mental spaciousness – that adult literary fiction seems to have turned its back on' (1998b, p. 44).

I could not ignore this phenomenon, and the students wanted to understand and learn more about it. I therefore included the authors Philip Pullman and J.K. Rowling in the course, but in the late 1990s, apart from a few newspaper articles and interviews there were very few, if *any*, literary discussions of either Pullman's or Rowling's work. Indeed, Fox (1998) referred to the surprising dearth of articles presented to the United Kingdom Board on present-day authors, including Michael Morpurgo, Anne Fine and Gillian Cross. I therefore had to write my own materials and critical analyses of the few works published so far. The students loved the course, saying at the end of it that they had seldom been so intellectually challenged. However, at the end of each of the seven years during which I taught the course, students complained that articles on contemporary children's books were scattered widely across a range of journals and book sources, and that texts which included ideas on *how* to teach children's literature in the classroom, combined with a deeper knowledge about contemporary authors, were virtually impossible to find. What was needed was a book that would do *both* in one text. This became the spur to the creation of this book. In addition, I knew many teachers who were valiantly attempting to meet the goals and targets of the literacy strategy but who were very hard-pressed to find the time to read children's books themselves, let alone acquire a deeper knowledge about them. Even more worrying were the numbers of teachers and students who frequently lamented to me that they found it difficult, if not impossible, to find the time to read longer works of fiction from beginning to end to their classes of children.

This book sets out to offer guidance to teachers working in primary and the lower years of secondary education, when the shackles of the National Curriculum and the constraints of the Literacy Strategy in particular are beginning to loosen in order to allow for more flexible approaches to teaching and learning. Current educational initiatives in primary education are giving teachers greater control over what and how they teach as well as urging them to give greater prominence to children's voices, responses and needs.

There are six chapters in the book; one of them looks at the genre of comic books and five of them examine contemporary children's book authors. The authors chosen are Anthony Browne, Michael Morpurgo, Jacqueline Wilson, Philip Pullman and J.K. Rowling. They have been selected because each of them is prolific and phenomenally successful. They have inspired thousands of children, teachers and students in recent years, and most people will have heard of their names even if they have not actually read their works. Comic books have been included because they are read widely by children but rarely examined critically; indeed, most of the authors chosen have themselves been inspired by the vibrant colours and complex narratives of the comic book. The book sets out to appeal to the widest constituency of readers and is written in the belief that it is more likely to be of interest if some knowledge about its content already exists. It is hoped that this book will extend and deepen that knowledge. More importantly, it aims to bring some remarkable contemporary writing into the heart of the classroom and inspire all those who work with children to find the time and confidence to tell, read and share some of the stories selected for examination in this book. To that end, this book is merely the beginning . . .

Acknowledgements

I should like to thank the headteachers of the following schools for so willingly allowing us to trial ideas for this book in the form of classroom workshops: Willen Primary School, Milton Keynes; Knebworth Primary and Nursery School, Hertfordshire; Hartsbourne Primary School, Watford; Nascot Wood Junior School, Watford; Preston JMI School, Hertfordshire; and Offley Endowed Primary School, Hertfordshire. I should especially like to thank the following class teachers for making the workshops so enjoyable and rewarding: Rosemary Williams, Vivienne Hollis, Stephanie Holder, Sally Meredith, Dave Allen, Lucy Barget and Hannah Warne. Sincere thanks are due to the children who took part in the workshop and whose reactions were so important to the book. Thanks to all the parents who kindly gave permission for their children's work to be reproduced in the book. Warmest thanks to Dave Allen for making such incisive and helpful comments on an earlier draft of the Philip Pullman chapter and for his wholehearted enthusiasm for the book and an unforgettable workshop. Very special thanks to Noel McHugh and Steve Springett for being so generous in providing contemporary information about teachers' and schools' needs with respect to the teaching of children's literature. Their support for the book throughout has been invaluable.

Sincere thanks to Andrew Charles, Watch and Clockmakers Ltd, Wymondley, for the kind loan of an antique chiming clock with exposable working parts for use in the workshop based on Philip Pullman's *Clockwork or All Wound Up*. The children were entranced by it. Thanks too to Frederick White for his immensely valued artistic advice and help.

Thanks of a very special kind to Tim Stafford and his unbounded enthusiasm for the book and for the strong contribution he has made to it. The warmest of thanks to my very special friend Melanie Bradley for her astute comments during the book's progress, for reading an initial draft of the introduction and for her ever-present, abiding faith in it. Most of all love and grateful thanks to Len, Joan, Marilyn, Jeanne and Graham for their loving support and interest in the book's progress and for so generously tolerating my virtual absence for several months.

Tim Stafford's acknowledgements

I should like to thank my parents and my grandparents. Thanks to Di for her faith in me, her sense of fun and for providing me with this thrilling opportunity. Finally, thank you to two special members of my 'family', Derek and Marina.

Introduction

Several writers and commentators have pronounced the past decade a new golden age for children's books. Perversely, however, the pressures of an overcrowded curriculum have made it very difficult for teachers or children to enjoy and savour the immense richness of literary wealth that is now available. Indeed, some writers (Pullman, 2003b; Morpurgo, 2004), for example, have commented that the National Literacy Strategy and the impact of testing and league tables on schools may be in danger of creating a generation of children 'who hate reading and feel nothing but hostility for literature' (Pullman, 2003b: 3). Despite the colossal effort and resources that have been invested in raising reading standards through the National Literacy Strategy, the interim findings of the Primary Review report (2007) conclude that the strategy has had a limited impact. One of the consequences of the ever-changing and increasing coverage demanded by the literacy strategy has been the creation of an 'extract culture' whereby children are introduced to sections of high-quality literature solely for the purpose of searching for word classes or examples of figurative language. As Pullman (1996) trenchantly puts it, 'We don't need lists of right and wrongs, tables of do's and don'ts: we need books, time, and silence. Thou shalt not is soon forgotten, but Once upon a time lasts forever.'

In response to the growing concern and dissatisfaction among teachers about the reductive content of the literacy curriculum, formerly known by the more inclusive titles of 'English' or, in the case of primary education, 'language', the Qualifications and Curriculum Authority (2005) launched a national consultation on how the subject of English should develop over the next ten years. Partly in response to the 'English 21' initiative and developments already taking place within the Primary National Strategy, renewed literacy and mathematics frameworks were introduced in 2006. One timely and significant feature of the new literacy framework is that on-screen texts now have parity with printed texts (Harrison, 2006).

The educational principles behind these frameworks make the reading of stories in ways that will help connect teachers and pupils to a broader and more spacious pedagogy a serious possibility. In addition, there are now several new initiatives that are encouraging a more coherent, systematic approach to learning which will help children to see the links with subjects and their own development as human beings through the curriculum of social and emotional aspects of learning (SEAL; see DfES, 2005b). The needs of children have been given a strengthened focus with the initiatives of Every Child Matters (DfES, 2005a) and the Primary Review (2006–2008) which is currently investigating the condition and future of primary education in England.

However, if we really believe in the principles behind these agendas for a more interrelated approach to children's education, then we need to care very deeply about the material we offer if we are to help children make sense of themselves and the world in which they live. Stories are one very important way of helping children connect with themselves, with others in their own lives and with those who live in imagined worlds who may see, think and feel in ways different from their own. There are many kinds of narratives: everyday gossip, mobile text messages, emails, blogs and chat rooms, television soaps, films, cartoon strips, celebrity gossip columns, written and oral stories. In their different ways, they unite us all as human beings and we have been compelled by them since humans first began to communicate with vocal sounds and paint with sticks and dye. The power of narrative is eternal, and children need the time, space and emotional quietness to soak up some of its immense diversity and richness. The intensity of the relationship that can exist between children, teachers and the reading of stories is mercurial and unknowable. But when children are spellbound by what they hear in the language, rhythm, pain, despair, love and laughter of others, something profound and lasting happens which is not immediately retrievable or measurable. As Pullman said in his Isis Lecture:

> Stories are written to beguile, to entertain, to amuse, to move, to enchant, to horrify, to delight, to anger, to make us wonder. They are not written so that we can make a fifty word summary of the whole plot . . . the true purpose of literature . . . [is] to delight or to console, to help us enjoy life or endure it.
>
> (2003c: 2)

This belief in the true purpose of literature forms the bedrock of the book at a time when the renewed literacy framework gives greater prominence to literature and narrative in *all* its forms, including screen and graphic texts. The importance of teaching children to engage in a critical understanding and fascination with the way in which film, comic books, picture books and written texts work is an important feature of the book. Indeed, one of the unifying features of the authors chosen for inclusion in the book is that their writing is informed by a love of comic and graphic narratives. Surreal art and brilliant graphic vibrancy radiates through all of Anthony Browne's works. Both Pullman and Morpurgo acknowledge the bold clarity of comic book pictures and the complexity of their narratives as an important influence on their writing. Wilson's books are enlivened by Nick Sharratt's powerful, cartoon-like pen and line drawings, and Rowling provided her publisher with immensely detailed pictures of the characters in her Harry Potter series. This is why the chapter on comic books written by Tim Stafford fits so well with the five authors chosen for examination. The chapter provides clear guidance to teachers using them for the first time, as well as a sharp and insightful discussion of the genre itself and the potential it offers for enriching children's moral and social understanding.

In recent years, many teachers have found it difficult to find the time to read longer works of fiction to children, let alone acquire a wider knowledge of children's books, which would make the sharing of stories a more interesting and enriching experience. This book, intended for children between Year 3 and Year 8 (7- to 14-year-olds), has deliberately set out to use material that is appealing, accessible and relatively short in length. Three of the teaching chapters have focused on one short story, while the other three have used picture books, comic books or, in the case of the J.K. Rowling chapter, short clips from two of the Harry Potter DVDs. It is hoped that having used the teaching materials, teachers, student teachers, classroom assistants and students following courses on children's literature will be sufficiently enthused to want to read on in order to gain deeper theoretical insights about the authors and their writing in Part 2 of the chapters.

How the book is organised

Contained in one book is a wealth of material based on five children's authors and the genre of comic books which does two things:

1   makes one or two books come alive in the classroom with a series of ideas and activities which can be used to plan a unit of work or a series of single interrelated lessons;
2   gives deeper knowledge about the author, their works, language, plots, characterisation, cohesion and intertextuality.

The book is divided into six two-part chapters. The first part of each chapter is concerned with classroom ideas and activities, and the second part with deeper, more theoretical insights about the author and her or his works. All the ideas contained in the Part 1 (teaching) sections of the chapter are based on recently conducted trial workshops in six primary schools. Some ideas worked extremely well, others less so. The activities set out in Part 1 of the chapters have taken serious account of the written and oral feedback so helpfully given by teachers and children at the end of each of the workshops. They are, I hope, a better product as a result. A 'diary' section is included which gives a verbatim record of children's and teachers' reactions to the workshop, the purpose of which is to give a grounded authenticity to the dynamic way in which the ideas and activities were conceived, trialled and developed.

The book deliberately sets out to focus on a specific group of well-known authors rather than offer a comprehensive overview of the range of genres and characteristic features of a broader range of children's fiction. This has already been done in a number of books, of which one particularly good example is *Exploring Children's Literature* by Gamble and Yates (2002). In each of the teaching elements (Part 1) of the chapters, the organisation is as follows:

Part 1

*   An introduction that sets out in brief terms the book/(s), film clips or comic book material the chapter is based on, the overarching objective, the year group used in the trial workshop and, where appropriate, ideas for heightening the atmosphere during the readings of the story.
*   A brief synopsis of the story where necessary.
*   Preparatory ideas and suggestions.
*   Activities which include some or all of the following: thinking and discussion; drama; and drawing, language work and writing in relation to written stories, film, comic and picture books. Activities suitable for social, emotional aspects of learning (SEAL) development have been included in the chapter on Jacqueline Wilson.
*   A model for questioning designed to prompt and encourage children to move from lower to higher levels of thinking and talking. Each of the Part 1 sections gives illustrative examples of the kinds of questions that could be used for the focus book or film clips.
*   Objectives and learning outcomes from which a unit of work or series of individual lessons can be planned. A unit of work can extend over half a term, a whole term or beyond. For example, as a result of the children's enthusiasm for Philip Pullman's *Clockwork or All Wound Up* in the spring term, one class teacher decided to do a play based on the book for a school performance at the end of the summer term.
*   Diary extracts which give an account of verbatim feedback from teachers, children and my own reflections at the end of the trial workshops.

- Examples of children's work arising from the workshop.
- A glossary of technical terms and/or new vocabulary.
- Teaching resources needed for the activities.
- Useful websites and additional sources of information.

Part 2

Each of the theoretical parts of the chapters includes some or all the following sections although not necessarily in the same order, since this depends on the genre and the particular nature of the author's works. Live interviews were conducted with Anthony Browne, Michael Morpurgo and Derek Watson, a comic book author.

- the writer
- her or his works
- genre
- intertextuality
- coherence
- themes, values, beliefs
- language
- plot
- characterisation
- live interviews.

In order to facilitate quick and easy access, the following icons have been used to identify specific types of activities and teacher instructions:

 Group discussion and interaction

 Examples of teacher questions and teacher instructions

 Drama activities

 Teacher instructions for drama activities

 Drawing, language and writing activities

 Film activities

 Activities suitable for SEAL development

PART I

Chapter I

Teaching Michael Morpurgo

The book chosen for this unit of work is *Kensuke's Kingdom*. For teachers who have not used this book with children before, it is a beautifully written and intensely moving island adventure story. For those who have, use the framework and ideas presented in Part 1 of this chapter with one of the other books discussed in Part 2. Few children will be familiar with the experience of living on a 42-foot yacht in the midst of seething, rolling seas, sharks and leaping dolphins. Even fewer will know what it is like to live on a deserted island with only a dog for company. Their imaginative involvement in the story will therefore be heightened by visual displays of photographs and paintings of island settings, oceans, large yachts and atmospheric pictures of storms at sea. The trial workshops took place with two Year 6 classes but the story is suitable for children within the Year 5 to Year 8 age range, though not exclusively so.

Synopsis of Michael Morpurgo's *Kensuke's Kingdom*

Michael is just 11 years old when his ordinary life suddenly becomes extraordinary. When both his parents lose their jobs at the local brickworks, his father scrapes together all his savings and, with a blind leap of faith, decides to buy a large yacht so they can sail round the world. All goes well until Stella, their pet sheepdog, bored with the sea and the restrictions of the boat, decides to chase Michael's football around the deck. He tries to coax her away from the bow, but she will not come. The boat lurches violently in a strong gust of wind and they are tossed into the towering waves. After a terrifying ordeal in the dark and freezing sea, Michael and Stella find themselves washed up on a deserted island. The island has a haunting, desolate beauty, but there is no water and no food, and thousands of eyes seem to be peering to Michael through the trees. They are not alone. This is Kensuke's kingdom and he hates intruders. He banishes Michael to the other end of the island and forbids him to make a fire to aid his rescue. What follows is a remarkable tale of sorrow, survival and forgiveness in which the solace of friendship becomes as important as the love of lost families.

Preparation

This story lends itself very well to cross-thematic work in geography, the natural world, marine animal life and conservation (Kensuke's love of the orang-utans and his protection of them from marauding hunters, for example, is a powerful theme in the plot). Some relevant classroom displays in advance of reading the story would make it possible for the children to make meaningful conceptual connections with the narrative, including a glossary of terms such as *winch*, *jib* and *rudder* (see p. 29). A display that includes a picture or poster of a large yacht with all the parts clearly labelled will help the children understand the realities of living at sea which Michael and his parents experienced. It will also help them to visualise just what it takes for Michael's family to keep the yacht steady in stormy weather. A large-scale map of the world on which the children can plot the voyage of the *Peggy Sue* as the story progresses will enhance their understanding of navigational geography and seafaring danger spots as well as helping them feel that they are part of *Peggy Sue*'s voyage.

Some time spent practising the different voices in the story will make the reading more dramatic and interesting. There are only five key characters: Kensuke, who speaks in broken English with a Japanese accent; Michael; Stella; and Michael's father and mother. Note that the name 'Kensuke' is pronounced 'Kenskee', not 'Kensook'. I had this point verified by Michael Morpurgo during one of his Children's Laureate lectures at the Royal Society of Arts. At a book signing event he met a Japanese child called Kensuke who explained to Michael how his name was pronounced. This chance encounter provided the idea for the title of the book.

Reading the story

Each time you assemble the class for a reading of the story, display on the interactive whiteboard one of the several screensavers indicated in the 'Teaching resources' section on p. 28. There are sufficient choices here for you to be able to vary them to suit the particular part of the story you have reached. They also come accompanied with atmospheric sound effects, which, if not too loud, will provide a dramatic soundscape to the reading of the story.

The story is sufficiently well signposted for you to know when to introduce knowledge about sailing a large yacht, the plotting of the *Peggy Sue*'s voyage and the unexpected weather changes that occur at sea. Many children will be interested too in Michael's log of the sighting of basking sharks, dolphins, water turtles and flying fish. This would be a good time to introduce further knowledge about these and other marine creatures.

Responding to *Kensuke's Kingdom*

The following activities can be done during the course of story reading along with the other cross-curricular work already mentioned, or after its completion. As is stated at the beginning of Chapter 2, teachers can make selections from the lesson objectives to plan individual lessons, a series of lessons or a coherent unit of work. The activities can also be done in any order, but my preference is to leave the writing and drawing activities until *after* the drama work. The quality of the stimulus and information given *before* the story will unquestionably heighten the children's ability to engage imaginatively and cognitively with its content.

The discussion on questioning written texts on pp. 82–3 in Chapter 3, Part 1 applies equally to this text. It is highly advisable to read it before selecting questions for the discussion activity. Encouraging the children to move gradually from reporting what happened in the story to an analysis of its deeper meanings, patterns and connecting themes is the key to ensuring that they gain greater insight and understanding about the book as well as the points it raises about the unfathomable bond that can exist between animals and human beings. The model for questioning written texts is presented here too, on this occasion with some exemplifications from *Kensuke's Kingdom*. You are advised to make a selection for any one session that follows progressively from the *content–narrative–structure* framework.

A model for questioning written text

1   Broad questions that focus on general impressions of the story as a whole. For example, What did you find interesting about the story? Which parts of the story did you enjoy most? Which parts puzzled you?

2   Questions about the characters and the parts they play. For example, Which character did you find most interesting? Who was the most important character?

3   Searching for puzzles in the story and those parts you did not like or understand. For example, Why did Stella seem to want to stay close to Kensuke even though she did not know him and he had just been very angry with Michael?

4   Questions about narration and point of view. Who is telling the story – the author or a character in the story? From whose perspective is the story written? Does it change or remain the same throughout the story?

5   Identifying patterns or links in the story. For example, Why does Kensuke hate Michael's presence on the island so much? Why is Michael so angry with Kensuke? What are the key differences between Kensuke's and Michael's relationship with the island?

Arrange the seating so that children are next to a partner they work well with for the group discussion and interaction activities. If an expectation of maximum pupil involvement is set from the outset, it will help to use a paired discussion strategy for the first two or three activities at least. In the first few teacher-directed questions, I have indicated where paired and whole class interactions might best take place. The remaining questions leave this to teachers' judgement and discretion.

◇   Why did you find the story interesting? Give at least two reasons. Discuss in pairs first. Share some responses with the whole class.

◇   Tell your partner why you enjoyed the story. Give three reasons. Share one or two different sets of reasons with the whole class.

◇   Which part of the story did you enjoy most and why? (Paired activity).

◇   Were there any parts of the story that puzzled you or that you did not understand?

◇   Do you think that Michael's dad was right to risk everything he had to sail around the world? Discuss in pairs or in small groups using evidence from the story to back up your opinions. Write down all the things for and against his decision. Share some of the responses with the class.

◇   Divide the children into small groups and assign each of them one of the following characters: Michael, Mother, Father, Stella and Kensuke. Each group is to contribute all they know from the story about their assigned characters. One person from each group is to share their knowledge of the different characters with the rest of the class.

◇   Which character interested you most? Give reasons for your choice.

◇   Who do you think is the most important character in the story?

◇   Do any of the characters in the story remind you of people you know in your life? If so, which character are you referring to and what qualities do they have in common?

◇   Who is telling the story? Does the same person tell the whole story from beginning to end or only parts of it?

◇   Why does Kensuke hate Michael so much when he first arrives on the island?

◇   What grounds does Kensuke have for claiming that the island is *his*?

◇   List the skills and qualities that enabled Kensuke to survive so well on the island.

◇   If Kensuke hated Michael's presence on the island so much, why did he care for him after he had been stung by the deadly jellyfish?

◇   What are the qualities in Kensuke's character that eventually led Michael to respect and like him?

◇   Michael and Kensuke gradually form a very close relationship with each other. What makes this happen? Think especially about what they *both* did to win each other's respect and friendship.

◇   What does the book teach us about friendship and trust? Think about the relationships between adults and children and humans and animals that are portrayed in the book. (A timed small-group discussion is suggested for this more challenging thinking and speaking activity).

◇   What were some of the thoughts that you think went through Kensuke's mind before he decided he would not go back to Japan?

◇   What is the story trying to tell us about responsibility and the choices made by the characters?

Drama activities

The following activities do not depend on the use of the school hall. A space created in the classroom by moving the furniture safely to the sides of the room is perfectly adequate.

Menu of activities

1 Warm-up
2 Individual character freeze-frame
3 Hot-seating
4 Group freeze-frame, 'On the *Peggy Sue*'
5 Group dramatisation, 'Man Overboard!'
6 Group dramatisation, 'Confrontation on the Island'
7 Cool-down

The following props are not essential but they will enhance the children's dramatic involvement.

Useful props

- A large, rough wooden stick for Kensuke.
- Golden Shores screensaver. This is a free screensaver that can be found on http://www. magentic.com/gallery/gallery. Click on the 'Oceans' screensaver menu on the left and open the one entitled 'Golden Shores'. It is an animated screensaver accompanied by the sound of ocean waves lapping against the cliffs, and can serve as a theatrical backdrop to the 'Island' dramatisation.
- 'Storm at sea' sound effect. There are any number of sea sound effects available for downloads on to a CDR or iTunes. The ones suggested give the required effects of lashing waves and the creaking sound of wood as a boat is tossed relentlessly by howling winds and a turbulent sea. Either one of the following two will provide the appropriate atmospheric sound for the 'Man Overboard' dramatisation. They are available for a small fee on http://www.sonomic.com/search. Put 'Storm at Sea' into the search box and click on 'exact match'. Four options will come up; the two most suitable are titled 'Boat large storm wind' 01G2 or 'Ship storm thunder' 01 PS.
- Lapping waves and seagull cries sound effect. Go to http://www.sonimic.com/search. Put 'Beach' 1028 2801 into the search box and click on 'exact match'. This gives the sound of waves lapping and seagulls crying overhead, which will provide an atmospheric soundscape for the 'Island' dramatisation.

Warm-up activity (six minutes)

If the children have had little experience of drama, then the following warm-up activity is a good way of breaking the ice. If children are comfortable with drama, proceed straight to the 'freeze-frame' activity set out in the next subsection.

Find a space on the floor.

When I say 'run' use all the spaces on the floor.

Freeze absolutely still on the command of 'freeze'.

Hold your position perfectly still.

When the children have done this once and got the hang of the idea, tell the children that you are going to ask them to make different movements on the command of 1, 2 or 3.

On the command of 1, sit down and freeze.

On the command of 2, lie down and freeze.

On the command of 3, stand on one leg and freeze.

The idea is to rapidly change the commands so the children have to run, sit, lie and stand on one leg in quick succession. Each time they are told to go again, they have to run using all the spaces without touching or bumping into anyone else. This will make demands on them to be aware of others and the space around them. It should get them out of breath, thinking quickly about what they have to do on a given command, and if they are panting, giggling and hot by the end, so much the better. Practise the different commands first.

Freeze-frame activity (ten minutes)

Before beginning this activity, it will be helpful to provide children with a list of the key characters and their role in the story either in the form of a photocopied sheet or displayed on the IWB. The idea of this activity is that children freeze in role on a given command.

> **The Characters in Kensuke's Kingdom**
>
> Kensuke, an old Japanese man who lives on the Island
> Michael, a young boy of eleven and ship's boy
> Michael's Mother, the skipper
> Michael's Father, first mate and handyman
> Stella, a black and white sheepdog, and the ship's cat

The children should sit in a space on the floor and choose the character they would like to be. Before beginning the activity, ask the children to:

Think carefully about who you are and what you might be doing. You can either stand still and mime an action typical of the character you have chosen or you can move around the room in role.

If you are moving in role, think about the differences in the way you would walk depending on whether you are Kensuke or Michael, for example.

On the instruction 'Go', the children move into role. On the command of 'Freeze', the teacher and any other adults in the room have to guess which character a chosen child is playing. Stress the importance of what each of the characters might be doing on the boat, for example hauling down the mainsail, steering the boat, looking out to sea with a pair of binoculars, and so on. The boat is moving all the time, so they will need to show how their bodies move when it pitches and rolls.

Repeat one more time, ensuring the children hold their action absolutely still on the command of 'Freeze'. Half of them watch while the other half mime a character different from the one they had chosen before. Tell the watching half of the class to concentrate on watching one or two children only.

 Go.

Freeze.

Selected members of the watching half try to guess which character(s) those they observed were playing.

Praise the children for what they did well and change over so that the watching half become the acting half. Repeat as above.

Hot-seating activity (fifteen minutes)

Children choose which character they would like to be in 'the hot seat'. You may need to remind the children of what was said in the discussion about the main characteristics of each of these before beginning the activity. Seat the children in a horseshoe shape with a chair in the gap of the crescent. Before beginning the activity, ask the children to:

 Think carefully about the character you would like to play and the kind of person he or she is.

Close your eyes for a minute or so and think about the role this character plays in the story in relation to the other characters.

Begin the activity by choosing a child who is reasonably confident about performing in front of others and who will be able to sustain credibility in their chosen role. This will set the tone for the others. Children and teachers then ask questions of the character in the hot seat in turns. Keep the pace moving and give as many children as time allows a chance to be in the hot seat. If children choose to hot-seat the same character as one that has previously been 'hot-seated', it is important to encourage children to ask questions *different* from those asked before, otherwise the activity will become tedious and undemanding for the new child in the hot seat.

Group freeze-frame, 'On the Peggy Sue' (fifteen minutes)

Children to work in groups of four with each child deciding which character they will be: Michael, the mother, the father or Stella. The idea here is that all the children perform an action in the boat which fits with their character. For example, Michael's mum might be taking a compass bearing. Michael could be at the wheel while his father is taking down the mainsail, and Stella is at the bow of the boat barking at something she has heard. At the command of 'freeze', the children hold their actions absolutely still as though frozen into a photograph.

In your groups, decide which character you are going to be.

Decide what action you will be doing on the boat. Imagine you are at sea and the boat is heaving up and down in a choppy sea.

Go into action.

Freeze!

Praise children for effective mime and for holding their movements still, whatever they were doing on the command of 'freeze'. Repeat, this time asking the children to be very clear about what they are doing in their mimed actions while at the same time trying to maintain their balance in rough seas. (You may need to coach how the body's weight will need to be distributed if they are not to fall over as the boat lurches from side to side.) After the groups have 'frozen' for the second time, share one or two of the group freeze-frames.

 Go into action.

Freeze!

Children to highlight examples of authentic mime and the quality of stillness in the group freeze-frame.

Group dramatisation, 'Man overboard!' (twenty minutes)

Building on the previous freeze-frame activity, the children are now going to work on two group dramatisations. In the first one, children form themselves into pairs. One of them is going to be Michael, and the other, Stella. They are going to enact in mime the scene where Stella is barking at the bow end of the boat without her safety harness. Reread the passage on pp. 42–4 from the words beginning 'It is so dark out there . . .' to '. . . open my mouth to scream.' Ask the children to close their eyes and imagine the events while you read the passage. Put up the following **sequence of events** on a flipchart or large piece of paper so the children can easily see it:

- Michael and Stella on board alone (*beginning*).
- Stella at the front of the boat with no harness; she will not come to Michael (*middle*).
- The boat lurches violently and Michael is thrown sideways (*middle*).
- Michael tries to grab the rail but the boat lurches violently again and both are thrown into the cold sea (*middle*).
- Both thrash around in the turbulent sea and are washed ashore (*end*).
- Michael and Stella lie still on the island completely exhausted (*end*).

Children might find it easier to read and remember if the above sequence is shortened to key words only. Stress the importance of the mimed sequence having a clear beginning, middle and end as indicated above.

 In your pairs, decide which of you is to be Michael and which Stella.

Read the sequence and think about how you are going to fill in the gaps between the six events.

> Discuss how you are going to mime the sequence. Remember that the boat is pitching and rolling more violently than usual. Remember how you showed this before by the way you moved your body and held your balance.

Give the children three to four minutes to discuss their ideas and begin to work out their mime. *Emphasise the importance of **not** attempting to lift Stella.* When you think the children are ready, give the following instructions:

 Go into your starting positions and hold your movement still.

Go into your first action.

Continue until you are both lying exhausted and still on the island.

When all the children are lying still, praise what went well in the mime and suggest, with the help of children's contributions, how it might be improved.

 Change over roles and repeat the sequence.

Now play the 'storm at sea' sound effect detailed on p. 9. If you have not got this sound effect, use the howling wind sound effect listed on p. 85 in Chapter 3, Part 1. Let the children listen to it first, while they imagine the scene they have just enacted. Make demands upon children to improve upon their first attempts.

 Change over roles again. Repeat the sequence and finish as before.

Tell the children what was better this time and what could still be improved. Repeat, again with changed roles. If there is time, share one or two effective dramatisations. Teachers can choose whether to develop the mime sequence into an improvisation that includes speech. Questions like the following will help the children devise their own speech: 'What would you say to Stella to coax her to come to you?' 'What does Stella do?' 'How would you show the fear in your voice when you realise that neither of you has a safety harness on and the storm is rapidly getting worse?'

Group dramatisation, 'Confrontation on the Island' (twenty minutes)

Working in the same pairs, the children decide who is going to be Kensuke and who Michael. In this mimed dramatisation, Kensuke angrily confronts Michael, who has lit a fire in order to try to attract passing ships and get rescued. Check that children understand that the Japanese word *Dameda* means 'forbidden'. Reread the passage on pp. 69–72 of *Kensuke's Kingdom* from the words beginning 'He was diminutive, no taller than me . . .' until halfway down p. 72, ending with the words 'Go, boy. No fire. *Dameda*. No fire. You understand?' Ask the children to close their eyes and imagine the events while you read the passage. Put up the following *sequence of events* on a flip chart or large piece of paper so the children can easily see it:

- A tired Michael starts to build a fire (*beginning*).
- After several attempts, it starts to burn (*middle*).

- The smoke from the fire attracts Kensuke, who approaches Michael, waving his stick in fury.
- They both argue, and Kensuke draws the shape of the island with his stick (*middle*).
- He angrily draws a dividing line that shows which is his end and which is Michael's, and walks away, leaving Michael desperate and devastated (*end*).

Before beginning the dramatisation, ask all the children to think about how Kensuke would walk, using the stick to help him. Even though he is old and bent, he is fit and strong.

Walk round the room in the role showing how you think Kensuke would move as an old, bent but fit man. How would he use his stick to help him walk?

What expression does he show on his face when he sees the smoke from Michael's fire?

How will you show the anger in your eyes when you approach Michael?

Now get the children to mime Michael collecting wood and building his fire.

Decide in the space close to you where you are going to build your fire.

Show in your movements whether the sticks of wood you are collecting are big or small.

Show by the way you are placing your sticks that your fire is of a large pyramid or wigwam shape. Light it using your piece of glass as Michael did, and show your pleasure when it catches fire and begins to smoke.

How will you react when you hear Kensuke shouting, 'Dameda, Dameda!'?

How will you show your fury and despair when Kensuke walks away having forbidden you to make a bonfire to aid your rescue?

The children can now work in their pairs to decide how they are going to act out the sequence of actions outlined above, remembering to think about the beginning, middle and the end. It would make sense in this activity for the children to use speech. Ask the children to come up with ideas for what Michael would say to Kensuke after he has forbidden him to light a fire. Stress that neither speaks the other's language, so they will have to depend more on signs and gestures, such as pointing, than on words. When the children have gone through their sequence once, put up the Golden Shores screensaver or the sound effect of waves lapping against a shore accompanied by seagull cries listed in the props on p. 9. Give the children time to go through the sequence at least twice with the suggested screen backdrop or sound effect. Give the following instructions in order to ensure a clear beginning and end:

Michael and Kensuke, go into your starting positions.

Show your first action in stillness.

Make sure you end by holding your last movement absolutely still.

Now go into role and enact the scene.

Divide the class into two, letting one half watch the other and then vice versa. Ask the children to concentrate on one or two pairs only and highlight what was good about the paired dramatisations they focused on.

Cool-down activity (2–3 minutes)

 Lie down on the floor and imagine you are on a peaceful island.

Think about all the sounds you can hear and all the things you can see on the island.

Enjoy the peace and warmth of the sun.

Slowly stand up, relax and breathe deeply.

Drawing, language work and writing activities

Maps are an integral part of the story of *Kensuke's Kingdom*, as they are in many of Michael Morpurgo's books. It is for this reason that the following activity interrelates with a visual and verbal narrative. The objective here is for the children to construct an island map of their choosing which gives a visual representation of a sequenced story about their first arrival on an unknown island. If the drama activities have preceded the drawing and language work, the children will already possess an experiential understanding of the importance of sequence. Teachers are advised to have a range of pictures, posters and photographs of islands to which children can refer and use as a source of ideas.

◇ Show children an enlarged photocopy of the map of Kensuke's 'kingdom'.
◇ Point out the importance of the *compass sign* and the *legend* at the top right-hand corner of the map and what this means with respect to the 'story' the map is communicating.
◇ Encourage the children to lead the questioning about the map so that they increase their understanding of its meaning with respect to the various symbols, track signs and sketches of boats.
◇ A key point to emphasise (if the children have not already worked this out for themselves) is the relationship of the map narrative to the 'island' part of the story.

When the children have reached a fuller understanding of the information conveyed by the map, ask them to work individually or in pairs to devise a narrative from which they can draw a map using the enlarged Kensuke map as a model. The following framework should help to shape their ideas and needs to be easily visible on an interactive whiteboard or large sheet of paper.

• You are on a boat and somehow you have ended up in the sea swimming for your life.
• What happened? Make it different from what happened to Michael.
• You land on a remote island. Are you on your own?
• What is the first thing you think when you look around you?
• What is the first thing you do?
• What is the first thing you see?
• You explore the island and find two more things of interest. What are they? Are they dangerous? Are they mysterious? Will they help you to survive?
• You find somewhere to sleep when night falls. Where and what is it?

- When you wake up in the morning, you discover you are not alone. What have you seen? Who or what do you think it is?

Give the children at least 15 minutes to think up a story around this structure. Share some of their ideas. Stress that the map they are going to draw will represent their story in pictorial symbols.

◇ Show the children a copy of a suggested map outline which they may use as a starting point for their own (see Figure 1.1).
◇ Decide on the shape of your island.
◇ Like Figure 1.1, it must have a legend, compass points and an island name.
◇ Mark your map with clear, easy-to-understand symbols showing where you landed, where you slept and the two other things you saw on the island (see the example of a child's work on p. 21).
◇ The symbols must be placed in your legend, like the sign of an 'x' on Kensuke's map to represent where Michael first landed.

Give the children at least 45 minutes to complete their individual maps.

Writing activity

The children will need access to their maps and the structured sequence on p. 15. Before they begin the written narrative, reread the passage halfway down p. 52 of *Kensuke's Kingdom* beginning 'The sun was blazing down . . .' as far as the sentence 'I was not at all downhearted . . .' on p. 53. The extract needs to be photocopied or shown on the interactive whiteboard so that the children can follow it during the reading.

◇ Ask the children to point out the parts of the extract that made it possible for them to see the island clearly in their mind. What phrases and individual words do this really well?

◇ What descriptive words and phrases made the colours and atmosphere of the island come alive as they were listening to and following the extract?

◇ Can they think of other descriptive phrases which would vividly describe the sea and the beach? Teacher to write their suggestions on the whiteboard or flip chart.

◇ Encourage the children to use all their senses when they describe their first landing on the remote island. What did they smell? What did they feel or touch? What did they hear? What did they see?

◇ Try to use as many interesting and unusual words as possible in your story.

◇ Follow the structure of the sequence, ensuring that it ties up with the 'story' represented on your map. Give your story a title.

Figure 1.1 Suggested map outline.

Children may need two or three extended writing sessions to complete their island stories.

Writing from another perspective in a first-person narrative

During the dramatic work, the children had to enact the scene between Kensuke and Michael just after Michael had lit the bonfire. As Kensuke walked back to his part of the island, they were both angry for different reasons. This activity requires the children to put themselves in the perspective of one of the characters and write down their thoughts, describing how they feel about what has just happened and why they dislike each other so much.

◇ Make a list of all the reasons why you are feeling angry and upset with Michael/Kensuke.
◇ List all the feelings you have. For example, are you enraged? Is your blood boiling? Are you close to tears? Is your heart thudding? Are you shaking with anger? Is your stomach churning? Be as clear as possible so that your readers will be able to share what you are feeling.
◇ Now put all your thoughts and feelings together and write your description in the first person so that you begin your writing with 'I . . .', as in *Kensuke's Kingdom*.
◇ Give your writing a title that fits closely with its subject matter.

Objectives and learning outcomes

Lesson/series of lessons/unit of work objectives

1 To deepen children's understanding, appreciation and enjoyment of Michael Morpurgo's *Kensuke's Kingdom*.
2 To develop children's understanding and knowledge of the importance of respect and trust in relationships as portrayed by key characters in the story.
3 To develop children's knowledge of natural life and the importance of respect for animals on the part of human beings, especially those belonging to endangered species.
4 To challenge children's understanding and thinking about the deeper meaning of the story, particularly with respect to narration, language use and characterisation.
5 To use the story as a basis for widening knowledge and understanding about geography, natural life, conservation and oceanic navigation.
6 To enable children to learn, use and apply some of the basic technical vocabulary associated with sailing.
7 To provide writing, drawing, drama and speaking and listening activities that will deepen and extend children's understanding of the story.
8 To extend and improve children's ability to write first-person narratives in a range of different writing forms based on models of writing provided by the text.
9 To sufficiently stimulate children's interest and understanding of *Kensuke's Kingdom* for them to want to read and enjoy other books by Michael Morpurgo.

Lesson/series of lessons/unit of work outcomes

By the end of the lesson, or unit of work, the children will be able to:

1 think and reflect more knowledgeably about the deeper meaning of the story;
2 understand the relevance of the story to geography, conservation, marine and animal life;

3 mime and act individually, and in small and larger groups, selected scenarios from the story;
4 write using first-person narration in a variety of different writing forms;
5 use vivid and accurate language in their writing;
6 draw a map of their own design in an imagined context that involves the use of a legend;
7 understand and use some basic technical language associated with sailing;
8 read a wider range of books by Michael Morpurgo with interest, enjoyment and appreciation.

Diary

Drama

It was clear from the outset that the children in the first of the two Year 6 classes were very unsure and self-conscious about drama work. The session began with two short readings from the book in order to get the children focused on the key differences between the characters of Michael and Kensuke before beginning the freeze-frame activity. This was a mistake because it meant the children had to sit still for several minutes. They clearly needed a simple, energetic and enjoyable warm-up activity that got them moving straight away. This is why the warm-up activity suggested on p. 10 is strongly advised if the children have not previously had much experience of drama. Even when most of them eventually became involved in the 'Man Overboard' and 'Island Confrontation' group dramatisations, very few wanted to share their work. This may be partly explained by their insufficient confidence in the work they had achieved and the fact that they had heard only part of the story when the workshop took place. They were not, therefore, sufficiently familiar with Kensuke to understand his anger with Michael.

Because of the diffidence of the first group, I decided that much more coaching of mime work associated with the differences in appearance, movement and emotions of Michael and Kensuke was needed with the second Year 6 class.

At least fifteen minutes was spent working on ways in which emotions such as surprise, anger, happiness, etc. could be communicated. This preparatory work certainly paid off in terms of their involvement in the freeze-framing and group dramatisations. Again, before beginning the 'Peggy Sue' and 'Island' dramas, the sequences were broken down into much smaller steps and coached with respect to movement, atmosphere, the communication of mood and the differences in the way in which Michael and Kensuke would walk. The whole sequence was only put together towards the end of the session and the quality of work was markedly better than that of the first group, despite the fact that we had to work outside in noisy and windy conditions.

Like other subjects, drama needs to be explicitly taught with respect to the skills of concentration, listening, remembering, moving, imagination and communicating feelings. Even with able and assured Year 6 children, too much too soon can be disheartening and not conducive to a positive and enjoyable learning experience. For these reasons, the drama activities outlined earlier have been very carefully designed and paced to ensure that each new activity builds on the previous one. It cannot be stressed too strongly that sufficient time needs to be allowed for children to acquire an internal visual and kinaesthetic 'script' of the sequence before they can put it together with any degree of confidence and dramatic involvement. It is also important to resist the temptation to move too quickly on to the next activity.

Drawing and writing activities

Both classes of children were fascinated and intrigued by the enlarged map of Kensuke's 'kingdom' and were very keen to ask questions about the meaning of the various symbols. It was clear that 'cracking the code' of the map and its legend gave them a symbolic representation of the story which enabled them to see it from a different perspective.

However, several children found the drawing of their maps and symbols a challenging and difficult experience as was similarly noted in the Philip Pullman workshop to be described in Chapter 3. They lacked the requisite drawing skills to do justice to the details they wished to include in their maps, such as boats, ruins and temples. The importance of simple, clearly presented pictures and photographs of island settings from which the children can glean ideas cannot be stressed too highly.

The writing activities

The quality of work demonstrated in the writing activities was of a reasonably high standard, given that it was their first draft. Several children who were reluctant to get involved in the drama work became intensely engaged in the island writing activity.

Using extracts from the book and highlighting examples of rich and vivid descriptions in Morpurgo's writing had a marked impact on the quality of their work, as can be seen by the examples of children's work shown below. Thinking and talking about the story they would represent before they designed their own maps undoubtedly served to clarify their thinking about the structure and organisation of their written narrative. This reduced the cognitive load demanded by this writing form, allowing them to focus more on language features.

Examples of children's work

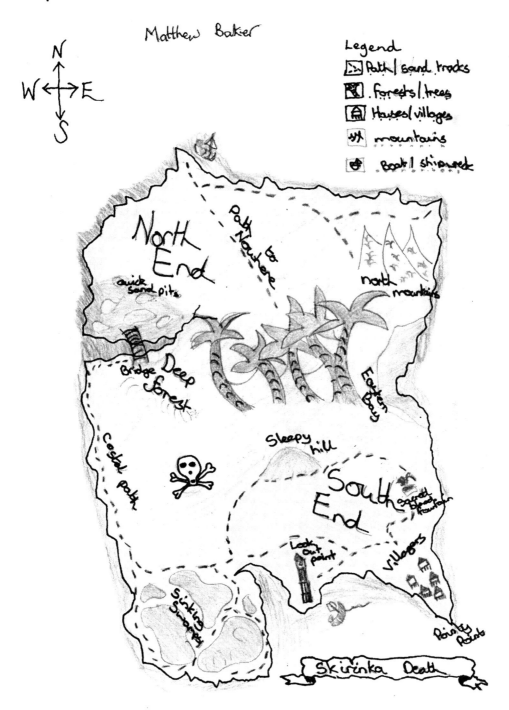

Figure 1.2 Work by Matthew (Year 6).

Creative Writing

13th April Day 2

Dear Diary.

We have been here one and a half days now on this strange and incredible place of a island. I remember when are yacht smashed into the rocks in the shallows, of this island which I call Skirinka Death and as the tide brought us back out we were beached, beached on a island in the middle of nowhere. Fortunately we managed to save some of the remaining food on board mosty containing baked beans and tinned grapefruit. Me and my fourteen year old brother Tom started to look around just to be walking in circles. I have noticed many strange things so far like this morning me and Tom noticed some dangerous quicksand pits down by the creak which we marked off with dead tree debris from the forest. I did think about venturing into the forest but my Dad said no and I see why with all the weird noises coming from inside. Last night me and mum noticed some smoke from the other side of the island that had appeared out of nowhere. This made me tremble inside and out.

Figure 1.3 Work by Matthew (Year 6).

Creative Writing

16th April   Day 5

Dear Diary.

Yesterday was a disaster. Mum was feeling ill and all the medicine and First Aid kits fell over-board when we smashed into the rocks five days ago. I know I will never forget that raing sunday afternoon with the fifteen foot waves and the heavy down-poors. Anyway I spent all yesterday afternoon comforting mum whislt Dad and Tom went looking for food, me and mum didn't get our hopes up. Thankfully they did find food. they found tones and tones of bananas also many berries to. Tom Brought me aside and said there is other people on this island. Tonight lets sneek out and go look for them.

Figure 1.3 continued

Creative Writing

17th April Day 6

Dear Diary

He's gone, Tom's gone. They caught him on their land. They were speaking some kind of different language, all they said in English was: Must leave or die. Strait away I sprinted home and told mum and dad everything. How we made are way through the jungle and how they saw us and how they caught Tom. I couldn't say my sentences right I was so scared and in shock. I couldn't believe they caught him and what will they do to him. Dad said he will look for him alone with no-one else. I told him the way through jungle and I warned him they had weapons. The last thing that I said to my dad was good luck.

Figure 1.3 continued

Figure 1.4 Work by Thomas (Year 6).

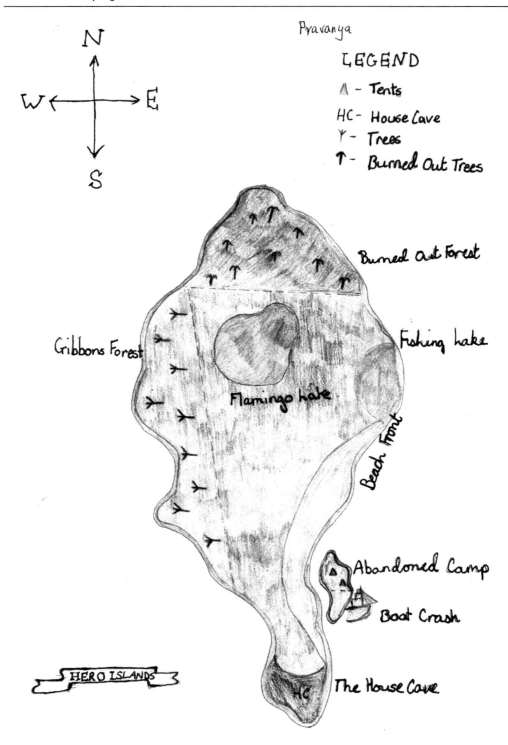

Figure 1.5 Work by Pravanya (Year 6).

Creative Writing

Monday 26th
June.

5th May 2003.   Day 1

Dear diary,

Earlier this morning my crew marroned me on this god forsaken island. I do not understand why but it may have been my decision to head west instead of East. All day I have just sat here on this beach thinking, shall I go further inland? or wait for a ship to pass by?. Soon I will go in search for food and water. This of coarse means I will have to go on a long search inland and I hope I will find something soon. If not I will surley perish

Tom xxx

6th May 2003   Day 2

Dear diary,

Today was a great success, I feel so elated, I have finally found food and water it happened late this afternoon I had been traveling for at least 11 hours and been walking at least 21 miles inland when I came accross 2 large trees and a plane had somehow crashed in between. I could find no one living inside; just 2 large skeletons sitting in the cockpit. To my surprise the plane was full of rice. I concluded, since the rice was cooked and there was burnt marks on the plane, that there had been some sort of fire. I load my bag full with all the rice I

Figure 1.6 Work by Thomas (Year 6).

could and searched the rest of the plane, inside I found 1 compass, 2 fountain pens and a box of matches. Afterwards I decided to head East and I came accross a small waterhole. At first I could not drink it for the risk it was poisonous, but the overwhelming urge for water was too strong for me. I took a handfull and gulped it down. The taste was so refreshing it made me feel strong again. Tommorrow I am hoping to find something which will help me on my journey.

Till Then

Tom xxx

31st May 2003   Day 27

Dear diary,

The last few days have been extremly tiring 2 days ago I finished my trip on the canoe and started treking through the forest the tribesman told me to keep heading west until I reached the lost temple of Azenton. The temple was about 60m high and it was covered in brambles also it had a strange red substance on it which looked a lot like eyes. As I stepped inside the temple I cold imediatly feel the change of climate, the air was cool and it was quiet. I then went through the left door and began to search for a bright blue glow, when I found it I went towards the wall it shined on and touched it the wall suddenly began to seppurate when it had finished I stepped through

Figure 1.6 continued

and there before my very eyes was a small, pocket sized, gold statue. I quickly grabbed it and ran back the way I came because I knew the temple would collaspe, and it did. When I got out I watched the building slowly fall to the ground afterwards I closely inspected the statue it was of a small tiger cub. Tommorow I will search for away to escape this island

with high hopes

Tom xxx

Figure 1.6 continued

A glossary of sailing terms used in *Kensuke's Kingdom*

Bow	The front part of a boat, ship or yacht, which is usually pointed.
Cockpit	An enclosure on a yacht or boat which contains the wheel or tiller.
Jib	A small triangular sail in front of the mainsail.
Knot	A unit of measurement for the speed at which a ship or aircraft travels.
Life jacket	A sleeveless jacket made of light material and filled with air so that it can keep someone afloat in the water.
Mainsail	The largest and most important sail on a sailing ship.
Rudder	A pivoting blade under the water that steers the boat or ship.
Sextant	An instrument that includes a telescope which is used to measure a ship's precise position in the sea by calculating the lines of latitude and longitude.
Ship's log	A dated and timed record of all the events that take place on a ship's or aircraft's journey.
Stern	The rear part of a ship or yacht, usually flattened in shape. The rudder underneath the water is attached to it.
Wheel	On a ship or large yacht like the *Peggy Sue*, the wheel is housed in the cockpit. It is attached to the rudder and helps to steer it.
Winch	A machine for lifting heavy loads with a rope or a chain which is wound round a wheel or cylinder. It can be turned by hand or by an engine.

Teaching resources

- Copy of *Kensuke's Kingdom*. The edition used for the workshop was M. Morpurgo, (1999) *Kensuke's Kingdom*, London: Egmont. At least two or three extra copies would be useful for children to refer to for help with the writing and drawing activities.

- Ocean and island screensavers. The ones suggested are titled Rippling Water; Golden Shores; Sailing a Clipper Ship and Tropical Island Shore. These are all free screensavers that can be found at http://www.magentic.com/gallery/gallery. Click on the 'Oceans' screensaver menu on the left, then click on the above titles. The last one in the list can be found at the same website under the 'Islands' menu. The screensavers can be used as a theatrical backdrop to suit the part of the story you are reading at the time. They can also be used to add atmosphere and mood to the drama activities.
- An enlarged photocopy of the map of Kensuke's 'kingdom'.
- Enlarged copies of the two group dramatisation sequence instructions.
- Enlarged version or individual photocopies of the island description, *Kensuke's Kingdom* pp. 52–3.
- Enlarged photocopy of Michael's ship's log, *Kensuke's Kingdom*, p. 25.
- Photocopies or word documents (saved to a memory stick for use on the interactive whiteboard) of the key characters in *Kensuke's Kingdom* and the framework for the map and writing activity.
- Clear and simple pictures, paintings and/or photographs of large yachts and island settings.

Useful websites and additional sources of information

For a comprehensive biography of Michael Morpurgo's life, his books, the ideas behind his stories and how he writes, see:

Fox, G. (2004) *Dear Mr Morpingo: Inside the World of Michael Morpurgo*, Cambridge: Wizard Books.

For a complete list of Michael Morpurgo's books, further details about his life and answers to frequently asked questions about *Kensuke's Kingdom*, visit his official website at www.michael morpurgo.org.

Michael Morpurgo, weaver of magic

The writer, the man and the child

Having listened to Michael Morpurgo several times in recent years giving talks and performing readings of his work, I have been struck by his consummate skill as a performer. He looks his audience in the eye and tells them stories without ever using notes. He holds their attention with his voice and commanding presence. He speaks with humour, conviction and sincerity, his clear, uncluttered prose moving at a swift pace. He is, in every sense of the word, a storyteller. He has an instinctive feel for the way language impacts upon the ear and the mind, giving sufficient but not too much detail. He has a finely honed sense of how to work the pace, cadence and rhythm of the story he wants to tell. The content of his narrative is sometimes comic and self-deprecatory but more often it is uncompromisingly tragic and poignant. The material he uses to craft his writing has always been meticulously researched, with much of it experientially grounded. His books are much loved because they have integrity, and believable characters who often find themselves faced with cruelty and terrifying ordeals with a resolution that holds out hope or some kind of personal reconciliation.

However, it is Morpurgo's talent as an actor, teacher and *teller* of stories that is the key to understanding his success as a writer. It is his ear that tells him whether the alchemy of his story will work or not. For Murpurgo, writing is not solely a matter of what many writers have described as an unreliable and indeterminate interaction of the pen and the mind; it is also kinaesthetic and aural. Morpurgo seems almost to 'feel' the story flowing from his mind through to his arm and fingers and on to the page (Morpurgo, 2000b). Once he has 'told' the story in a first draft, he reads his work into a cassette recorder, letting his ear dictate the changes he will make (Kellaway, 2002). Before he begins to write, however, he has a well-worked-out sense of the structure and the form of narration it will take. The most difficult and lengthy part of the writing process is its incubation, or what Morpurgo calls his 'dreamtime'. This can take anything from two or three weeks to several months. During this period, all the various strands of the plot begin to cohere and he, the actor within, breathes life into his characters, mostly by becoming them himself. It is not until he has had all the time he needs to reach this point that he can bring his dream to paper and write his story. He then writes at great speed, quickly bringing the reworked draft to completion. However, the actual reality of this process is probably far less tidy and linear than this account would suggest. His wife, Clare, has always been the first reader and critic of his stories, and, after his writing career of some thirty-three years, continues to be the first to pass judgement on his latest creation, a moment of reckoning that Morpurgo still dreads, even with a publishing track record of 107 books (Morpurgo, 2007a).

Success, however, has been hard won, and as a child he hated reading, loathed school and was often only really happy when playing sport or outside exploring bombsites or foraging in the marshlands and seashores of Essex. It is hard to believe that a writer whose books have enthralled so many children once found books a source of dread and active dislike (Fox, 2004). The cause of some of this may be located in his uneasy relationship with his stepfather, Jack Morpurgo. Michael Morpurgo was born in 1943 in the shadow of the Second World War. At the end of the war, his natural father, Tony Bridge, returned home to find that his wife had fallen in love with another man. He quickly saw the way things were and decided it was best for his two sons if he simply moved away so that his wife could build a new life with Jack Morpurgo. Tony therefore disappeared from his sons' lives at a time when they had scarcely begun to know him, and during their childhood years it was as though he had never existed because they were they not allowed to mention his name in front of their stepfather (ibid.).

Morpurgo's stepfather was a gifted, ambitious man of iron discipline and with an enormous capacity for hard work. He had high expectations of his son, which Michael found very difficult to live up to (Fox, 2004). Their relationship for much of Morpurgo's life was tense and uneasy, eventually leading to feelings of crippling inadequacy that took years to overcome.

Yet despite the austerity of the post-war period and the distance that both Michael's parents kept between themselves and their children, there were also times of great delight and happiness in his childhood. Some of the seeds of his later love for poetry, song, music and the rhythm of language were sown by his mother and grandparents, who entranced him with their readings of Edward Lear, Rudyard Kipling's *Just So Stories*, and the nonsense poems of Lewis Carroll. His maternal grandfather was a Belgian poet, his grandmother an opera singer and his mother an actress, all of them used to performing and using their voices to bring the music of language alive. Acting was also present on his paternal side in his natural father, Tony Bridge, whom Michael saw by chance one day on television playing the part of Magwitch in Dickens' *Great Expectations*. In his adult life, when Michael was able to develop a close relationship with his father, he saw him in several stage performances. His family's history is steeped in acting and performing talent. This probably explains why performing comes so naturally to Michael and why he listens so intently to the language, rhythm and tempo of his stories before writing them.

These magical times of story reading with his mother and grandparents ended all too soon when he was sent away to boarding school at eight years of age. Not only was he desperately homesick, but lessons and anything to do with book learning were a cause of great anxiety. Given the need for physical affection, which Morpurgo craved in his early childhood, and the forced and tense relationship he endured between himself and his stepfather, it is not surprising that his stories

> frequently depict lone male protagonists who are self-reliant and resourceful. They have to find their way out of danger and fear and in so doing, frequently forge intensely close relationships with older people and animals, with trust, friendship and loyalty remaining paramount, regardless of the great cost and personal sacrifice this often means.
>
> (Duncan, 2007: 274)

Morpurgo's first attempt to write stories of his own happened once he had met Clare, the love of his life and current wife, with whom he has had three children. When he first started writing children's books, in 1974, he was immensely dissatisfied with them and almost gave up. Fortunately, at this point in his life he met Ted Hughes, who was a neighbour of his in Devon. Ted Hughes became Morpurgo's mentor and gave him his first real encouragement after he had shown him *War Horse*, of which he was immensely proud and which Clare believes remains his best story to this day. The idea for the creation of a Children's Laureate to reward a lifetime's contribution to children's literature was the brainchild of Ted Hughes and Michael Morpurgo, the latter becoming the third Children's Laureate in 2003.

Children have always been at the centre of his life. In addition to his own family of children and grandchildren, Morpurgo is often to be found working with them in schools, inspiring them and giving them the confidence to write. As a result of a legacy left by Clare's father and their belief that many city children were deprived of the opportunity to experience nature, animals and farming life, they set up a charity called Farms for City Children, which they have run since 1978. Public recognition for this pioneering work came in the form of an MBE, which they were awarded in 1999. Many of Morpurgo's stories concern the close and often inexplicable bond of trust that can exist between children and animals. Much of the source for these books comes from his close, careful observation of children in these rural settings over many years, as does his vast knowledge of both farm animals and those that live in the wilds of the countryside.

Michael Morpurgo's works

The first of his phenomenal output of books over thirty-three years was *It Never Rained: Five Stories*, published by Macmillan in 1974, and his most recent, *Born to Run*, was published by HarperCollins in 2007. His latest book, like many others, explores a familiar Morpurgo theme: that of a child protagonist forming an inseparable bond with an animal. A greyhound puppy is rescued from drowning in the local canal by Patrick on his way to school. After pleading with his parents, he is eventually allowed to keep one of the litter he has saved, and names him 'Best Mate'. Best Mate is Patrick's closest companion until one day he is stolen by dog thieves. This is the start of Best Mate's life on the race track and its associated cruelty, but he is a survivor, a graceful racer and a fiercely loyal companion.

What is moving about these stories is the way in which Morpurgo compels his readers to believe absolutely in the strong but unsentimental reciprocal affection that can grow between an animal and a human being. This relationship is often tested to its limits by acts of selfish, brutish behaviour on the part of adults, but these are usually balanced by acts of kindness and generosity, often from people who have suffered loss and loneliness themselves. The form of narration in the storyline is a familiar one: a mixture of third- and first-person narratives that glide fluidly one from the other. Four main voices tell Best Mate's story: Morpurgo's third-person narration focused through the characters of Patrick, Becky and Joe, and the fourth, first-person narration through the eyes and ears of Best Mate and his subsequent renamings of 'Brighteyes' and 'Paddywack'.

Mythological and sentient forms of animal life speak powerfully in many of Morpurgo's books, one of the most poignant being Joey, the farm horse who is sold to the army for use in the cavalry during the First World War. Morpurgo has acquired a deep knowledge and respect for animals during his working life on farms, so there is no room for sentimentality in his animal stories. This is handled particularly well in *The Last Wolf*, when in 1746, after the battle of Culloden Moor, Robbie McLeod flees for his life, having witnessed the killing of what was thought to be the last wolf in Scotland. A day later, hearing the piteous yelps of a wolf cub, Robbie befriends and feeds him. He disguises him by shearing his long coat and eventually flees by ship to America, taking the now fully grown 'Charlie' with him. He builds himself a log cabin and carves out a life for himself in the wilds of Vermont. Charlie gradually becomes restless as he hears the howling of neighbouring wolves. Robbie realises, with a heavy heart, that he must let Charlie go in order to be with his own kind. When, some months later, Charlie returns with a mate and family of cubs, it is clear that he recognises Robbie. While, longing to reach out and touch Charlie, Robbie does not; the wolf stands, meets his eyes and then lopes off with his family. Robbie's love for Charlie had not changed, but he respected his need to be wild and apart from humans.

Many of Morporgo's stories feature close relationships between the young and old, often serving to relieve the tense and occasionally dysfunctional and abusive relationships between parents and their children, especially fathers and sons, as featured in *Waiting for Anya* and *Why the Whales Came*, for example.

For a writer who found no joy in books until he came across Robert Louis Stevenson's *Treasure Island*, his prodigious creativity is impressive. He has published a steady flow of books from 1974, with as many as four publications each year and a remarkable *eight* in 2006. He has also written his own screenplays and libretti for opera. Morpurgo has won countless awards and was awarded an OBE in 2006 for services to literature. His stories have strong, fast-moving plots, which makes them attractive to film, stage and television directors. Five of his books have been made into films, including *When the Whales Came*, starring Paul Schofield and Helen Mirren. There have also been television and stage adaptations of his stories, including *Kensuke's Kingdom* and, more recently, *Private Peaceful*, which enjoyed two sell-out seasons at the Bristol Old Vic in 2005. *War Horse* was adapted for stage by Nick Stafford at the National Theatre in October 2007. The stage version is a remarkable feat of imaginative genius in which life-sized horse puppets are puppeteered in association with the Handspring Puppet Company. This highly acclaimed and enthusiastically reviewed stage version departs from the book in places, but the heart of the story and the way in which the horse 'narrates' the terrors of the Great War come across as powerfully and as poignantly as in the novel. In the same year, a concert of music and readings was given at the Royal Academy of Music based on the 'The Mozart Question', and in his Platform talk at the National Theatre, Morpurgo (2007a) announced that the film rights had been bought for *Kensuke's Kingdom* and *Private Peaceful*.

The stunning success of Morpurgo's work and the increasing media attention it is receiving have brought his stories to audiences of both children and adults. It is a remarkable fact that in a fast-moving digital age where tastes, fashion and image change on an almost weekly basis, Morpurgo's writing has delighted children from the mid-1970s into the first decade of the twenty-first century. What is the magic that he weaves? What are the sources of his ideas? What is it about his work that lights up the imagination of children, stage and film directors?

Some of these questions are addressed in a live telephone interview with Michael Morpurgo:

Telephone interview with Michael Morpurgo on 19 December 2007

Preamble: A few weeks prior to the following interview, I had sent Michael a copy of an article I had written on the relationship between the biographies and writing themes of Philip Pullman and those of Michael Morpurgo (Duncan, 2007). The conversation began with a response to the article:

MM You've set yourself a tough assignment with your book project. Which other authors feature in the book besides Philip Pullman and me?

DD Anthony Browne, Jacqueline Wilson, J.K. Rowling and the genre of comic books. I wanted to write a book on the teaching of children's literature which included contemporary best-selling children's book authors which most teachers and student teachers would have heard of and would know something about. I was also very keen to include graphic texts because they are such compelling and complex narratives – which is why I was keen to have a chapter on Anthony Browne's picture books and comic books.

MM I am pleased and interested to see that you have included comic books. In France, where I spend quite a bit of time, they are taken much more seriously than they are over here. French bookshops have a special category for them called *Bande Dessiné* (crudely translated as *drawn strip*). A cultural coldness has closed over teachers in England with respect to literature. One of the effects of the many changes to the National Curriculum has been the loss of stories which are read to children for pleasure and enjoyment. The current emphasis on breaking up texts for dissection, investigation and examination for verbs, adjectives and so on has reduced the opportunity and space for enjoyment. This will take some time to overcome.

DD I have recently been to see the breathtaking stage adaptation of *War Horse* at the National Theatre. I thought it was a magnificent and heart-stopping portrayal of your story – in fact, one of the most moving and compelling pieces of theatre I have ever seen. I was as enthralled by the life-size puppets of the horses, Joey and Topthorn, as I was by the total commitment of the puppeteers to portray the life and spirit of the horses. Did you share my enthusiasm for the production?

MM I thought the National Theatre did an extraordinary job. A stage performance of a book can be very disappointing, and I was unsure and rather nervous about what they would do with it. So I spoke to Philip Pullman, who had already had the experience of working with the National Theatre on the staging of *His Dark Materials*. 'The National Theatre is so good. You have to trust them, Michael,' he said. The first review performances were awful. To begin with, the play just didn't gel, but then it did. Once it gelled, it was stunning. I was delighted too that the directors didn't talk down to the audience. Terrible things happened in the First World War and they didn't shrink from showing some very traumatic scenes. What I didn't want was a view of the Germans as terrible people. The story isn't about who won the war but about the appalling tragedies which took place on both sides through the eyes of Joey, the horse. They succeeded in putting this across.

DD At the end of the play, I noticed, as did two of my friends who went to see it on different nights, that many of the adults around me were in tears, but not the children. They were captivated and enthralled but not crying. Can you explain the difference in the reactions of adults and children to the play?

MM I think adults feel what they and their relatives went through in this war, even if for many people the First World War is now a distant memory or an album of old photographs. Children just see it for what it is. They have no experience of this war. They just want to know what happens next. As you know, I love Robert Louis Stevenson. If I read it now I read it differently from the way I read it as a child. When I revisit now, it is with an adult's experience and a different understanding. I think something similar accounts for the differing reactions of adults and children to the play. The important thing is that the greatest children's literature stretches both children and adults.

DD   I am very pleased to hear that owing to overwhelming demand for seats, the National Theatre will be running a second showing of *War Horse* towards the end of 2008.

MM   Yes, and there will be a musical version of *War Horse* on Radio 2 on November 11th 2008. There will also be a festive musical adaptation of my retellings of Aesop's Fables on Radio 4 at 2.15 p.m. on Christmas Eve, 2007.

DD   You mentioned in your Platform talk at the National Theatre on October 26th, 2007, just before the performance of *War Horse*, that the film rights had been bought for *Kensuke's Kingdom* and *Private Peaceful*. Are you able to give any more details about these forthcoming films?

MM   Yes. Frank Cotterill Boyce is writing the screenplay for *Kensuke's Kingdom* and Simon Reade for *Private Peaceful*. Pat O'Connor will be directing *Private Peaceful* and the films should be on release at some point in 2009. In fact, the film crew is coming to Devon tomorrow to look at possible locations for *Private Peaceful*.

DD   In my chapter on your work, I have written a section on the role of women in your stories. They are seldom the central protagonists but they provide an important counterpoint to some of the impetuous, highly active, brave and resourceful boys in your stories. The women are often intelligent, quiet, attentive, tenacious and also very resourceful – like Allie in *Alone on a Wide Wide Sea*, Laura in *The Wreck of the Zanzibar*, Millie in *The Butterfly Lion* and Clemmie Jenkins in *Why the Whales Came*. How far have you drawn on the love and storytelling ability of your actor mother and the lifelong support of your wife, Clare, for your female characters?

MM   In the world I grew up in, men were the most important members of the family. But in many ways, my stepfather was [only] superficially dominant. My mother was really the central character in my life. The relationship between a mother and her child is unbelievably strong. My mother, a fine actor, suffered from feelings of very low self-worth. She played a secondary role in the running of the family. My stepfather was louder and stronger. But my mother had a subtlety and a way of dealing with pain which I admired. I think women are much better than men at dealing with pain. They stick at things and stay the course. My mother was named Kippe by my Belgian grandfather to mark the victory of the Belgian Army in retaking the hamlet of De Kippe in 1918. My mother often wept when she talked about the war, especially when she spoke about my Uncle Pieter, who was shot down in 1941, two years before I was born. Her pain taught me a great deal about emotions and how women deal with it. Towards the end of her life, she talked to me a lot more about herself and her feelings. I sometimes have moments of darkness but my wife, Clare, my soulmate, always sees the positive side in life. The ongoing work for the charity City Farms for Children is mainly done by her. She went to a Quaker school which taught her about the capacity we all have to enrich other people's lives. My daughter has also opened my eyes to the strength that women have, and the voice of Allie in *Alone on a Wide Wide Sea* is that of my granddaughter.

DD   In *Alone on a Wide Wide Sea*, the technical knowledge of sailing a 33-foot ocean yacht and the unpredictable behaviour of the sea suggests to me that you have a deep knowledge of the sea and sailing. Am I right?

MM Not really. I know a bit about the sea, but most of the story was based on detailed research. I got the email narration from my granddaughter, who emails us regularly. I learned about the immediacy of email language from her. I like endings which are hopeful. Some terrible things happen but life goes on.

DD The story in beautifully interrelated with Coleridge's 'Rime of the Ancient Mariner'. Which came first, the story or the poem?

MM I read about a story of two old Australian guys who wanted to sail around the world. I followed their journey with intense interest. These guys were fantastic sailors, and one night they saw what they thought was a moving light. It was the International Space Station. They had sat phone and internet technology on the yacht and they communicated with NASA. The astronauts were up there in space on their voyage and they were on theirs on the ocean below. I was inspired by these two ancient mariners and the fact that they were able to communicate to American astronauts somewhere above the planet. When they eventually docked in Falmouth at the end of their voyage, the American astronaut they had spoken to was waiting with his wife to greet them. The story is based on a real voyage. As for 'The Rime of the Ancient Mariner', I have grown up with this poem and it seemed to fit so naturally with the story. I wanted the boy (Allie's father), who was sent to Australia after the Second World War and so brutally treated by a God-fearing working farm owner, to have a positive ending to his life. I love stories which are circular.

Nine years ago, I met a lady in Australia who had set up a farm to show others how the first people who settled in the bush lived their lives. She was eccentric and dedicated to her purpose. She started adding to her project by rescuing marsupials from the pouches of injured kangaroos and wombats which had been run over by trucks. She eventually had a menagerie of rescued animals living on her farm, which she released into the wild once she felt they were strong enough to cope on their own.

The brutal treatment of British orphans who were shipped off to Australia for almost twenty years after the Second World War was one of the several strands to the story that eventually became *On a Wide Wide Sea*.

DD I think this relatively recent and quite lengthy book is a remarkably successful story which uses myths and poetry to make a story about voyage and self-discovery, a story of our times. You must have spent years on the research.

MM You can't write stories unless you have your heart, eyes and ears open. You also need to be living an interesting life. The culture of reading is not soaked into us. Stories have to be part of your world, and enjoyment of them must come first.

DD Finally, Michael, you have been writing books for some thirty-three years. There are numerous books reviews and website articles about your books, but I have had difficulty in tracking down any serious academic discussion of your work. In the last ten years or so a growing body of academic criticism and analysis has amassed on the various themes and issues associated with the writings of Philip Pullman and J.K. Rowling. I think your work should be part of this interest and debate. I would be interested in your comments on this point.

> **MM** My book sales have been a slow burn for me. The academic world is also not paying sufficient attention to writers like David Almond and other superb writers I could mention. I think *Singing for Mrs Pettigrew* is a really interesting book about the craft of writing [I agreed], but it contains lots of short stories, which the booksellers tell me don't sell well. Interestingly, the French academics have engaged more critically with my work than they have in this country. Recently my book sales have increased and I have been more lucky.

The rest of this chapter will be devoted to an examination of Morpurgo's selected works and, in particular, of the way in which the plots, ideas, characters and themes interrelate to make his stories live and breathe.

Themes and values

Most of the themes that pervade Morpurgo's writing can be traced to his life experiences from childhood onwards. One of these is endurance and resilience in the face of harsh social circumstances, as portrayed by the orphan Arthur Hobhouse, who is banished to Australia only to find he has to work in conditions of brutal captivity on a working farm. Less harsh, but just as terrifying and wretched, are the forlorn, bleak and unhappy experiences of young boys at boarding school. The execrable food, bullying and canings, so much a part of Morpurgo's school life, are lived out again in the characters of Michael in *The Butterfly Lion* and Toby Jenkins in *The War of Jenkins' Ear*. Another common motif in his books is fathers and sons living in tense and volatile relationships with each other. In *War Horse*, for example, the uneasy relationship between Albert and his father is tested to the limit in fierce and violent arguments about how Joey, the farm horse, should be treated. In *Why the Whales Came*, Daniel Pender confronts his abusive father head-on when the islanders come to claim the narwhal as theirs, believing its determined and desperate saviour, the 'Birdman', to be half-mad and a likely spy for the Germans in the First World War. Risking a public beating by his enraged father, Daniel defies him vehemently and implores him to listen to what the Birdman has to say. The motif appears again in *Waiting for Anya*, when Jo's father returns from a Nazi prison camp to find that the farm has been managed well in his absence. Traumatised by his brutal treatment in the camp, he feels useless and distant from his family. His brewing anger erupts when he believes that Jo has befriended the German soldiers billeted in the town, and Jo is knocked sideways as his father punches his face. A similar 'war' of difference is waged between Billy and his father in *The Wreck of the Zanzibar*, leading to Billy's escape from Bryher, one of the Scilly Isles, to try his luck on the open seas with the dubious and untrustworthy Joseph Hannibal. The distance between many of the fathers and sons (not, interestingly, between daughters and their fathers or mothers) may have its source in his own deeply ambivalent relationship with both his stepfather and his natural father. The boy protagonists in his stories often crave understanding and affection from their fathers, which when denied is sought elsewhere and often found in wise, kind-hearted grandfathers and old men who are eccentric or outcasts in some way. Morpurgo's writing is uncompromising in its portrayal of taut and troubled relationships, but often his stories allow the psychological space needed for the possibility of forgiveness and renewal.

A further interesting feature of Morpurgo's writing is that over the course of the story, readers are able to observe their protagonist developing from childhood to old age. This accords with his strongly held view that children are able to identify closely with older people. He believes that adults and children struggle with the same questions about the nature of why we are here. He never patronises children, and while he is concerned not to thrust tragedy and violence in their faces, he is convinced that adults and children have similar experiences about the perennially disturbing and dislocating emotions of suffering, isolation and loss (Travis, 2006).

In a different way, emotional, physical and mental endurance, sometimes of the most extreme kind, is a strong theme in his island and voyaging stories. In these tales, the protagonists have to find extraordinary courage and resilience in order to survive the ordeals that cruel and unpredictable seas can wreak upon even the most experienced and hardy sailors. In *Kensuke's Kingdom* and *Alone on a Wide Wide Sea*, the reader lives with these ocean explorers throughout their worst ordeals of survival against the odds. These two particular stories are given a heightened immediacy through the reporting devices of a ship's log and email accounts of their day-to-day experiences. These stories go further than a simple recounting of dangers and near-death encounters; they also concern equally interesting journeys of self-discovery. In this sense, they are deeply moral stories that yield considerable psychological insight about their characters and how they deal with both physical and emotional crises. Part of their appeal is that, in common with all good writing, they enable us to learn more about what it is that makes us human as well as extending our horizons of imagined experience.

Two central themes in Morpurgo's writing concern his preoccupation with war and the fragility of the natural world. Old men who live simply in harmony with nature are powerfully and movingly portrayed in *Kensuke's Kingdom* and *Why the Whales Came*. In the latter, it is the Birdman's passionate concern to save a pod of narwhals from fatally beaching themselves on the shores of Bryher at the time of the outbreak of the First World War, and in the former, it is Kensuke, an old Japanese man shipwrecked on a Pacific island at the end of the Second World War. His love and care of the endangered orang-utans matters so much to him that he chooses to spend the rest of his life protecting them rather than return to his homeland. A similar motif is present in *The Wreck of the Zanzibar* when a young girl, rather than the usual boy protagonist, does all she can to save a stranded leatherback turtle from swiftly gathering gulls and their lacerating beaks. However, it is her frail grandmother who saves the turtle from almost certain death by finding blue jellyfish, the only food that will provide the weakened turtle with enough strength to find its way back to the relative safety of the sea.

With the deep social unease that exists today about the safety of children, many parents are too afraid to allow their children the freedom to explore the countryside and open spaces that so many generations of children before them had. Despite this socially imposed curfew and the lack of opportunities to explore wildlife and observe the ways of animals for themselves, many of them are, nonetheless, profoundly concerned about the increasing threat to endangered animal species caused by global warming, profligate hunting, destruction of natural habitats and climate change. Morpurgo's stories speak to children with an informed authority about ecological concerns. They need to read about strong, morally committed people who are prepared to take risks to protect and save animals from harm and potential extinction. Morpurgo's writing on this theme hits a vital nerve for many children. His stories provide them with the hope that if it is possible for characters in imagined contexts to perform brave and courageous acts, then they too might be similarly inspired. As Morpurgo himself said in an interview with Simon Hodgson,

What I have discovered over my time as both a parent and a teacher was how important this link is to the natural world we come from and how separate we seem to have become from it; an extraordinary cut off between ourselves and what it is that nourishes us and gives us our life.

(Morpurgo cited in Hodgson, 2006: 1)

A recurring theme in Morpurgo's books is the two world wars. War is the setting for the main storyline in several of his books, and where it is not, it is often a backdrop. The First World War is the context for Millie and Bertie's story about the white lion in *Butterfly Lion*; in *War Horse*, its terrors are seen through the eyes of a courageous and magnificent red bay horse called Joey; and in *Private Peaceful*, the love of Charlie for his injured younger brother, Tommo, prompts him to disobey a vindictive sergeant's command to leave him, even though he knows that his defiance may cost him his life. In *Why the Whales Came*, the First World War is the background to the story. In *Kensuke's Kingdom*, *Waiting for Anya*, *The Amazing Story of Adolphus Tips* and 'The Mozart Question', the stories are centred on the Second World War. These include a personal account of one man's experience of Hiroshima in *Kensuke's Kingdom*. *Waiting for Anya* depicts life in a rural village in occupied France where people risked their lives to help Jewish children escape over the border into Spain. *The Amazing Story of Adolphus Tips* recounts the effects on the villagers of Slapton Sands, Devon, when told they have to evacuate their homes so that Allied American troops could prepare for a seaborne attack on northern France prior to the D-Day landings. 'The Mozart Question' is a story of indescribable beauty and unbearable pain that features the appalling experience of a group of Jewish musicians who are forced to play Mozart to calm the thousands of Jewish families who are led from the cattle trucks to their deaths in the gas chambers. The darkness and light of this harrowing story are superbly captured by Michael Foreman's illustrations in the latest edition (the 2007 reissue).

Why is war such a predominant theme in Morpurgo's books? The source, as is the case with so many of his stories, is to be found in his personal life history. In an interview with Spiers (2006), he tells her that war is very much a part of him. He was born in 1943, just before the war ended. Some of his earliest memories were of what the war had done to London. He played on bomb-sites and wanted to understand what had happened to the people who had once lived in the wrecked shells of buildings that had once been family homes. He tells Spiers, 'There was this loss and this grief that they were living through. And I suppose these things never leave you. . . . War really gets under the skin, and so I think it's important to write about it' (ibid.: 1). One such searing memory was a picture of his young and handsome Uncle Peter looking out at him from a silver-framed photograph on the mantelshelf of his grandparents' home. He was killed when his bomber crashed, after he had ensured that his fellow soldiers had parachuted to safety. Morpugo has been exploring both world wars ever since.

The other, equally interesting question is why children reading his books in the twenty-first century, who have no vicarious experiences of either world war, find his unsparing details about their atrocities and devastation so compelling. Let us examine one of Morpurgo's war stories, *War Horse*, in order to find some possible answers.

War Horse

Morpurgo often refers to this book as being his first accomplished and successful piece of writing. It grew out of several long conversations with octogenarian First World War veterans over pints of beer in a pub in his home village of Iddesleigh. Two things touched him deeply. One was the recounting of an old man who had served in the Devon Yeomanry and who, after showing him his trenching tool, told him that 'I was there with the 'orses. I used to feed the 'orses and talk to them' (2007a). The other was of another veteran telling him with tears in his eyes that 'We were so frightened that we did not dare to talk to each other about being frightened' (ibid.). Finding a picture in the *London Illustrated* of horses charging into barbed wire and research in the Imperial War Museum which revealed that over 10 million soldiers and over 2 million horses (an imprecise and possibly conservative figure) were killed in the First World War all combined to make him very angry and moved him to write *War Horse*.

Characteristic features of Morpurgo's plots are their simplicity, an avoidance of long descriptions, and a fast-moving storyline that begins in the very first lines. At the start we are told of a dusty painting of a horse in a village hall, possibly the one in Iddesleigh, and immediately the reader not only has a clear picture of what Joey looked like but learns that there was something very special and extraordinary about him:

> He stands, a splendid red bay with a remarkable white cross emblazoned on his forehead and with four perfectly matched white socks. He looks wistfully out of the picture, his ears pricked forward, his head turned as if he has just noticed us standing there. . . . Some in the village, only a very few now and fewer as each year goes by, remember Joey as he was. His story is written so that neither he nor those who knew him, nor the war they lived and died in, will be forgotten.
>
> (Morpurgo, 1982: 1–2)

The reference to this picture, painted in 1914, draws us into the picture to look Joey in the eye. We long to know more about him. A page further on and we hear, in Joey's voice, of his first terrifying experience as a young colt being sold off at an auction to Albert Narracott's inebriated father. Joey is dragged off with a rope round his neck, screaming for his mother, from whom he has been separated. He is sweating with fear as he is led roughly into a stable at the farm. Ted Narracott beats him with a stick as he slams the door shut, and Joey is left trembling in its solitary darkness. Albert loves the horse the minute he sees him, and calms him by stroking and talking to him. When Albert leaves the stable, Joey says, 'I knew then that I had found a friend for life, that there was an instinctive and immediate bond of trust and affection between us' (Morpurgo, 1982: 10). This is a familiar motif in many of Morpurgo's stories, but in *War Horse* it is all the more poignant because Joey shows such courage and skill during the horrific ordeals of exploding shells and flying shrapnel on the front line. Initially, the horse causes increasing conflict between Albert and his father, who threatens to shoot or sell Joey unless Albert can train him to plough. Albert trains him well, and the horse responds to his firm kindness. But because of shortage of money, Ted Narracott sells Joey to the army. He is bought by a Captain Nicholls, who admires him and promises to look after him. Captain Nicholls is a man with a good heart who knows how to handle a horse, and Joey quickly learns to trust him.

Much of the rest of the story follows Joey's encounters with the terrors of war and Albert's desperate search for his beloved friend. Tragically, Captain Nicholls is killed at an early point in the war, and Joey finds comfort in his new friend, Topthorn, a majestic black stallion, the only horse who can outrun him. A sickening climax is reached when our two hero horses are led, with hundreds of others, at full gallop towards the barbed wire separating the English from the German front line. In eloquent, direct and graphic prose, Morpurgo takes us into the heart of the horror:

The bedlam of battle had begun. All around me men cried and fell to the ground, and horses reared and screamed in an agony of fear and pain. The ground erupted on either side of me, throwing horses and their riders clear into the air. The shells whined and roared overhead and every explosion seemed like an earthquake to us. But the squadron galloped on inexorably through it all towards the wire at the top of the hill, and I went with them.

(ibid.: 65)

Joey and Topthorn survive, unlike many of their fellow creatures, who are so badly mangled in the barbed wire that they have to be shot. Ironically, it is their very stamina and agility that bring them into enemy territory so that both horses become the property of the Germans. Luckily, the German soldier charged with their care admires their beauty and lavishes them with affection.

Choosing to narrate the entire story through Joey's experience means that partisan concerns about which side wins the war are not the point. Horses do not care whether their riders are German or English; what matters is that they are respected and well looked after. Webb makes the point well when she points out that behind the grey and khaki uniforms 'are men who understand animals; each extends a sympathy and humanity to the trapped and suffering animal. Men and horse [are] equally imprisoned by circumstances not of their making and beyond their control' (2005: 3). In this story, Joey and Topthorn are the heroes in a war where the cavalry was utterly useless against an armoury of gunfire and tanks. Millions of horses died unnecessarily, as did their riders. Even more tragic was that at the end of the war, the army decided that these faithful horses would cost too much to be shipped back to England. The brutal fact is that thousands were sold off to French butchers, and without the intervention and humanity of British soldiers, the fierce determination of Albert and the compassion of an old French farmer, the indomitable Joey might well have suffered the same fate.

Children are captivated by *War Horse* and Morpurgo's other war stories because the action is fast, the plot well crafted and the story beautifully written. Most importantly, *War Horse* deals with the enduring and potent themes of the agony of loss alongside love, compassion and humanity. Central to many of these stories is the protagonist's abiding love for an animal. In *Waiting for Anya*, it is a bear cub; in *The Amazing Story of Adolphus Tips*, it is a much-loved cat; in *The Butterfly Lion*, it is a rare white lion; and in *Kensuke's Kingdom* it is the orang-utangs, who come to trust Kensuke as their protector. The story of *War Horse* has inspired leading stage directors to mount one of their most ambitious projects of ensemble puppeteering, with the demand for seats being so overwhelming that a return season has been scheduled for autumn 2008.

The role of women in Morpurgo's stories

While most of Morpurgo's protagonists are young males, women occupy an important place in his narratives, sometimes taking the lead at crucial moments. They are often presented as strong, resourceful and intelligent. They are shrewd and attentive listeners who provide a balancing counterpoint to male dominance and, at times, reckless irresponsibility. For example, in *Why the Whales Came* it is Clemmie Jenkins, Gracie's mother, who confronts the crowd of islanders waiting to bludgeon the stranded narwhal to death. She berates Tim Pender for being a bully and a coward, telling him that he has allowed years of rumour to influence his opinion of the Birdman. She silences the crowd by telling them of the Birdman's unobtrusive kindness to her, and turns their impending violence into constructive action. The narwhal is saved and the curse on the island of Samson resulting from of a previous cull of narwhals is lifted. In *The Wreck of the Zanzibar*, Laura saves the day by taking her injured father's place on the gig to save the shipwrecked sailors. With unflinching courage she proves her skill as a powerful oarswoman in the teeth of a ferocious Atlantic storm. All the sailors are rescued, as are her brother and the cattle that the *Zanzibar* brought with it. Bryher becomes a thriving island once more and its people are saved from starvation.

Storytelling magic, bravery and belief in the value and power of books are invested in the librarian in 'I Believe in Unicorns' (Morpurgo, 2006a). Clever, strong and indomitable women are to be found in Michael's seafaring mother in *Kensuke's Kingdom* and the veterinarian mother in *Dear Olly* (Morpurgo, 2000).

Perhaps the strongest female role of all is the fearless and determined Allie, who helps her father build the bright yellow *Kitty Four*. After her father's untimely death, she sails it single-handed across the oceans in search of her father's long-lost sister, Kitty. Despite raging seas, a broken finger and the loss of the beloved albatross that had sailed with her throughout her voyage and in whom she believed her father's spirit has come to rest, she finally makes it to England, where she is reunited with her family and the elusive Aunt Kitty. Her fortitude, optimism and buoyant spirit make her perhaps one of Morpurgo's finest female characters. What is remarkable about this story is that interwoven as an intertextual refrain is Coleridge's 'Rime of the Ancient Mariner'. The Mariner's guilt as a result of shooting an albatross is mirrored in the guilt that Allie experiences when she awakes one day to find that hers has become strangled in the fishing line she had inadvertently left over the side of the boat. Her remorse is all the greater because she believes that with the death of her albatross companion she has also lost her father's much-needed presence. However, she learns through her suffering and torment to come to terms with tragedy and to hold steadfast to her purpose and quest. On this voyage, she learns as much about herself as she does about the unpredictable rhythm and temperament of the sea.

In these women characters, there may be resonances of the role that Morpurgo's mother played in his life and that of his wife, Clare, whose steadfast, loving strength as guide, critical friend and inspiration has mattered so greatly (Duncan, 2007).

The magic that Morpurgo weaves in his stories has several sources, none of which entirely explains the potency and power of his storytelling. Three things stand out. The first is the immense care he takes to bring his characters to life. He spends weeks and sometimes years thinking himself into their lives, so that by the time he is ready to write, they are an organic part of the embryonic story. He endows them with the kind of truth and credibility that make them live in the mind long after the book has been closed. Second, he researches his material assiduously, often travelling abroad to spend time in archives, record offices and museums to seek out the finer points of detail that make his stories so compelling and vivid. Third, it is strongly evident from the many stories he writes about the sea, sailing and horses that he has an immense and intimate knowledge of each of them. However, the mysterious alchemy that makes his stories so magical, tightly interwoven and coherent is inherently mercurial. As Morpurgo astutely writes, 'The secret once revealed, may spoil forever the trick, may lobotomise the spell. We may, by robbing the story of its essential mystery, invalidate it quite and its creator with it' (1993a: 235).

Chapter 2

Teaching Anthony Browne

One of the most important outcomes of this unit of work or series of lessons is that teachers and children engage with the warmth, humanity and compassion of Anthony Browne's work. The objectives and learning outcomes used for the workshop are given at the end of the section on teaching activities. The trial workshop took place with a Year 4 class, but could just as easily be used with Year 3, 5 or 6 children, although the demands and activities for older pupils would need to be more complex and challenging. You can pick and choose from these objectives to plan single lessons or use them all to plan a coherent unit of work. Towards the end of Part 1 is a *diary* section that gives selected extracts from the children and teachers' responses to the workshop, including some of my own reflections. This is followed by some examples of work done by the children during the workshop, the teaching resources needed for the activities, and some further useful sources of information. The three books chosen for the teaching activities are *Gorilla*, *My Dad* and *My Mum*.

Preparing the children for the lesson(s) or unit of work

It would help the children begin to explore some of the distinctive characteristics of Anthony Browne's work if, a week or so before you begin the lesson(s) or unit of work, there was a display of some of his books in an 'Author of the Week' focus, excluding the books detailed in the list of resources (p. 69).

Introduction

Ask the children about their reactions to the Anthony Browne books they have looked at in the display. For example:

◇ Why did they find the story interesting? Give at least two reasons. Discuss in pairs first. Share some responses with the whole class.

◇   Tell their partners why you enjoyed the story. Give three reasons. Share one or two different sets of reasons with the whole class.

◇   What are the particular things they have noticed about his books?

◇   Which books of his have they read and what did they like about them?

◇   What have they noticed about the colours and characters in his books?

◇   What makes his books different from other picture books they have seen?

◇   What would help them to understand and appreciate Anthony Browne's books more?

Pull together and summarise some of the main characteristics of his work that they have identified verbally or recorded on a whiteboard or flip chart. Introduce the children to Browne's main interests and influences: his fascination with gorillas and his love of sport (especially rugby) and art, for example. His love of art is central to his work, and many well-known paintings feature in his pictures as another connecting narrative. For a very informed and interesting account of what motivated Browne to write *My Dad* and *Gorilla*, it is worth reading the *Guardian* interview of Anthony Browne by Julie Eccleshare on 21 July 2000 (see p. 69).

When focusing on specific pictures for analysis in *Gorilla* and *My Dad*, you need to adopt a questioning strategy that will help children begin to develop an ability to 'read' visual narratives. I have exemplified a detailed set of questions for two pictures in *Gorilla* to help teachers achieve this objective. However, you may choose to ignore these and frame your own questions. The suggested questions do not need to be followed slavishly, because of the need for sufficient flexibility and scope for children to be able to state what interests and intrigues them about the pictures. I was surprised and sometimes disarmed by the children's responses to the workshop, which often revealed features, and even absences, in the picture narratives which had not occurred to me. It is therefore very important that the interactions between you and the children give space for their ingenuity and perspective. The following model of questioning is designed to prompt and encourage children to move from lower-order to higher-order thinking and talking. The same broad model can be adopted for the other pictures selected for focus:

A Model for questioning

1   Broad questions on whole-picture impressions (e.g. What is happening here?)
2   Predominant features of colour and tone (see p. 68)
3   The use of colour and its relationship to mood and atmosphere
4   The characters on the page
5   The expressions on their faces and relationship to tone and mood
6   Space and positioning of the protagonists

7 Size of picture, single-page or double-page spread and its significance to the narrative
8 Other details worthy of note or interest (e.g. features of cohesion and intertextuality; see p. 68)
9 Inferring meaning from the visual text
10 The relationship of elements within the page to the page as a whole
11 The relationship of the focus page to other pictures within the book and other books by the same author

Before reading *Gorilla*, seat each child with a partner he or she is happy to work with. Talking in pairs before sharing discussion points with a larger group or the whole class is an important learning strategy for achieving exploratory discussion and focused thinking from the maximum number of children.

Reading *Gorilla*

Read *Gorilla* as a story, showing the pictures as you read it. Ask the children to think about the things that interest or puzzle them as they listen to the story. Provide them with paper or notebooks or mini-whiteboards to make brief notes as they listen. This could be just one or two words to remind them about what to say or what questions to ask after the story has been read. The children's observations and verbal interactions with you and with each other are vital to the quality of their engagement with the picture narrative. Ask the children to talk to each other in their working pairs about the things that interested or puzzled them. Share some of the pair responses with the whole class and deal with the comments and queries raised.

Focusing on selected pictures

Now that the children know the structure of the story, it is important that you move up a gear and insist on deeper, more perceptive thinking and responses. Tell them that you want them to be detectives and to search for clues in the pictures in order to find out more about what Anthony Browne is communicating to his readers through his use of colour, mood, atmosphere, expressions on the characters' faces and how they are positioned in the picture frame.

Before you begin to talk about the pictures, it is important that children have ready access to the pictures you are focusing upon in book form, as enlarged colour photocopies or good-quality reproductions on the interactive whiteboard.

◇ Show children the picture of Hannah and her father eating breakfast (see Figure 2.1).

The following questions are in no way exhaustive; rather, they are a guide to the kinds of questions that will prompt children to strive for higher-order thinking and discussion. I found it essential to give the children time to respond, and it helped the children to begin to articulate their thoughts by starting with paired discussion. If the children are reasonably confident about talking in front of the class, move to whole class discussion halfway through the following questions:

Figure 2.1 Illustration from *Gorilla* by Anthony Browne.

Reproduced by permission of Walker Books Ltd.

◇   What do they notice about the colours used in the picture?

◇   Why do they think the author has chosen these particular colours and what kind of mood is suggested by them?

◇   Who is dominant in the picture? Whose face can they see, or not see?

◇   What kind of expression is on the father's face?

◇   What might this tell them about the father?

◇   What other details are in the picture and what do they tell them about their relationship to the characters?

◇   What do they notice about the way space is used (for example, bare, uncluttered surfaces and the distance between Hannah and her father across the table)?

◇   Why do they think the kitchen tiles are black and white on one side and blue and white on the other?

◇   Is there anything else they notice about the blue and white floor tiles?

◇   Why do they think that Anthony Browne added this feature?

◇   What else helps to communicate the mood of the picture?

◇   What does the picture tell them about Hannah and what she might be thinking?

◇   What is the significance of the warmer-looking wood of Hannah's chair and the colour of the jumper she is wearing compared with the cold, clinical appearance of the rest of the picture?

◇   What is Anthony Browne trying to tell them about Hannah and her father which is not part of the written text?

◇   Can they see anything interesting about the cereal box?

◇   Why does a gorilla make an appearance on this page?

Come back to this last point later on when you help children begin to develop their understanding of the term 'visual cohesion' (see p. 68).

◇   Now compare Figure 2.1 with Figure 2.2. It will help to make the comparisons easier for the children to observe if they can see both pictures side by side so that they are in relation to each other.

◇   What do they notice about the difference in colours between this and the previous picture of Hannah and her father?

◇   What is the difference in the mood, tone and atmosphere in this picture and how is it conveyed?

◇   How does the use of space compare with the previous picture? What, for example, is the difference in the distance between the gorilla and Hannah?

◇   What is the difference in the way that Anthony Browne has drawn the tables?

Figure 2.2 Illustration from *Gorilla* by Anthony Browne.

Reproduced by permission of Walker Books Ltd.

◇   How does the expression on the gorilla's face compare with her father's and what
     part of the face in both pictures tells them most about the character's mood?

◇   As in the previous picture, they can still only see the back of Hannah's head, so
     what kind of expression might she have in this picture? If they think it is different,
     why is that the case?

I suggest that you frame your questions for the rest of the pictures using the model for questioning outlined on pp. 45–46. I hope that in so doing you too will be surprised and intrigued
by the many layers of meaning embedded in Anthony Browne's pictures. In each of the following
picture narratives I will highlight features of particular interest that are worthy of discussion
and further exploration.

◇ Move now to the picture of Hannah sitting on the floor in the corner of an empty room
   watching television.

Figure 2.3 Illustration from *Gorilla* by Anthony Browne.

Reproduced by permission of Walker Books Ltd.

This is a very revealing picture of Hannah's perspective and contains a number of interesting features. Browne often allows for a range of 'readings' of his picture narratives so the children may rightly have a variety of viewpoints in response to it. The location of Hannah at the corner of an empty room marooned in a vast space of bare floorboards and a large expanse of wall on either side of her communicates a particular view of Hannah and how she is feeling. The children might consider *why* Browne has positioned her in this way and why there is a map of Africa on the wall. There is a cohesive link here with the first picture in the book which the children can be prompted to discover. Much of both walls is in shadow, with one bright arc of light surrounding Hannah, and there is a difference in the patterning of the wallpaper on the left wall. The visual richness in this picture offers considerable potential for higher-order questioning.

◇   Compare the picture of Hannah and her father at work in his study with that of him wishing Hannah a happy birthday and inviting her out to the zoo.

◇   What do they notice about the differences in the tone, mood and use of space in these pictures?

In Figure 2.4, note the heavy curtains and sombre tones of the father's study in contrast to the colours Hannah is wearing. The viewer can see only the backs of the two protagonists. The pictures on the desk and wall are significant in terms of what they are communicating about the father and to Hannah. In Figure 2.5 the colours are in stark contrast to the previous picture. There are also several cohesive elements within it – for example, the dancing gorillas on the birthday cake, which also appear in previous pictures. The child's picture on the wall is also significant and worth discussing in terms of the deeper understanding it offers of Hannah's view of the world.

Figure 2.4 Illustration from *Gorilla* by Anthony Browne.

Reproduced by permission of Walker Books Ltd.

Art and surrealism in *Gorilla* and *My Dad*

Anthony Browne is a remarkably gifted artist whose richly subversive, witty and poignant pictures display the human condition in its many forms. Before you introduce the children to

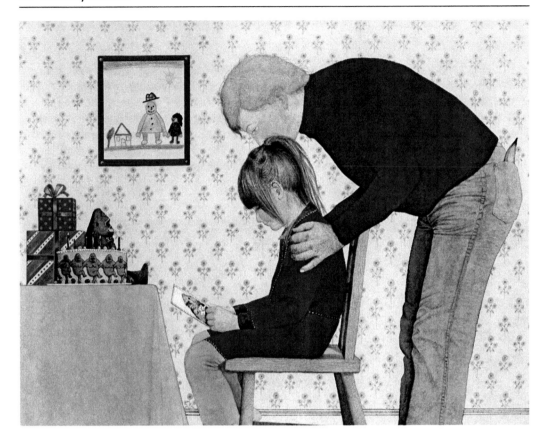

Figure 2.5 Illustration from *Gorilla* by Anthony Browne.

Reproduced by permission of Walker Books Ltd.

some of the influences he draws upon in his illustrations, it would be useful to read selections from some of the websites listed at the end of Part 1 of this chapter, which discuss his love of art and his interest in surrealism in particular (see p. 69).

René Magritte (see p. 68) is one of Anthony Browne's favourite surrealist painters, and it is Magritte's version of surrealism that is focused upon in this chapter. Two striking examples of Browne's use of surrealism are to be found in his books *Voices in the Park* and *Willy the Dreamer*. In the latter, children will love the way bananas become boat sails, cloaks, cushions and ballet shoes.

◇ Show the children some selected pages from these books in order to illustrate Magritte's influence on his work.

There are elements of surrealism in *Gorilla*, as in the emerald-green dancing sequence on p. 24, for example. There are also intertextual references to works of art, as instanced in *Whistler's Mother* on p. 12 and Leonardo da Vinci's *Mona Lisa* on p. 7 – both, of course, portrayed as gorillas!

◇   Show children the pictures by René Magritte suggested in the resource list at the end of the chapter, giving them time to talk to each other about what they find interesting and strange in his pictures.

◇   Share some of their responses.

Reading *My Dad*

My Dad is a much simpler text than *Gorilla*, but, because it is based on Browne's own father, it is profoundly moving. The children need to know what prompted Browne to write the book so many years after his father's death. Browne's starting point was the discovery of his father's old dressing gown, which smelt like his father and reminded Browne of how his father was as a man and a parent.

◇   Read it with the children in the same way as *Gorilla*, showing them the pictures as you do so. Ask them to continue being detectives, this time looking for examples of Magritte's influence.

◇   Ask the children to talk together in pairs about what they have observed in the book which reminds them of Magritte's pictures.

◇   Did they notice examples of visual cohesion in the book?

◇   Ask the children to give you some examples of what they noticed.

The colours in the dressing gown are one example, but there are other, more subtle examples within the individual pictures.

Focusing on selected pictures

◇   Look closely at the picture of the bad wolf slinking out of the front door with his tail literally between his legs.

The children will see for themselves the reference to the folk tale of Little Red Riding Hood. References to folk tales, fairy tales and nursery rhymes are a strong and characteristic feature of Anthony Browne's work. Another example of visual and literary intertextuality can be found in the picture of Dad jumping over the moon. There are further instances of recurring motifs (see p. 68), surrealist and intertextual features in the pictures of Dad on a tightrope, eating like a horse and being fantastic at football (see Figures 2.6–2.8). Questions that enable children to

Figure 2.6 Illustration from *My Dad* by Anthony Browne, published by Doubleday.

My dad can eat like a horse,

Figure 2.7 Illustration from *My Dad* by Anthony Browne, published by Doubleday.

Reprinted by permission of The Random House Group Ltd.

He's fantastic at football,

Figure 2.8 Illustration from *My Dad* by Anthony Browne, published by Doubleday.

Reprinted by permission of The Random House Group Ltd.

identify and comment on these visual narrative features will help them to understand these terms and apply them in their responses. It is important to encourage children to try to use these terms accurately, using visual evidence to justify their points.

Motifs and symbols

Bananas, gorillas, hats and clouds are frequently used motifs in Anthony Browne's work. They are also another form of cohesive device serving to unify the book as a whole. The sun and Dad's dressing gown are motifs that repeat in different forms throughout the book. The sun motif also represents the mood of happiness and the sunny disposition of Browne's father's personality. The motif, then, is also a *symbol* (see p. 68), in so far as it stands for or represents something else beyond the object. Explain the word *motif* and ask the children to find an example of one. Prompt the children to notice how the sun motif changes throughout the book, appearing in several different guises. There are other examples of Magritte's influence in the book which the children can be encouraged to find for themselves in a paired activity.

Drawing and writing activities

◇ Make a four- to six-page picture book based on *My Dad* or *My Mum*.

Teachers will need to decide how many pages of illustrations children will be able to manage and sustain, depending on their age, ability and interest levels. One of Anthony Browne's latest books is based on his brother, Michael, and is entitled *My Brother*. Some children may prefer to make their picture book on their brother or sister rather than on one of their parents. Teachers will be aware of the need to give careful thought as to how best to approach this activity with those children who have separated parents, whose parents may have died, or who live with carers other than parents. A picture book on a brother or a sister may be a useful alternative in these cases.

◇ Spend a few minutes showing the children Anthony Browne's book *My Mum* and take them through the pictures and the text, avoiding the detailed analyses of the previous two books.

The heart motif is obvious in the book even though it appears in various guises.

◇ Ask the children to talk in pairs about whether their picture book will be based on their mother, father, brother or sister.

Some children may need some support in deciding who their book will be based on.

The first picture

◇   What is your first picture going to show your Mum, Dad, brother or sister doing?

◇   Return to the first pictures of *My Dad*, *My Mum* and *My Brother*.

◇   Look closely at the clothes the various characters are wearing, what they are doing and what the motif is.

◇   Talk together in your pairs about the details your first picture is going to show.

Share one or two ideas in order to help those children who may be struggling with their initial ideas.

◇   What clothes would they be normally be wearing?

◇   What motif might you have on your first page?

◇   Which room will your first page be focused upon: the kitchen, bedroom, dining room, lounge – or perhaps the garden or garage?

◇   Which part of the room will be the most important – a chair, table, settee, floor, desk, window or door?

Share one two of their embryonic ideas and pull together key features of interest.

The first page of a potential picture book has already been modelled by three of Anthony Browne's books. It would help too if you told the children who *your* character would be and what would be included in the first page, including the motif. My example was of my father painting a picture of a bear. He is very good at painting with water colours and likes painting bears, so a bear was my motif.

◇   Give out the photocopied sheets with the first line on the bottom of the page which has been taken directly from Browne's *My Dad*: 'He's all right, my dad.' And from *My Mum*: 'She's nice, my mum.'
◇   Tell the children that they can alter the line at the bottom of the page if they wish. If some children wish to base their picture book on their sister or brother, they can make up their own line or use the one at the beginning of *My Brother*.

Encourage the children to fill the page with their first drawing (from just below the top of the page until roughly 2 centimetres from above the printed sentence) and to keep it simple and clear. It may help the children to have access to the picture books focused on so far.

Children will need at least 20 minutes for this activity. Give them time to work out their ideas and to discuss their ideas in progress with you and any other adult who is available in the classroom.

◇ At the end of this time slot, ask three or four children to volunteer to show their pictures and explain to the rest of the class what is in their picture and why they have chosen their particular motif.

Storyboard activity

The aim of this activity is to get the children to sketch out in simple detail what is going to be included in their next three pictures. You will need to explain to the children what the purpose of a storyboard is (see p. 60). The children have already completed their first picture, so the three storyboard frames are numbered 2–4 (see Figure 2.9).

◇ Tell the children that it is important not to use too much detail in each frame. The basic outline of what their father, mother, sister or brother is doing in each of the three pictures is all that is required.
◇ To keep things simple, it is helpful to use matchstick people to represent their characters.

However, unless the children have done matchstick men before, you will need to show them how to do this successfully. Either do a simple one yourself to model the idea or show them an enlarged copy of Figure 2.10.

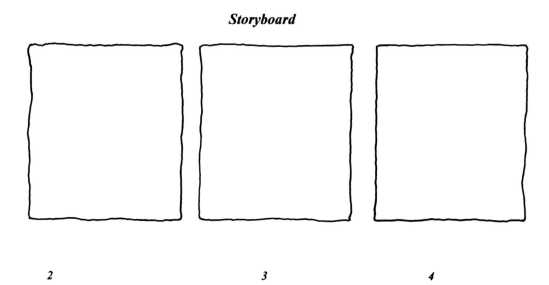

Storyboard

2   3   4

Figure 2.9 Storyboard frames.

Storyboard

My Dad is a brilliant painter.   He loves music and plays the   But he's like a bear with a
                                       piano fantastically.   sore head when he has to cook!

2   3   4

Figure 2.10 Example of completed storyboard frames.

◇ Point out that the matchstick 'Dad' is represented doing a different action in each of the three frames.

◇ Only essential detail is needed for the action with a clear picture of the context. For example, in Figure 2.10 it is the easel, the piano and the oven.

The motif in the three pictures is clearly the bear, but in the third one it appears in the text rather than in the picture. It is not essential for the motif to appear on every page.

◇ In your pairs, tell each other what might be in your next two pages. Help each other with ideas.

◇ Think about what sentence you will write under each picture.

Refer them to Figure 2.10 for an example of what the sentences might include.

◇ Show them once more how Anthony Browne does this in *My Dad* with one sentence for each page, sometimes at the top and sometimes at the bottom of the page.

◇ It will save time to have a photocopied A4 page (landscape style) with three blank frames in which they can draw their pictures and write their sentences, as in Figure 2.9.

◇ Allow children 20–30 minutes for this activity.

◇ Share some of the children's storyboards, picking out the strengths of those storyboards that are more successful in terms of simplicity and clear sequences of picture and text narratives.

◇　Give children time to return to their storyboards in order to improve upon them where this is necessary.

You can decide to finish the sequence of lessons/unit of work at this point or develop it into an art and English activity by getting the children to turn their storyboard into three large, detailed colour pictures so that they complete a short picture book comprising four pages. It could also be developed into a longer picture book which the children can publish as books, complete with covers, story blurb and author details, for other classes of children to share. Alternatively, the finished products can be published on the school's intranet or more widely onto an inter-school website.

Due regard needs to be taken with material of a sensitive nature if it is being published on a school website.

Objectives and learning outcomes

Lesson/series of lessons/unit of work objectives

1　To deepen the children's interest and understanding of picture narratives through a detailed focus on two selected books by Anthony Browne: *Gorilla* and *My Dad*.
2　To help the children begin to develop and apply the ability to 'read' colour, mood, pattern, space, meaning and inference by focusing on selected pictures from *Gorilla* and *My Dad*.
3　To provide opportunities for the children to derive pleasure, enjoyment and intellectual challenge by treating Anthony Browne's picture narratives as 'puzzles' in order to make demands upon them to look beyond the surface and probe for deeper meaning.
4　To introduce children to the work of René Magritte and its influence on Anthony Browne's work.
5　To introduce children to the concepts of *surreal, surrealism, symbol and motif, visual cohesion* and *intertextuality*.
6　To apply their understanding of the concepts introduced in the above objectives through:
　　–　thinking and talking activities;
　　–　practice in the reading of picture narratives;
　　–　drawing and writing activities;
　　–　the creation of a storyboard based on Anthony Browne's *My Dad* and *My Mum*;
　　–　the creation of their own picture book using selected books by Anthony Browne as models.

Learning outcomes

By the end of the lesson/series of lessons/unit of work, the children will be able to:

1　listen, think and discuss in pairs, groups and the whole class their reactions and responses to *Gorilla* and *My Dad*;
2　listen, think and discuss their reactions and responses to the work of René Magritte and his influence on the work of Anthony Browne;
3　sustain a developing ability to probe for layers of meaning within and between selected picture narratives;

4 demonstrate a beginning understanding of the concepts of colour in relation to mood, atmosphere and tone and the meanings they convey;

5 demonstrate a beginning understanding of the concepts of space, visual cohesion, motif, intertextuality, surreal, surrealism and symbol;

6 use and apply visual narrative terminology with greater accuracy and understanding;

7 use and apply the above concepts through the activities of thinking, talking, listening and discussion, showing increasing evidence of higher-order thinking and talking;

8 apply the above concepts by making their own storyboard of a picture narrative and a picture book of their own;

9 read a wider range of Anthony Browne's books with deeper appreciation, enjoyment and insight.

Diary

The children in the Year 4 class that took part in the workshop were described by their teacher as unresponsive and unforthcoming in discussion activities, and she was not confident that they would be especially interactive.

When asked about what they had noticed about the classroom display of a selection of Anthony Browne's books which the teacher had used as an author focus for two weeks or so, the children gave very generalised responses: for example, 'He paints very bright pictures' and 'There are more pictures than words in his books.' Hardly any children appeared to have picked up on his fascination with gorillas and chimpanzees, or his depiction of children as sad, bored or frightened.

I told the children that I wanted them to understand more about Anthony Browne's books and that I was going to read them *Gorilla* and *My Dad*. I wanted them to see the pictures as puzzles because not all the meanings were immediately obvious, so they would have to search for them like detectives. They warmed to this idea and listened intently to *Gorilla*. At the end of the story I asked them to discuss in pairs what they had found strange and interesting about the book. They liked the fact that Hannah loved gorillas, but found her father's indifference to Hannah's need for his company difficult to understand.

When the children were asked to focus on the difference between the first two pictures in *Gorilla* (Figures 2.1 and 2.2), they initially said things like 'The gorilla looks happy and the Dad looks sad.' When pressed to think more deeply about how Browne communicated mood through colours, use of space and positioning of the characters in the picture, the children responded with comments like 'The reds in the picture of Hannah and the gorilla make you feel that it's a happy picture.' One child said, 'You can't see Hannah's face but you guess she's happy because the gorilla looks happy and she's eating lovely food.' It took some time, however, for the children to make a connection between the colours in the first picture and the mood it conveyed, although one or two recognised that there were lots of blue and lots of empty spaces. Eventually one or two recognised that the blue colours were cold and sad in contrast to the warmth and happiness conveyed by the reds and oranges of the 'gorilla feast' picture.

One little girl, Francesca, volunteered that she thought that Hannah was a bit rude and spoiled for throwing her present of a toy gorilla into the corner with her other toys.

I replied that I thought she had made a very interesting point and to hold on to it until we had finished looking at the other pictures. The class then looked at the picture of Hannah on her own watching the television in a dark, empty room (see Figure 2.3). After some thought, Tom responded that 'She looks as though she's trapped in her own emptiness.' When the children were asked to look for the differences between Hannah's dad working in his study and the one with Dad wishing her a happy birthday (see Figures 2.4 and 2.5), they began to make more references to tone and colour. Several children pointed out the dark and gloomy colours of Dad's study with his back towards her, and one child astutely noted that the diploma on the wall showed that this room was external to Hannah's world. In the other picture there was more warmth, with Dad in a red sweater and jeans 'with something poking out of his back pocket' which the children thought could have been a pencil or a banana. They also began to relate clues in this picture back to other pictures in the book, such as the gorillas on Hannah's cake and her birthday card with those on her bedroom lamp. They also picked up on the child's picture hanging on the wall, noting a house, a Dad and the little girl out for a walk together while the sun was shining. At this point, a quiet girl, Rachel, who had not yet contributed, put up her hand and said, 'I've got a question but it's not about anything we've just talked about . . . it's about the fact that there's no mummy in any of the pictures.' When the rest of the class were asked why this might be, various suggestions were made. For example, some thought that the mummy might be away on a visit somewhere or working away from home. When we returned to the child's drawing in the last picture, they agreed that the absence of a mother figure suggested that there was no mummy for whatever reason. One child then suggested that the Dad might be depressed because his wife was no longer with him. When asked if the children knew what being depressed meant, Rachel said, 'It's when you're sad for a long time and you don't get over it and you might need tablets to help you feel better.'

They were now really beginning to probe below the surface of the pictures for deeper meanings. It would seem that children need practice and time to see the less obvious and more subtle features of picture narratives. They also need to know that you will not simply accept their first thoughts as the best they can offer.

When I returned to the earlier comment made by Francesca about Hannah being spoiled and rude for throwing her gorilla into a corner, she said, 'If she was really feeling alone and feeling empty because her dad couldn't find time to spend with her, you can understand more why she threw her gorilla on to the floor.'

I then gave the children some personal details about Anthony Browne's favourite pastimes and why he liked gorillas so much. I also told them that something very sad happened to him when he was only 17 years old which I would share with them later. This connection between Browne's biography and his books was *very* important to the children.

The children were extremely interested in his love of art and of surrealism and were fascinated by Magritte's dreamy, bizarre pictures of fish, fleecy clouds and apples filling up the entire space of a room. When I showed them some examples of Magritte's influence in *Willy the Dreamer* and *Voices in the Park*, they caught on very quickly and started to see other things in Browne's pictures that they had not noticed before. They seemed to have little problem in understanding the concept of surrealism.

Just before *My Dad* was read to them, one of the children pointed out that I had not yet told them about the sad thing that had happened to Browne as a teenager. I told them how his father had died of a heart attack just after he had returned home from watching Anthony and his brother playing rugby. I added that the picture of King Kong falling from the Empire State Building (on the wall of Hannah's bedroom on p. 10 of *Gorilla*) was really an expression of how Browne's world had crashed when he saw his father dying in front of him. The children were saddened and captivated by this biographical information. When the children were asked to work together in pairs to talk about the pictures selected for special attention, one of the boys remarked, 'This is not just about Anthony Browne's dad. It's about all dads. We all want our dads to take an interest in us and do things with us.'

At playtime a group of children stayed behind to ask me how old Browne's father was when he died and what the name of Browne's brother was (see the interview with Anthony Browne on p. 71). Anthony Browne's personal life story and its influence on his books mattered greatly to the children and unquestionably increased their interest in the workshop.

Children's responses to the first drawing activity

One child said that her mother loved hearts and she, the child, had drawn a picture of her using a heart as a motif. There were hearts on the necklace, on her T-shirt and on the wallpaper around the room. A boy had drawn his mother surrounded by handbags and shoes (two of her passions). He had depicted her against dominant bedroom wardrobes with plain, hook handles and asked, 'What do I do to make the bedroom cupboards more interesting?' I asked him to imagine he was Anthony Browne and to think what he would do, given her interest in handbags and shoes. As he looked at his simple hook handles, he suddenly said, 'I could make one of the hook handles into a handbag, what a brilliant idea!' He couldn't get back to his work fast enough! Later he called me over to his table again and asked, 'Shall I put handbags on all the cupboard handles?'

Again, I referred him back to Anthony Browne's books and the fact that you really had to search for the puzzles in his pictures, to which he replied, 'Hmmm . . . it wouldn't be very subtle, would it, if I put handles on all the doors, so I will just choose one.' This was just one example of the deeper learning going on in terms of what the children had begun to understand about motifs and their need to be so well blended into the rest of the picture that the reader really had to search for them.

The storyboard

The idea of a storyboard definitely needed explaining to the children, and the decision to show the children how to draw matchstick people was vindicated. The children worked at this activity with genuine commitment and produced some interesting results (see p. 67). However, it needed at least thirty rather than the twenty minutes we had allowed. The difficulty for the children was keeping the pictures in the story frames simple with only the most essential of details, but by the end of the session, most children had begun to grasp the main principles of storyboarding.

The more that was demanded of them, the more insightful and thoughtful their comments, questions and observations became. The links they were able to make with Anthony Browne's books and his personal life made it possible for them to engage fully with the warmth, compassion and humanity of his work. The pupil evaluations indicated that the children had grown to enjoy Browne's books, especially the ones with gorillas in them. They liked the fact that they were funny and based on some of his personal childhood experiences. Apart from two boys who wrote that they preferred longer books, most commented that now they knew more about the way he wrote and painted, they would be reading other books by AB. The class teacher was pleased to see how well all the children engaged with the activities and surprised at how insightful and mature some of the children's responses had been. She also noted their obvious excitement and increasing involvement about what could be learned about visual texts.

She's nice, my mum.

Figure 2.11 Work by Kelly (Year 4).

Figure 2.12 Work by Jordan (Year 4).

Figure 2.13 Work by Jordan (Year 4).

Figure 2.14 Work by Dylan (Year 4).

Simple explanations of new vocabulary and visual narrative terminology

Explanations are set out in the order in which they appear in the text

Visual cohesion	The way in which the pictures and the elements within them repeat, interconnect and work together to form a united whole.
Tone	The general effect of colour, light and shade in a painting or photograph. In Anthony Browne's pictures the sombre or, conversely, vibrant tones of his colours serve to convey a particular mood and atmosphere.
Intertextuality	The way in which references are made between the picture narrative and that of another literary text, picture, work of art, comic strip or film. For example, in the picture of Hannah at the cinema, the gorilla appears as Superman, the Statue of Liberty and as a member of the audience (*Gorilla*). Thus, in the same picture there are references to film, comic books and statue icons. It works at both conscious and subconscious levels of thought for the writer and the reader. Children can recognise the deeper significance of a picture without always being able to work out exactly what it is they have recognised. It is a strong and characteristic feature of Anthony Browne's work.
Surreal	Having dreamlike qualities or character. Bizarre, strange landscapes and distorted objects are often associated with surrealism.
Surrealism	A twentieth-century movement of artists and writers who used fantastic images in unusual, incongruous, dreamlike settings in order to represent unconscious thoughts similar to those we have in dreams and nightmares.
René Magritte	A Belgian artist who loved the strange, the dreamy and unreal, frequently putting bizarre and odd things together in the same picture. A clear instance of this is in his picture, *Presence of Mind* where he paints a bowler-hatted, formally dressed man alongside a vertical fish and large bird of prey.
Motif	Repeated designs, shapes or patterns which occur in art, craft and architecture, for example. The sun and dressing gown in Anthony Browne's *My Dad* are examples of motifs.
Symbol	Something that stands for or represents something else beyond the object itself. For example, the sun motif in *My Dad* represents warmth and happiness.
Storyboard	A storyboard is a set of simple sketches arranged in sequence in a series of panels or frames which will later make up a story to be filmed, drawn, painted and/or written.

Teaching resources

- Copies of *Gorilla*, *My Dad* and *My Mum*. It is useful, though not essential, to have at least three or four copies of each text so that children can look closely at the illustrations.
- Enlarged, photocopied pictures (A4 size) from *Gorilla* and *My Dad*. The ones used in the workshop are detailed on pp. 47, 49, 50, 51 and 52. They can also be scanned on to an interactive whiteboard from a memory stick, but unless you have a very high-quality IWB you may find that the illustrations lose some of their intensity and vibrancy.
- A selection of René Magritte's pictures. Browne is very fond of surrealism, and Magritte is an important source of inspiration in his work. There are several websites showing examples

of Magritte's work. The one that I used can be found at http://interiors.intendo.net/magritte.html. Examples of those that most obviously connect with the books above are *Presence of Mind*, *The Big Family*, *Empire of Lights*, *Personal Values* and *The Listening Room*. These can be printed off, photocopied and enlarged for ease of viewing.

- Photocopies of A4 sheets with the sentences. 'He's all right, my dad' and 'She's nice, my mum' written at the bottom of the page. You will need sufficient copies for the children to be able to choose from (see examples on pp. 65–66).
- Photocopies of a blank storyboard with three frames numbered 2 to 4.
- One photocopy of an exemplar storyboard (see p. 60).
- A list of the new vocabulary and concepts to be taught: Magritte, motif, surreal, surrealism, symbol, visual cohesion, tone, mood and atmosphere. These can be produced in large print on the interactive whiteboard (I used font 48) or photocopied sheets sufficient for one per table or simply written on a whiteboard.

Browne, A. (2002) *Gorilla*, London: Walker Books.
Browne, A. (2001) *My Dad*, London: Picture Corgi.
Browne, A. (2005) *My Mum*, London: Picture Corgi.
Browne, A. (2007) *My Brother*, London: Doubleday.

Some useful websites

Eccleshare, J. (2000) 'Portrait of the artist as a gorilla', *Guardian Unlimited Books*, 29 July 2000, http://books.guardian,co.uk/departments/childrenandteens/story/0,6000,348137,00.html (accessed 22 January 2007).

Rabinovitch, D. (2003) 'Author of the month: Anthony Browne', *Guardian Unlimited Books*, 27 August 2003, http://books.guardian.co.uk/departments/childrenandteens/story/0,,1030200,00.html (accessed 2 February 2007).

http://www.booktrusted.co.uk (for several short articles on Anthony Browne and his books).
    http://interiors.intendo.net/magritte.html (accessed 2 February 2007).

René Magritte Online, http://www.artcyclopedia.com/artists/magritte_rene.html (accessed 13 September 2007).

The art of Anthony Browne's picture books

The author and the man

Anthony Browne is an internationally acclaimed author and illustrator who has been delighting audiences with his dazzling artistic genius for over thirty years. His work is probably best known for his portrayal of gorillas and chimpanzees, often set in close, if not always comfortable, relationships with human beings. The beauty of these creatures and their proximity to human beings are powerfully created by his meticulous brushwork, rich, bold colours and technical mastery. When asked what they most like about Anthony Browne's books, children's first responses are usually the gorillas, who appear in several of his books, and his Willy series, which features a vulnerable young chimp who has to learn to triumph in a terrifying world of gorilla tormentors. Whether the central protagonists are gorillas or children, his books deal with serious and challenging social themes, and Browne is uncompromising about the uneasy messages his books often communicate in his firm belief that children are wholly capable of understanding complex ideas. Within family relationships, children are portrayed as bored, angry, resentful, anxious, lonely and quarrelsome, with parents often falling short of being the kind of the people they crave and need. A distinguishing characteristic of Browne's work is the way in which reality and illusion interconnect in a clever interplay between image and words to provide an incisive social commentary on aspects of contemporary life. Social complexity, moral dilemmas and conflicting perspectives are revealed through densely textured, vibrantly coloured, cleverly crafted visual narratives that have to be worked at in order to reveal their deeper layers of meanings. These serious messages have power and resonance for children because they touch on both the reality of their inner fears and dreams and the reality of the world in which they have to live. The success of much of Browne's work derives from the fact that he is able to embed moral and social complexity without contrivance or overt didacticism. Children are compelled by the stunning vibrancy of Browne's illustrations because his humour, playful puns, jokes and witty text make them laugh at the same time as making them want to understand more about the puzzles and intriguing insights contained in his work.

Numerous websites detail Anthony Browne's career and biographical details, some of which are listed in the bibliography. He has also been extensively interviewed by book editors, journal and newspaper reviewers, all of whom have a similar commentary on his life.

He was born in 1946 in Sheffield, Yorkshire, to warm and loving pub-owning parents, Jack and Doris.[1] His father, a big, powerful man who had been a boxer and saw armed combat in the Second World War, also read poetry, loved drawing for his sons and would like to have been an artist. Browne loved the combination of toughness and gentleness in his father's physicality and, as a small boy, thought the sun (one of Browne's recurring leitmotifs) shone out of him. It does not take much of a leap of the imagination to see the autobiographical links with Browne's fascination for the fiercely powerful physique of gorillas, with their gentle–tough behaviour.

Books were an important part of Browne's life, especially folk and fairy tales. *Alice in Wonderland*, particularly its illustrations by Tenniel, and 'Hansel and Gretel' have remained special favourites, and two of Browne's folk-tale retellings, with newly worked original and provocative illustrations, concern these two tales. Comics were also a source of inspiration for Browne, and his detailed drawings of soldiers, knights on horseback, 'red Indians' and cowboys, often depicted in battle scenes with captions and jokes, revealed a nascent sense of narrative. His first important introduction to surrealism, a distinctive feature of most of his picture book creations, was not through art but through the writings of Harold Pinter and Samuel Beckett. Browne's encounter with Beckett's plays in his teenage years was akin to finding surrealism in painting, something with which he felt intensely familiar.

At 17, nothing had prepared him for the sudden and tragic loss of his father from a fatal heart attack, and for several years he was profoundly affected by his father's dislocating absence from his life. While not necessarily the result of a conscious decision on Browne's part, there is a dark undercurrent that runs through much of his work expressed through recurring images of isolated, solitary children in relationships with parents, especially fathers, who are distant, cold, inattentive and absent, albeit in a psychological sense. When asked about this feature of his work by Rabinovitch (2003a), Browne responded, 'I've heard people say that you're angry with the parent who dies too soon. I don't remember feeling angry but maybe that's how it's come out – that I show cold fathers. Which is the opposite of what mine was, actually.' However, Browne's protagonists usually find ways of facing fear, jealousy and unhappiness with resourcefulness and ingenuity, and there is often as much sun, warmth and optimism in his picture books as there are expressions of the darker side of the human condition.

As was discussed in Part 1 of this chapter, children are sharp observers of what is both absent and present in his books. Extracts from a telephone interview with him began with my request for his comments on the view expressed by some of the children who took part in the trial workshop, that the dad in *Gorilla* might be depressed because his wife had left him (see the Diary, p. 63).

Telephone interview with Anthony Browne on 20 July 2007

AB I am very interested in the children's responses but not surprised by them. When challenged and prompted, children frequently offer mature and sophisticated reactions to my books. However, I am not naturally drawn to depression, but I do have an empathy with gorillas and with the underdog. My response to Rachel and the other children about the absence of the mother would be one of interest and enthusiasm. I would hate to be prescriptive about my books and welcome any interpretations, especially from children.

DD I am often struck by the lustrous, thick hair of most of your child characters and how almost every strand is carefully painted. Is this because you like painting the texture of hair?

AB There's not too much difference between animals and human beings as far as fur and hair are concerned.

DD Writers on your work frequently comment that intertextuality and the way it is played out in both picture and text narratives is one of the key strengths and most interesting aspects of your work. Would you agree with this view?

AB   I don't consciously think about intertextuality when I'm painting or writing. It is one of the aspects of the way I work. I am interested in surrealism, and surrealism is magical and strange. In that sense, surrealism is intertextual.

DD   Before reading *My Dad* to the children they were very interested in your biography. They were particularly fascinated to learn that it was when you found your father's dressing gown that all the memories of his presence came flooding back. They were very saddened by the fact that your father had died in front of you and your brother just after he had been to see you both play rugby. In fact, they identified very closely with *My Dad*. They knew you were 17 years old when your father died but they wanted to know the name of your brother and how old your dad was when he died.

AB   My dad was 47 years old and my brother's name is Michael. In fact, I've recently written a book about him called *My Brother*, which will be published later this year.

DD   Was there a similar inspiration for the book about your mother, *My Mum*? I didn't think it had the same impact as *My Dad*.

AB   I didn't really want to do this and initially resisted the request to some extent. My mother died when she was 84. I was less confident in the drawing because it wasn't new to me.

DD   Some time ago I shared your book *Voices in the Park* with a very bright group of Year 6 children. They were disarmingly perceptive about the mood, atmosphere and hidden meanings within the pictures. They talked about it for at least an hour and were disappointed when the session was over. One of the things they were puzzled about was the autumnal tree bursting into flames as Victoria, Charles and his mother walk out of the park gates. They thought it was because the mother had left a bad and destructive atmosphere behind her in the park. Can you talk me through the conception of this book and the reason for the burning tree?

AB   The idea for this book was based on a previous book of mine called *Walk in the Park*. I was not happy with the pictures and was struggling for an idea. What happened was that two little ideas came together to become a big idea. The tree on fire is trying to feel like the woman (Charles's mother), who is burning with anger. It's a bit like remembering a dream.

DD   Was this how the idea for *Voices in the Park* came to you?

AB   I'm really talking about the creative process in general rather than a particular book. Sometimes an idea comes to me, like a dream. Later perhaps I can try to interpret it.

DD   What are your next projects?

AB   I'm currently working on a book called *Little Beauty* which should come out in 2008. It's about gorillas in captivity and is loosely based on the tale 'Beauty and the Beast'. I'm also working with my son, Joseph, on a book about my memoirs. It's a long piece of prose which I was finding difficult to write, partly because it was too self-conscious. My son is now interviewing me, and the writing is being filtered through him. This is working well and the writing is now far less self-conscious.

Anthony Browne's work

The first of Browne's thirty-eight books, *Through the Magic Mirror*, was published in 1976. It featured a child called Toby who is bored with everything, including his parents. He escapes through the landing mirror into an internal world of dreams and fantasy before returning to the physical world. The text has a simple storyline but the pictures portray a more complex psychological reality that reveals Toby's state of mind. As in most of Browne's books, it is in his pictures that the more interesting and richer narratives reside, drawing the reader into a world of fantasy and dreams that uses surrealism 'as its visual language' (Doonan, 1999: 31). His latest work, *My Brother*, was published in 2007 as a picture book for young readers. It is based on his memories and perceptions of his brother, Michael, as a child, and while its simple text, arrowed labelling and uncluttered action paintings will have a strong appeal to young children, it does not have the densely textured narratives of much of his previous work.

In between his first and his most recent book, Browne has published two book series: the Willy series and the Bear series. There are six Willy books and four Bear books, the latter initially written for younger readers and his daughter, Ellen. He has illustrated eight books in collaboration with several notable authors. Included in his illustrated works is a highly original version of Lewis Carroll's *Alice's Adventures in Wonderland*. Two books come under the heading of 'retellings'. One is of a folk tale, *Hansel and Gretel*, and the other is *King Kong*, from the story conceived and adapted for film by Edgar Wallace and Merian Cooper. King Kong is Browne's idealised father, and in the dedication are the words, 'In memory of my dad; for me, the original Kong. A.B.' A substantial part of his work includes eighteen picture books, each of them different in scope, form and conception but all traceable to his first book.

Over thirty years, Browne's books have made a significant contribution to the establishment of picture books for older children (Eccleshare, 2000). Browne's steady stream of publications since 1976 have been internationally recognised, valued and commended, and he is the recipient of numerous awards. However, his struggle for formal acclaim was not achieved easily in the early years because his illustrations were distinctly different from what had become the recognised pattern and style in British children's picture books at the time. As he says in his own words,

> I've always felt that I was a bit of an outsider to the British children's-book illustration scene, because I don't work in line and wash. I work in watercolour and sometimes gouache, so obviously my books look very different from the line work of Cruickshank, Ardizzone or Shirley Hughes, who are thought of as the great British tradition.
>
> (Eccleshare, 2000)

His first breakthrough in glittering prizes came in 1983 with the publication of *Gorilla*, which, among several other awards, won him the prestigious Kate Greenaway Medal (awarded to an artist who has produced the most distinguished work in the illustration of children's books) and the Kurt Maschler Award (for excellence in both illustration and text).[2] He won two more Kurt Maschler awards, for *Alice's Adventures in Wonderland* in 1989 and for *Voices in the Park* in 1999. In 2000 he won the coveted Hans Christian Anderson Illustration award (the highest international recognition given to authors and illustrators for their entire body of work and its contribution to children's literature).

Reading Anthony Browne's picture books

The picture book differs significantly from an illustrated text or a literary narrative that makes use of occasional line drawings to enliven it (as, for example, is the case with Michael Foreman's elegantly simple, black-and-white shaded pictures of Michael Morpurgo's stories). It has been described as a totality of design and as an art form in itself. Bader writes that 'it hinges on the interdependence of pictures and words, on the simultaneous display of two facing pages, and on the drama of the turning page' (1976: 1). Picture books tell stories through a combination of visual and textual narrative. Sometimes almost all the story is narrated through the pictures with only minimal text to support it; in other cases there is more text than pictures. The central point about picture books is that text and illustration work *together* to convey the narrative. The one is not in the service of the other, as is the case with illustrated books. Image and text can be in a particular relationship with each other, as can image with image, depending on the type and style of picture book. In Browne's picture books the text and picture can be in ironic relation to each other or in counterpoint with each other (where two different messages combine with one another or where the two work in contrast with each other). They are, in Nodelman's words, 'unlike any other form of verbal or visual art' (1988: vii).

One of the compelling things about Browne's picture books is that they can be read and enjoyed at a surface level for their simple storyline and sumptuous visual display of colour, drawing and vivid characterisation. However, they can also be read as highly complex and dense narratives. Working out what is left unsaid and implied by the codes within the pictures is one of the most rewarding intellectual aspects of picture book analyses, and, as I have shown in Part 1 of this chapter, children quickly warm to it once they are shown *how* to look and how to access the codes. One of the difficulties here is that children in their junior years who are able readers and enjoying the challenges of substantial works of fiction often see picture books as insufficiently worthy of their serious attention and fit for young readers only. At the level of anecdotal evidence, this is also the view frequently expressed by adults. Hunt makes the point well:

> The picture-book genre is a paradox. On the one hand it is seen as children's literature's one truly original contribution to literature in general. . . . On the other, it is seen as the province of the young child and is therefore beneath serious critical notice.
>
> (1999: 69–70)

The question, then, is how to give picture books the status and serious critical attention they deserve in ways that are engaging, challenging and enjoyable to children. One obvious answer is that the way in which picture books work in terms of design, frame, format, size, font type and the meanings embedded in them has to be learned as a specific form of image- and word-related critical analysis. Our knowledge and understanding of the way in which picture books work have been greatly advanced by the substantial body of academic scholarship and interest that now exists within this particular form of children's literature (see, for example, Nodelman, 1988; Doonan, 1986, 1999; Lewis, 2001; Watson and Styles, 1996; Arizpe and Styles, 2003). Some of this work includes classroom research and children's responses to specific types of the genre, both of which have made a strong contribution to the insights and expertise that teachers are now able to draw upon.

The rest of this chapter will be devoted to an examination of how to read Anthony Browne's picture books by using some of the analytical tools and frameworks from the academic literature mentioned above. Three specific examples of his work will be examined in relation to the themes that recur throughout his body of work, along with the significance of art, surrealism and intertextuality within his pictures. Some of the terminology and concepts associated with the acquisition of a visual literacy have been drawn from artistic, cultural and literary criticism. A very useful list of visual terminology drawn from these perspectives is offered by Graham (2005), and a selection of those terms most applicable to the reading of Anthony Browne's books are listed in the following box.

Endpapers
The pages which are immediately inside the front and back covers. The story in a picture book often starts or ends here.

Format
The physical size and shape of the book.

Frame
The border around an illustration, which may simply be the white margin of the page or can be a printed line, a drawn free-hand line or a decorated band. When a picture bursts through a frame ('breaks' the frame), extra momentum and significance is added.

Page turn
Turning a page in a picturebook is a different experience from turning over the page in an unillustrated text; it requires the reader to pause and peruse the picture.

Tone
The level of brightness, lightness or darkness in coloured images.

Viewpoint
The position from which the reader views the illustrations.

(Graham, 2005: 213–14, cited in Reynolds, 2005)

Some of these terms will be used in the course of developing a deeper understanding of how narratives work in Browne's picture books but it is important to bear in mind that while greater skill and facility can be acquired in the reading of pictures, there are no definitive or 'correct' meanings that have the ascendancy over others. One of the central characteristics of picture books, and in particular those of Browne, is that they contain many meanings and a variety of 'voices' or points of view. The fact that they are both polysemous and polyphonic means that the narratives conveyed in his picture texts are, by their very nature, open to a number of interpretations and meaning possibilities. The two types of Browne's picture narratives chosen for close examination are a folk tale retelling and a picture book of which Browne is both author and illustrator.

Examining social relationships, art and surrealism

Hansel and Gretel (1981)

This early work of Browne's has been chosen because of the way in which his highly original and visual reconceptualisation of this familiar folk tale reveals the psychological reality of separation, abandonment and betrayal in a modern setting. Unusually, there is a complete absence of jokes and humour in this sombre retelling because Browne has been more concerned to re-present this tale in a way that will reach out and connect with the innermost fears and desires of today's children. It is particularly remarkable for the way in which he succeeds in combining aesthetic and emotional values, which is, according to Doonan, 'the mark of a fine illustrator' (1983: 124).

The front cover is an extraordinary painting of technical accomplishment which, even without prior knowledge of folk tales or its intertextual art references, powerfully communicates a dramatic intensity that foregrounds the content of the story. Two dejected children are seated huddled together against the foot of a gnarled tree with Hansel's bespectacled face cast downwards while Gretel gazes forlornly into the middle distance. They are clothed in modern dress, Gretel in green and red, and Hansel in Browne's beloved Fair Isle striped jersey which children will recognise from the Willy series. Bright green grass dotted with redcap toadstool contrasts with the menacing gloom of the forest behind. Painted into the bark of the tree roots is a version of Edvard Munch's *The Scream*, which is repeated as an intratextual motif at least five times. Munch's anguished expression of isolation and fear mirrors the children's internal state of hopelessness and despair. Munch depicts his cry of anguish against a blood-red sky, which may account for the frequent use of red in the cover picture. Blood seems to be leaching from the bark of the tree and from the profile of a despairing face etched into the tree roots, possibly echoing the plight of the children's father. Before the cover is opened to reveal the first page, the reader is left in no doubt that the lives of these two small children are endangered. The opening endpaper shows a small, framed picture of a white, densely caged bird set against a white background, while the final one depicts a similarly framed grey mouse who is running free. It can be inferred from the end papers alone that the caged bird symbolises the psychological and physical caging of the children. However, despite their relative powerlessness in the face of their stepmother's blatant self-interest and cruelty, they manage to free themselves by the end.

The first four pages of the book show the poverty of the exterior and interior of the house. The modern, bleak suburban house of the poor woodcutter and his family is in sharp contrast to the romanticised woodland cottage usually portrayed in classical fairy-tale versions of the story. However, its dismal 'edge of industrial housing estate' resonance may be far more familiar to children and therefore more potent in terms of the way it draws the children into the psychological reality of this dysfunctional family. In the first whole-page illustration, Browne uses a film-maker's technique by giving us a long shot of the living room which takes the eye straight to the mirror hanging over the mantelpiece on the far wall (Doonan 1983: 124). The stepmother is seated watching television, in the only armchair, and even in a modern, short-sleeved top and contemporary hairstyle she bears many of the signifiers of the stepmother trope: dark hair, red lips and hard, cold eyes that are consciously averted from the children. The father, Hansel and Gretel are seated together at the table; the father has the appearance of a beaten and defeated man as he looks at the newspaper while the children sit facing each other, their young faces devoid of expression, both doing and saying nothing. One leg of the table is propped up on a book, and on the tattered, faded carpet lie Gretel's doll and red ball. In one of his characteristic cohesive devices, the doll and the threesome at the table are united visually by their striped clothing (ibid.: 126). The stepmother is an outsider who nonetheless wields considerable power over her husband and children.

Another commonly used motif in much of Browne's work is that of the cage, bars, tightly bounded spaces and other signifiers of entrapment. This is a dominant feature of *Zoo* and it also figures in *Gorilla*, *King Kong*, *Into the Forest*, *Voices in the Park* and even in his monochrome illustrations for Ian McEwan's *The Daydreamer*. However, they have, as Doonan (1983) comments, been used with particular ingenuity in this book. From the beginning endpaper onwards, the bar motif is present in the backs of chairs, the bed heads and the back door, and continues until the height of tension is reached with Hansel padlocked in a wood and metal cage awaiting his fate. The six pages depicting characters looking out of bars in various settings emphasise the hopeless, poverty-entrapped circumstances of this deeply fragmented family. The mirror is also a familiar trope within the folk and fairy-tale genre, and Browne has used it to extend and expand his pictures. Continuing from the mirror motif in the living room, Browne takes us into the bedroom via a large dressing-table mirror reflecting the sleeping figures of Hansel and Gretel and the father and stepmother. In the following full-page picture is a large wardrobe mirror that shows the reflected image of the stepmother standing over the sleeping children in a pose of calculated malignancy. Somewhat incongruous in this chilling scene are two of Browne's recurring leitmotifs: his father's dressing gown and a pair of red high-heeled shoes decorated with pompoms. Cosy familiarity and designer shoes are shown alongside an impending act of criminal negligence and potential murder. The stepmother's witch-like stance is echoed by sharp-edged witch hat shapes in the way the curtains are drawn back, in the pointed turret of a picture on the wall and in a mouse hole in the skirting board. Browne's inventive use of mirrors in this way not only gives the pictures and the reader an unusually interesting perspective but also serves to take us 'inside the emotional event, not the woodcutter's cottage. The three mirrors have taken us in' (ibid.: 125).

The story of Hansel and Gretel is a poignant one that touches powerfully on the unconscious and conscious fears of all children from their darkest terrors (parental loss, abandonment, betrayal) to their brightest hopes (love and fulfilment). What Browne has succeeded in doing in this provocative retelling is to put 'into visual language the nature of these emotions' (Doonan 1983: 123). The hope towards the end of the story is symbolised by a white cat, a white dove, a white songbird and a white duck, which eventually take the children home across a lake beneath a rainbow-arched sky. The story ends with another film-maker's shot, this time from behind the father, who is framed by the front, bending down to greet his lost children. One of Browne's much-loved, Magritte-inspired blue, fleecy clouded skies is reflected in the window pane of the front door, and in the darker recesses of the hallway a brown plant pot shows the first green shoot of a single seedling. A symbolic journey from passive dependence to resourceful independence has been taken.

Voices in the Park *(1998)*

The idea for this more recent work of Browne's was based on a book he wrote twenty-one years previously, entitled *A Walk in the Park*. As he mentions in the interview reported earlier in this chapter, he was not happy with the drawings and was looking for a way of reworking the material. The result is a polyphonic narrative in which four different voices each describe their perspective on a walk in the park. They are distinguished by different font styles, styles of writing and seasons of the year. The four protagonists – Mrs Smythe, her son, Charles, Mr Smith and his daughter, Smudge – are all trapped in their particular social circumstances. The theme of caging, both physical and psychological, which so powerfully impresses itself upon the reader in *Hansel and Gretel* and *Zoo* is repeated in this work with different signifiers. The lives of these characters are bounded by social class, and the distinctive differences between Mrs Smythe and Mr Smith are shown through the semiotics of clothing, facial expression and body language. On the opening page, for example, Mrs Smythe is portrayed leaving her white-fenced, New

England-style house set in large, well-manicured grounds with Victoria, the Labrador. She is dressed in a large-brimmed red hat, brass-buttoned navy blue coat and black gloves and boots. The lines are harsh and severe, as is her expression. Cut to Mr Smith, who is slumped in an armchair in grubby dungarees. A grey-green shadow surrounds his chair and he looks depressed and lifeless. He is unemployed, and ensnared by the poverty and hopelessness of his predicament. The differing social positions of Mrs Smythe and Mr Smith are revealed in the text and, surrealistically, in the picture narratives. Early in the book, Mrs Smythe is shown seated at the far edge of a wooden park seat with her face turned away from Charles, who sits apart from her with his arms folded, looking the other way. Their closed and distanced body stances are suggestive of a relationship where power and oppressive control severely limit warmth and spontaneity. A crocodile-shaped shadow falls from one of the trees, signifying a dangerous and predatory presence. Annoyed by the 'frightful type' sitting on the same bench as her, the 'scruffy mongrel' chasing her 'pedigree' Labrador and the 'rough-looking child' playing with her son, she decides to leave the park. Her furious shouting for Charles is mirrored in the open mouths painted into the autumn trees behind her. Her anger is visualised by a tree bursting into flames as they leave the park, and a trail of fallen leaves scatters in their wake.

A wintry, bleak urban scene shows Smudge, her dad and their dog, Albert, on their way to the park. They are depicted in front of a drab, municipal wall on top of which are jagged pieces of glass with closely meshed wire rising high above it. Behind it are two dismal tower blocks, their stark lines broken only by the barren branches of nearby trees. Propped up against the wall in the lower foreground, alongside a drawing of a cracked heart, are paintings of Frans Hals' *The Laughing Cavalier* and Da Vinci's *Mona Lisa*. They rest on broken paving stones, their enigmatic smiles replaced with weeping countenances. In the gutter, a rat forages in the litter, and a beggar dressed up as Father Christmas is appealing to the passers-by to help support his 'millions of children'. Drained of light and colour, this picture poignantly visualises the destitution and distress that are the lived as well as the psychic reality of Smudge's father. The same picture is transformed into a scene of glittering radiance on their return home. Smudge's bubbly chatter about the fun she had playing with Charles cheers her father up. His dejected, downward gaze has become a warm smile as he listens to her, and there is a suggestion in his stance of a lighter step. The dismal tower blocks are lit up, there are snow crystal lights in the trees, the street light has become an art deco lamp in the shape of a snowdrop and the 'Laughing Cavalier' is dancing with 'Mona Lisa'. From one of the tower-block roofs, King Kong reappears in a gesture of power and strength, while the Father Christmas beggar pirouettes below. The entire picture symbolises a moment of bright happiness, renewed hope and inner strength. This 'reading' of the two contrasting pictures is a clear example of what happens when we 'experience' picture books. In Doonan's words, we 'put together the story told by the text and the story told by the pictures, whereupon an expansion takes place. What emerges is a composite text: the one which exists not on the page but in the head' (1986: 164).

The third voice is that of Charles, who is shown walking up a long, winding path in the park. As the path stretches into the distance, his small, hunched figure appears to be paralysed by the dominating shadow of his mother. The fine-hatched shading of her shadow extends across the path and falls diagonally across Charles's back. Even as he looks away from her to watch Albert and Victoria bounding across the grass, the sky, trees and lamp-posts all reflect the shape of her hat. Her presence, surrealistically represented, surrounds and engulfs him.

Smudge is our imaginative, resilient and ebullient fourth narrator, whose sunny personality brings some rare fun and spontaneous happiness into Charles's confined and heavily censured access to the world. Her sun-drenched park is a fantasy of fruits, jewels, purples and golden yellows. Initially seeing Charles as 'a bit of wimp', she ends up by enjoying his company. The children's palpable happiness is playfully reflected in the trees, which become gorilla profiles and grow multicoloured trunks with a whale's tail sprouting from one and its water jet from another. Before Charles is once more in the shadow of his domineering mother, the book comes to an iridescent climax with the children somersaulting on an exquisitely executed bandstand. The kaleidoscopic colours and design of the canopied bandstand give intense visual pleasure, as does the harmony of its setting: a greenish, cobalt blue, starlit sky above the canopy and below it a cloudy, daylight sky with a deep emerald green circle of grass at its base. The source of inspiration for this simultaneous juxtaposition of night with day is René Magritte's *The Empire of Lights*. The vibrancy and energy of the colours reflect the joyful abandonment of the children and their leaping dogs.

This extraordinarily accomplished picture narrative succeeds in bringing together an aesthetic visual experience that encapsulates a serious commentary on social class divisions and the impact of differential social circumstances upon and within family lives – although in this narrative, Smudge displays a greater resourcefulness and resilience than her socially more privileged counterpart, Charles. Browne has managed to construct a densely textured narrative based on anthropomorphised gorillas and chimpanzees which never once slips into sentimentality and whose psychological reality we are so drawn into that we forget they are gorillas or chimps and believe in them as recognisable human beings. The entire text is redolent with links to previous books, art and surrealism as well as to themes and motifs that recur throughout his body of work.

What will be clear by now is that reading picture books is a very different act from reading a verbal text. As Hunt (2001) points out, picture books are read not at word speed but at picture speed. It is a slower process, and one that involves as much turning back as it does turning forward. Making demands upon children to look longer and deeper into the pictures gives them opportunities to operate at a higher cognitive level and it is then possible for them to be taught how to identify the codes and signifiers of meaning. When they are engaged at this more reflective and probing level of analysis, they are learning a form of '*visible thinking*' (Arizpe and Styles 2003: 229) that involves them in a conscious metacognitive activity in which deductions and hypotheses can be made and tested like scientific reasoning. While not actually using the vocabulary of intertextuality, children have an implicit knowledge of how each newly turned picture page is influenced by the one before. They can then be taught to see the relationships within the picture (intratextual), between the pictures (intertextual) and with other books by the same author and the wealth of prior knowledge that children bring to the picture reading process (extratextual). This prior knowledge will, in most children, include a facility with non-linear screen forms of literacy such as computer games, online chat rooms, film, television cartoons, advertisements and the strip comic. Children often recognise icons and the smallest detail in a picture, which adults, who have been largely educated on a diet of linear text forms, may miss. The reading of pictures is also a social and cultural act in so far as children's responses are, to some extent, socially constructed by their immediate world and by the shared beliefs and values within which they and their families live. These social and cultural understandings will have some part to play in their interpretation of Browne's pictures, as will the scope of their knowledge of such diverse matters as moral and environmental issues, the welfare of animals, art and the literary forms of the folk tale and fairy tale. Some children may therefore have greater access to the codes in Browne's pictures than others. Reading picture books is not only about understanding the meanings within the symbiotic relationship of words with images, but also concerned with what the reader brings to the picture narrative. Browne's metafictive picture books (types of fiction that self-consciously address the devices of fiction) 'prise open the gap between the words and the pictures, pushing them apart and forcing the reader/viewer to work hard to forge the relationship between them' (Lewis 1990: 41).

Considerable research evidence of children's responses to picture books at Key Stages 2 and 3 (see, for example, Tulk, 2005; Arizpe and Styles, 2003; Watson and Styles, 1996) suggests that even for children who have literacy difficulties, reading picture books *can* advance their thinking and enable them to move from lower to higher levels of thinking and analysis if they are taught *how* to look. Browne's picture books give us, in Nodelman's eloquent words, 'what all good art offers us: greater consciousness – the opportunity, in other words, to be more human' (Nodelman, 1988: 285).

Chapter 3

Teaching Philip Pullman

The book chosen for this unit of work is *Clockwork or All Wound Up*. It is one of Pullman's shorter books and should not take more than a fortnight or so of short story-reading sessions. It is a strange, spooky and thrilling story that should have most children sitting on the edge of their seats. The trial workshop took place with a challenging Year 6 class, who were gripped by the story from start to finish. In order to heighten the atmosphere, every time the story was read, the class teacher dimmed the lights, closed the blinds and put a screensaver on the interactive whiteboard which depicted a large Gothic fireplace with crackling logs and a grandfather pendulum clock that ticked in real time. The class was also supplied with an antique chiming wall clock with a glass panel so that its cogs, wheels and working parts could be seen. The screensaver and antique clock unquestionably helped the children to feel and sense the atmosphere and historic setting in which this breathtaking folk tale is set. The format for Part 1 of this chapter follows the same pattern as that for the previous chapter.

Synopsis of Philip Pullman's *Clockwork or All Wound Up*

It is the day before Karl, an apprentice clockmaker, is supposed to unveil his personal addition to the great clock tower in Glockenheim. But despite the intense anticipation of his master and the townspeople, he has created nothing, and the next day will be a day of humiliation rather than triumph. A sinister figure steps right out of the story that Fritz, a local storyteller, is relating to his audience and offers Karl a clockwork knight so exquisitely wrought that it looks almost real. The trouble is that the knight will seek out and kill anyone who utters the word 'devil', and Fritz, who began this story, has not worked out how to end it. However, once a story has been wound up, it must continue ticking to the end. Will Karl sell his soul to the devil and accept the deadly knight to get him out of trouble? The implications of his actions have terrifying consequences for Gretl, the brave daughter of the innkeeper, who tries to save the young prince whose clockwork heart is winding down. Like all good folk tales, this story has suspense, terror, tragedy and a magical ending.

Preparation

Some time spent on practising the different voices in advance of reading the story will pay off. The most important ones are those of Fritz, Karl, Gretl and Dr Kalmenius.

Reading the story

Establish a routine for reading the story that is different from usual. For example, set the Gothic Fire screensaver on the interactive whiteboard (for details, see the 'Teaching resources' section, pp. 102–3), which will become the cue for the children to stop what they are doing, sit down quietly and wait for the story to begin. So, as in the idea behind the story, when one thing happens, something else follows on. After the first twenty pages or so have been read, this would be a good time to show the children the antique clock if you have managed to acquire one because by this time they will *want* to know what one looks like and how it works.

About halfway through the story, ensure that the children understand that the mechanical parts of a clock, and the Glockenheim Clock itself, act as a *metaphor* for the way in which a story works: 'Stories are just as hard as clocks to put together, and they can go wrong just as easily – as we shall see with Fritz's own story in a page or two' (Pullman, 1997b: 18). The idea that Pullman had for this story was that every part should fit together like clockwork in a very tight and connected way.

◇ As the children are listening to the rest of the story, get them to think about whether the parts, characters and storyline do fit together as Pullman intended.

Responding to *Clockwork*

The following activities can be done during the course of reading the story or after it has been read. My preference is for the latter since I think children are able to make more sense of the story once they have heard how it begins, develops and ends. As in Chapter 1, teachers can make selections from the lesson objectives to plan individual lessons, a series of lessons or a coherent unit of work. The activities can also be done in any order but I chose to leave the writing and drawing activities until *after* the drama activities in the belief that the children's understanding and appreciation of language and characterisation would be heightened through their involvement in role play and other dramatic activities. As a consequence, their engagement with writing and drawing would be greater and the quality of work higher (see the Diary extract, pp. 93–5).

In any individual lesson you may choose to focus on a discussion, writing, drawing or a dramatic activity. My preference is for there to be at least two different, but linked, activities in any one session. Arrange the seating so that children are next to a partner they work well with for the group discussion and interaction activities. Every class is different, as are children's respective levels of confidence. Unless otherwise indicated, teachers therefore need to make their own judgements about when a directed question needs to be part of a paired or whole-class discussion. If an expectation of maximum pupil involvement is set from the outset, it will help to use a paired discussion strategy for the first two or three activities at least. In the first few teacher-directed questions, I have indicated where paired and whole-class interactions might best take place. The remaining questions leave this to teachers' judgement and discretion.

It is important to give the children sufficient space and time for their own reflections and judgements and *not* to feel it necessary to go through *all* the questions suggested. Getting to the heart of the text and its meanings is the primary goal, and this is more likely to occur when the interaction between the teacher and the pupils is one of mutual enquiry and an openness of mind, and where there is a serious interest in what children have to say. The principles behind the model for questioning picture books in Chapter 2, Part 1 are broadly the same for written texts: that is, the questions should make demands upon children to move from lower- to higher-order levels of thinking and talking. What this means with respect to written texts is that the children gradually move from simple reporting of events without explanation to what Chambers calls 'speculation about meaning' and a search for the patterns and connections within the story (1995: 159). In the model below, the first two items will prompt reporting of the story's content, but increasing emphasis on 'why' questions will make demands upon children to think harder about the text. Item 3 challenges the readers to dig deeper into the text in an attempt to try to resolve the puzzles the story raises. Items 4 and 5 demand responses that focus on narration (the person/character telling the story), the way the story works, pattern links and the deeper meanings within it (its structure). The outline framework of the model is thus *content – narration – structure*.

The group discussion and interaction questions suggested after the model broadly follow this framework, but you will note that I have introduced 'why' questions at an early point in the questions because the Year 6 children in the workshop were used to having to justify their opinions and viewpoints. You are advised to make a limited selection for any one session which follows progressively from the *content – narration – structure* framework.

A model for questioning written texts[1]

1 Broad questions that focus on general impressions of the story as a whole. For example, What did you find interesting about the story? Which parts of the story did you enjoy most?

2 Questions about the characters and the parts they play. For example, Which character did you find most interesting? Who was the most important character?

3 Search for puzzles in the story and those parts you did not like or understand.

4 Question about narration and point of view. Who is telling the story – the author, a character in the story, more than one person?

5 Identify patterns or links in the story. In *Clockwork*, for example, What is the meaning of the clockwork metaphor for the story as a whole? What does the story have to tell us about responsibility, the nature of goodness, evil, reality and fantasy?

◇　Why did you find the story interesting? Give at least two reasons. Discuss in pairs first. Share some responses with the whole class.

◇　Tell your partner why you enjoyed the story. Give three reasons. Share one or two different sets of reasons with the whole class.

◇　Which part of the story did you enjoy most and why? (Paired activity).

◇　Were there any parts of the story which puzzled you or which you did not understand?

◇   Divide the children into small groups and assign each of them one of the following characters: Gretl, Karl, Fritz, Prince Otto, Prince Florian, Princess Mariposa and Dr Kalmenius. Children in each group to contribute all they know from the story about their assigned characters. One person from each group to share their knowledge of the different characters with the rest of the class.

◇   Which character interested you most? Give reasons for your choice.

◇   Who do you think is the most important character in the story?

◇   Do any of the characters in the story remind you of people you know in your life? If so, which character are you referring to and what qualities do they have in common?

◇   Who is telling the story? Does the same person tell the story all the way through?

◇   What part do the framed captions and pictures play in the unfolding story? Whose voice is behind the words?

◇   As you listened to the story, did you think that the various parts fitted together like clockwork? Give two examples from the story where this happens.

◇   Philip Pullman was interested in the idea of a clock working as a *metaphor* for the way in which the various parts of the story mesh together to work as a whole. Find examples of where Pullman uses clockwork metaphors to refer to the way his story works (there are three on pp. 8–9 and another on p. 92). Either read these sections again or display the passages on the interactive whiteboard. What is the difference between the way the metaphor 'wound up' is used at the beginning of the story and the way it is used at the end of the story?

◇   What is the story trying to tell us about responsibility and the choices made by the characters?

◇   What does the story tell us about the nature of goodness and evil?

◇   Does this folk tale, set in an old German town when 'time used to run by clockwork', have anything to tell us about our lives in *our* time?

Drama activities

The following activities do *not* depend on the use of the school hall. A space created in the classroom by moving the furniture safely to the sides of the room is perfectly adequate. The following props are not essential but they greatly enhanced the quality of dramatic involvement of the children who participated in the trial workshop.

Menu of activities

1   Individual character freeze-frame
2   Hot-seating
3   Group dramatisation. Fritz tells his story
4   Whole-class dramatisation. The entry of Dr Kalmenius
5   Whole-class dramatisation of both scenes
6   Whole-class dramatisation. Dr Kalmenius offers Karl a solution
7   Whole-class dramatisation. Sir Ironsoul
8   Group dramatisation. Putting it all together: Dr Kalmenius, Karl and Sir Ironsoul

---

Useful props

- A hooded garment. This can be any garment with a hood, to be used for the part of Dr Kalmenius. A long garment with a hood would fit more closely with the historic period in which the story is set. One will suffice, but if you wish several children to play the part of Dr Kalmenius simultaneously, you will need more.
- A blanket. To be used to cover Sir Ironsoul.
- Howling wind sound effect. There are any number of sound effects available for downloads on to a CDR or iTunes. The one used for the workshop had exactly the kind of authenticity and 'scare factor' that I was looking for. It is available for a small fee on http://www.tradebit.com/filedetail.php/830973. The use of this sound effect unquestionably increased the children's involvement and engagement with the drama activities.
- A tape recording of the haunting tune on p. 38 of *Clockwork*. This simple three-bar tune can be played on a descant recorder or picked out with one hand on a piano. If you can hum or play the tune without having to record it, so much the better. You can, of course, make up your own haunting tune.

Freeze-frame activity (ten minutes)

Before you begin this activity, it will be helpful to provide children with a list of the key characters and their role in the story, either in the form of a photocopied sheet or displayed on an interactive whiteboard. The idea of this activity is that children freeze in role on a given command.

The characters in *Clockwork*

Gretl, the little barmaid and the landlord's daughter
Karl, the clockmaker's apprentice
Fritz, the writer and storyteller
Prince Otto, father of Prince Florian
Prince Florian
Princess Mariposa, wife of Prince Otto and mother of Prince Florian
Dr Kalmenius, a brilliant clockmaker and a kind of philosopher
Sir Ironsoul, a clockwork knight in armour made by Dr Kalmenius

The children should sit in a space on the floor and choose the character that they would like to be. Before beginning the activity, issue the following instruction.

Think carefully about who you are and what you might be doing. You can either stand still and mime an action typical of the character you have chosen or you can move around the room in role.

If you are moving in role, think about the differences in the way you would walk if you were Karl or Princess Mariposa, for example.

On the instruction 'Go', the children move into role. On the command of '**Freeze**', the teacher and any other adults in the room have to guess which character a chosen child is playing. Repeat one more time, ensuring that the children hold their action absolutely still on the command of 'Freeze'.

Now split the class into two. One half watch while the other half mime a character different from the one they had chosen before. Tell the watching half of the class to concentrate on watching one or two children only.

Go.

Freeze.

Can you guess which character(s) they were playing?

Praise the children for what they did well and change over so that the watching half become the acting half. Repeat as above.

Hot-seating activity (fifteen minutes)

Children choose which character they would like to be in 'the hot seat'. Limit the choice of characters to Fritz, Karl, Gretl, Dr Kalmenius and Prince Florian. You may need to remind the children of what was said in the discussion about the main characteristics of each of these before beginning the activity. Seat the children in a horseshoe shape with a chair in the gap of the crescent. Before beginning the activity, instruct the children as follows:

Think carefully about the character you would like to play and the kind of person he or she is.

Close your eyes for a minute or so and think about the role the character played in the story in relation to the other characters.

Begin the activity by choosing a child who is reasonably confident about performing in front of others and who will be able to sustain credibility in their chosen role. This will set the tone for the others. Children and teachers then ask questions of the character in the hot seat in turns. Keep the pace moving and give as many children as time allows a chance to be in the hot seat. If children choose to hot-seat the same character as one that has previously been 'hot-seated', encourage children to ask questions *different* from the ones asked before (otherwise the activity will become tedious and undemanding for the new child in the hot seat).

Group dramatisation: Fritz tells his story (fifteen minutes)

Scene: The White Horse Tavern. Fritz is in full flow, telling his story to a rapt audience in the warm and cosy inn. He reaches the point in his story where he says, 'And that was the man who . . .'. Tell the children they are going to work in groups of three or four, with one of them playing Fritz and the others playing members of his audience. To help the children get into the mood and atmosphere of the scene, read from the second paragraph on p. 27 of *Clockwork or All Wound Up* beginning 'Dr Kalmenius could . . .' to the top line on p. 29 beginning 'And that was . . .'. Get all the children to think about how they will put Fritz's story into their own words. It does not matter if they forget parts and have to make up their own lines. The important thing is that they remember the last line: 'And that was the man who . . .'. At this point, Fritz stares in horror at the door and everyone else follows his gaze in terrified silence.

Get into groups of three and four and sit in different spaces in the room. Decide which of you is to be Fritz.

Fritz sits in the middle of the group on a stool or chair. The other three arrange themselves around him in various positions. You can be seated, standing, leaning against the bar or the fireplace.

You are all drinking ale out of large mugs. Some of you are smoking a pipe, some of you have your arms folded, chin cupped in your hands, leaning forwards or backwards as you listen attentively to the story.

Discuss with the group how each of you is going to behave in the scenario.

After a count of three, move into your positions and go.

Fritz begins his story and carries on until he reaches the line about Dr Kalmenius.

The teacher knocks three times on a hard surface to announce the entry of Dr K. This is the cue for Fritz and his audience to react in horror as above.

Repeat the procedure in the same groups with another person playing the part of Fritz. Tell the children what they have done well and encourage them to say how the dramatisation might be improved.

Whole-class dramatisation: The entry of Dr Kalmenius (ten minutes)

In this activity, all the children are going to be Dr Kalmenius. Display the following on the interactive whiteboard while you read it to the children:

He was very tall and thin, with a prominent nose and jaw. His eyes blazed like coals in caverns of darkness. His hair was long and grey, and he wore a black cloak with a loose hood like that of a monk; he had a harsh grating voice and his expression was full of savage curiosity. And that was the man who. . . .

Imagine how you are going to portray Dr K. How would he walk? What expression would be on his face?

He pulls a sledge in the freezing cold wind with his cloak wrapped tightly around him. He knocks on the door of the tavern, bows and speaks in a harsh and grating voice with the words 'Dr Kalmenius of Schatzberg, at your service. I have come a long way tonight, and I am cold. A glass of brandy!'

Practise saying these lines in a harsh and grating voice two or three times.

Think about how you are going to pull the sledge in a freezing cold wind.

Think about how you are going to communicate an air of menace and mystery.

Play the tape recording of the howling wind sound effect while the children listen. The children then go into role to the accompaniment of the sound effect.

 You walk, pulling the sledge until you come to the door of the inn. Knock on the door three times and say the words 'Dr Kalmenius of Schatzberg at your service . . .'.

Repeat, this time thinking carefully about how you would walk in the howling wind while pulling your sledge.

Show one or two examples of effective mime. Say what worked well and how it might be improved.

Whole-class dramatisation of both scenes (twenty minutes)

Choose one child to play Fritz and another to play Dr K while the rest of the class act as members of Fritz's audience in the White Horse Tavern. Use the Gothic Fire screensaver as a backdrop. The child playing Dr K is to be given the hooded cloak or garment to wear.

The following is an outline of the action:

*   Fritz is telling his story to a rapt audience in the White Horse Tavern.
*   Continue until the line 'And that was the man who . . .'.
*   The howling wind sound effect is to start just before the line above.
*   The teacher knocks three times, loudly.
*   Dr K enters, bows and speaks the line, 'Dr Kalmenius of Schatzberg at your service . . .'.
*   Fade the wind sound while the above line is being spoken.
*   Fritz reacts with a horrified look.
*   The rest of the audience follow his gaze towards the door.
*   The audience gradually leave, showing varying signs of fear and terror (some crossing themselves), without looking at Dr K until the White Horse Tavern is emptied, leaving only Fritz and Dr K.

Whole-class dramatisation: Dr Kalmenius offers Karl a solution (twenty minutes)

Scene: Karl has had too much to drink and is leaning miserably against the bar. Dr K approaches him with the lines:

I think I have something that will solve all your problems. What you wish for is right here (points to blanket on sledge). Uncover it! Take off the canvas!

Karl is very afraid, but he slowly unties the ropes holding the blanket in place on the sledge. He tremulously pulls back the blanket to reveal the clockwork knight. He walks round the figure slowly, looking in wonder at its perfection. He kneels to look closely at his sword. He touches it and it cuts his finger. He snatches his hand away with the lines:

> It's like a razor . . . And how does he move? What does he do? He does work by clockwork, I suppose? Or is there some kind of goblin in there? A spirit or a devil of some kind?

Display both sets of lines on an interactive whiteboard and let the children read them to themselves two or three times. Choose one child to play Karl while you, the teacher, go into role as Dr K. Place the blanket on the floor close to Dr K.

The following is an outline of the action:

- Begin with Karl leaning miserably against the bar while Dr K looks at him with a glass of brandy in his hand.
- Dr K speaks the lines as above.
- Karl responds as indicated.
- The children say what worked well and how it might be improved.

Every child is now going to play the part of Karl while you, the teacher stay in role as Dr K.

Find a space on the floor.

Imagine you have the sledge and blanket close by you. Kneel down by the sledge and mime the action of untying knots in a wet rope two or three times until I can see the knots on the rope untying one by one.

Practise slowly uncovering the blanket to reveal the exquisite clockwork knight.

Walk round slowly, looking at it in wonder.

Kneel, touch the sword and draw back quickly as the sword cuts your finger.

Practise saying the line 'It's like a razor . . .'

Now you, the teacher, go in role at Dr K, beginning as before and ending with Karl's lines '. . . a devil of some kind?'

Whole-class dramatisation: Sir Ironsoul (fifteen minutes)

Play the three-bar tune which is the cue to stop Ironsoul from killing his prey. This can be sung or played, but during the role play of Dr K it will be easier to sing it because it saves the action from being interrupted. If you cannot remember the tune well enough to sing it, make up a haunting tune of your own. All the children are to play Sir Ironsoul.

Lie down in a space on the floor.

Imagine you are Sir Ironsoul clothed in armour with your sword at your side.

When you hear the word 'devil', you tick and whirr into life. You slowly get up, turn your helmeted head towards an imaginary Karl, raise your sword and walk towards him with the intention to kill.

The teacher speaks Karl's line, 'Is there some kind of goblin in there? A spirit or a devil of some kind?'

All the children mime the actions above. When all the Sir Ironsouls are walking towards their imaginary Karls with their swords raised, the teacher, in role as Dr K, sings (humming or la, la la-ing) the haunting tune.

 Immediately you hear me singing the haunting tune, freeze and hold your movement absolutely still.

The children will need to practise moving like clockwork with their head turning towards Karl, sword raised, arms, legs and torso following, all with jerky, mechanised movements. Make demands upon the children to think carefully about how they will do this. Practise two or three times. Demonstrate effective actions by choosing one or two children who have begun to get the idea by sharing their mime with the rest of the class.

Repeat once more and then go through the sequence again.

Group dramatisation: Putting it all together: Karl, Dr Kalmenius and Sir Ironsoul (twenty minutes)

Depending on the time available and the children's level of involvement and interest, divide them into groups of three with one playing Karl, another Dr K and the third, Sir Ironsoul. Ensure that both Karl's and Dr K's lines are displayed again. If the children can manage without them, reset the Gothic Fire screensaver. Go through the entire sequence beginning with Dr K's line 'I think I have something that will solve . . .' to the point where Dr K sings the haunting tune to stop Sir Ironsoul from killing Karl. All children freeze at various points in their group work. When all the children are completely still, bring the session to a close with further praise and a cool-down activity.

Drawing, language work and writing activities

Drawing and language work

The objective of this part of the session is to draw a picture of Dr Kalmenius. Return to the description of Dr Kalmenius on p. 87. Display it on an interactive whiteboard. Ask the children to read it to themselves again while thinking about how they portrayed him in the drama sessions.

◇   Get the children to talk together in working pairs to describe the key features of Dr K – for example, 'He was very tall and thin with a prominent nose and jaw.'

◇   Tell each other what you think is meant by the word 'prominent' and discuss how you might show this feature in your drawings.

◇ Share with the class and check that the meaning of 'prominent' is secure.

◇ What were his clothes like? What would he wear on his feet?

◇ Think about Pullman's simile 'His eyes blazed like coals in caverns of darkness.' What does it mean and how might it be shown in your drawings?

◇ What does the phrase '*savage* curiosity' mean? What kind of expression would communicate a '*savage* curiosity'?

Illustrations of figures in long, hooded gowns from history books or from paintings will provide useful models to which the children can refer during the drawing activity. Use A4-sized paper for the drawing of Dr K and encourage children to fill the page from top to bottom.

Writing activity

The drawing activity focused the children's attention on the outward appearance of Dr K. The writing activity makes demands on the children to think about the inner motives and feelings of the man. The following are some questions to stimulate and direct the children's thinking:

◇ Think about the man and what drives him or makes him 'tick'.

◇ What powers does he think he has which other people do not possess?

◇ What do other people think of him? Are they afraid or in awe of him? Does he care what they think?

◇ How did he know that Karl would need his powers to help him out of trouble?

◇ Think about the simile that Pullman uses to describe Dr K's eyes: 'His eyes blazed like coals in caverns of darkness.' Can they think of a simile they might use to describe his inner thoughts and feelings?

◇ Brainstorm ideas in pairs and share ideas with the whole class.

◇ Write five or six sentences that give a description of Dr Kalmenius from his point of view, beginning with 'I . . .'.

◇ When the drawing and pieces of writing are completed, share selected examples with the whole class.

Use and application of new vocabulary

There are a number of words and concepts in the story that may be new to the children, for example, apoplexy, implacable, inexorable, artifice, illusion, congenital and malign. Some brief, simple definitions of the above words are given on p. 102.

◇ Give some textual context for these words and ask the children to try to work out what they mean.
◇ After brief discussion, give some short, exemplified meanings of the words. This activity need only take five or ten minutes.

Writing and drawing activity

Give the children an opportunity to choose another character in the story which particularly appeals to them. The children in the workshop were particularly fascinated by Princess Mariposa, and several chose to draw and write about her (see the Diary, pp. 94–95). This time the writing should come before the drawing. As above, ask the children to write five or six sentences about the character, using similes and/or metaphors, including one or two words from the list above where appropriate. As with Dr K start the sentences with 'I . . .'.

◇ Encourage the children to refer back to the story text in order to reread the descriptions Pullman gives of their chosen characters. Some additional information is given in the framed captions, so these should be included in their revisiting of the text.
◇ Ask the children to use their written descriptions and knowledge gained from the text to draw a picture of their chosen character with the same care and precision of detail that they used for the drawing of Dr K.

Objectives and learning outcomes

1   To deepen children's understanding, appreciation and enjoyment of Philip Pullman's story *Clockwork*.
2   To develop children's understanding and knowledge of how Philip Pullman achieves coherence in *Clockwork* via the concept of his 'clock' metaphor.
3   To enable children to use, understand and apply some of the following concepts and vocabulary: metaphor, narrative, apoplexy, congenital, implacable, malign, inexorable, artifice and illusion.
4   To challenge children's understanding and thinking about the deeper meaning of the story, particularly with respect to metaphor, coherence and narration.
5   To provide writing, drawing, drama and speaking and listening activities that will deepen and extend their understanding of the characters in the story as well as how the characters change and develop.
6   To extend and improve children's ability to write descriptions of two characters involving the use of figurative language based on models of language provided by the text.
7   To sufficiently stimulate children's interest and understanding of *Clockwork* for them to want to read other books by Philip Pullman.

Lesson/series of lessons/unit of work outcomes

By the end of the lesson/unit of work, the children will be able to:

1   think and reflect more knowledgeably about the deeper meaning of the story;
2   understand how metaphor works to achieve coherence in a story narrative;
3   mime and act, individually in small and larger groups, selected scenarios from the story;
4   describe at least one character, in their own words, using Pullman's description of Dr Kalmenius as a model;
5   use vivid and accurate language in their writing;
6   draw accurately at least one character from the story using the text as a source of reference;
7   read a wider range of books by Philip Pullman with interest, enjoyment and appreciation.

Diary

The observations of the children throughout the day's workshop were sharp, perceptive and, at times, disarming. Yet the children were described to me by their very able and experienced class teacher as 'not easy to enthuse', 'difficult to motivate' and 'definitely not high-flyers'. None of these descriptors applied to the workshop and it was evidence, if such evidence is needed, of the power of the story to unlock the extraordinary and unusual in children.

Reading the end of the story

The workshop began with a reading of the last twenty pages of the story. When the screensaver was put on to signal that it was time for the story, the children rushed forward to sit on the carpet. I had practised reading it with different voices for all the characters. The dramatic and expressive reading, the screensaver and chiming clock unquestionably enhanced the atmosphere and increased the children's involvement in the story.

Class discussion and interaction

The responses to the questions indicated in the teaching activities sessions showed that the concepts and ideas the children were asked to grapple with were well within their capabilities.

Indeed, their responses showed both insight and wisdom. For example, when asked what they understood by Dr Kalmenius's line 'The heart that is given must also be kept', one boy said, 'It means that she gave her love and affection to Prince Florian, but kept her heart, meaning that she did not physically give her heart like Prince Otto did.' A girl then said, 'Do you think that Gretl actually fancied Florian?' A very articulate boy quickly responded, 'No! She was only about 11 or 12, she couldn't have fancied him. I think she just loved him like a responsible older sister would.' Most of the class agreed with this viewpoint.

Freeze-frame activity

At the beginning, the children needed some encouragement to be clearer in their actions and the way they walked in character. Demonstrating one or two effective frozen frames quickly improved their work. I was interested in the number of children (including boys) who chose to mime Princess Mariposa combing her hair, trying on jewellery and looking at herself in the mirror. One boy ably portrayed Karl, leaning against the bar and morosely drinking one drink after another. The children clearly enjoyed this activity and would happily have gone on with it for longer.

Hot-seating activity

I was amazed, as was their class teacher, by the feisty and robust way in which the children defended their characters, whether questioned by teachers or by children. Indeed, a very shy Asian boy, who normally did not like drama, had chosen to be in the hot seat as Karl. When asked by his class teacher about how he felt about choosing to keep Sir Ironsoul as a way of making money while consigning Prince Florian to chains and fetters inside the Clock Tower, he was unrelenting in the defence of his actions. He was pressed further by his teacher: 'Don't you feel bad in any way about what you've done?' The boy was not in the least fazed by the question, stuck to his chosen 'guns' and expressed no remorse whatsoever.

The most interesting thing about this very familiar drama warm-up activity was the seriousness and relish that the children displayed in their involvement. They had clearly internalised the various characters' personalities during the reading of the story. They really knew them, understood them and enjoyed the opportunity to give voice to their feelings about them. Their responses to the questions put to them by both adults and children were informed, confident, assertive and unselfconscious. Again, they did not want to 'wind this activity up'.

Group and whole-class dramatisations

The children loved acting the part of Sir Ironsoul. I did not accept their first enactments of the clockwork knight coming to life and insisted that they think very carefully about precisely how a clockwork figure would move. After the third attempt, the children clearly wanted to get it right and enjoyed doing so.

When I was in role as Karl and spoke the word 'devil', the children walked inexorably towards me with their swords raised! I had not anticipated this and as they moved in unison in my direction, I broke into fits of giggles, as did they. According to their class teacher, it was their enjoyment in getting better at playing Sir Ironsoul that made their involvement in the drama so intensely rewarding for them. A comment made by the class teacher in his written workshop evaluation is worth quoting: 'Many teachers tend to rush through drama activities and move the children on far too quickly. They need time to develop and rehearse their performance and their interpretation of the character. This is what gives them the confidence to improve.'

Drawing and writing activities

What was revealing about the drawing task was that I thought it would be relatively unproblematic, given the stimulation they had been given in the drama activities and the constant references to the text. Not so! The children were keen to do the drawing of Dr K but did not have the requisite drawing skills to do justice to it. Some really struggled to get their drawings right, especially the way in which the cloak draped over Dr K's tall, thin body. Some children became visibly disheartened with their efforts and frequently asked for help. The few drawings that showed vitality and confidence were those done by children who went to voluntary art classes after school or whose parents encouraged them to draw at home. The class teacher commented that unfortunately the constraints of the National Curriculum gave them little time to practise and gain confidence in drawing skills. Several children were particularly interested in the character of Princess Mariposa, who featured significantly in their drawings and writing. Some children commented that they thought she was a shallow character who was not in the least interested in her child, Prince Florian, seeing him as a mere accessory to her self-interested life. Perhaps the children were making a connection here with the cult of celebrity glamour and image projection which is currently so pervasive in television programmes and the popular press.

Language work and writing activities

The children had no difficulty in grasping the central meaning of the clockwork metaphor or the way in which Pullman sustains it throughout the story. They also demonstrated a beginning understanding of new vocabulary and concepts (see the examples of work on pp. 99–102). However, the writing they produced was unremarkable, given all that they had experienced during the day. Interestingly, several children produced drawings and writing of a markedly higher quality at home later that day. This was entirely unsolicited by either the class teacher or myself.

The important point of pedagogical interest here is this: they had given so much to the drama and the discussion following the story that they were tired by the time the writing and drawing tasks took place. They needed time and space to let the experience sink in and assimilate with prior knowledge. When they had the benefit of some hours' distance from the workshop, they were able to produce work that demonstrated clearly how much they had gained from the story, the discussion and the drama activities.

As can be seen from the following examples of work, the quality is unremarkable, but it was their first effort and considered to be of a higher standard than usual by the class teacher. The most important outcome was the degree of energy and enthusiasm that the children showed in their reaction to the story and the work following from it. Several of them have since been inspired to read other novels by Philip Pullman. On the day following the workshop, a mother of one of the boys in the class commented to the teacher that her son, who would not normally talk about school at all, had been so motivated by the drama that 'he would not stop talking about it'.

Examples of children's work

Dr Kalmenius

Figure 3.1 Work by Amber (Year 6).

Isabelle

Marapossa

Figure 3.2 Work by Isabelle (Year 6).

Dr Kalmenius

Figure 3.3 Work by Georgina (Year 6).

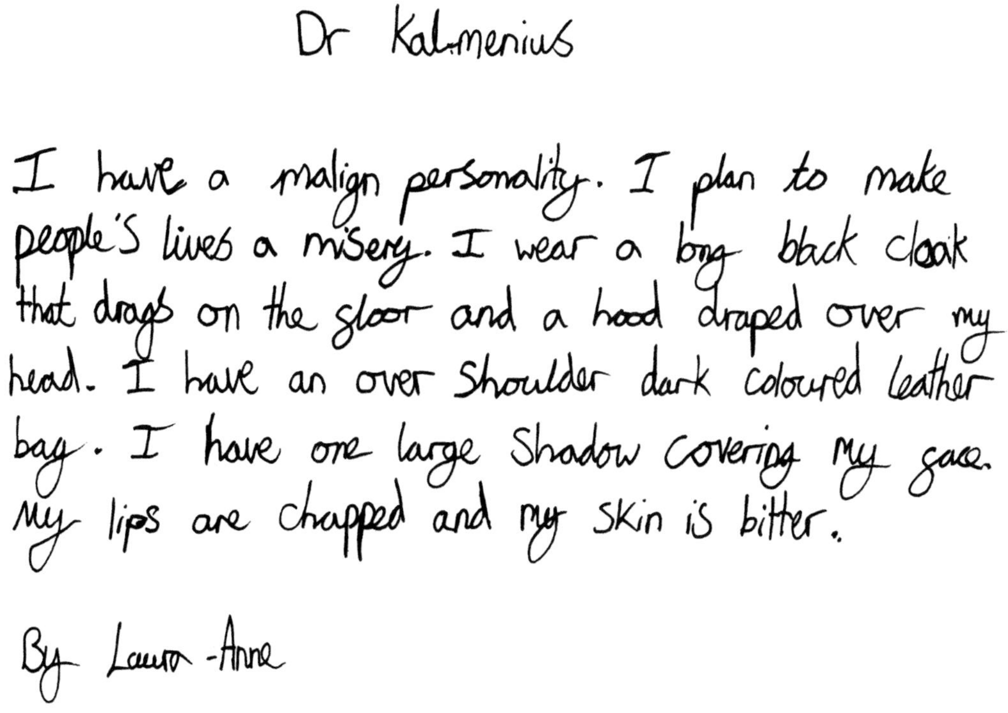

Dr Kalmenius

I have a malign personality. I plan to make people's lives a misery. I wear a long black cloak that drags on the floor and a hood draped over my head. I have an over shoulder dark coloured leather bag. I have one large shadow covering my face. My lips are chapped and my skin is bitter.

By Laura-Anne

Figure 3.4 Work by Laura-Anne (Year 6).

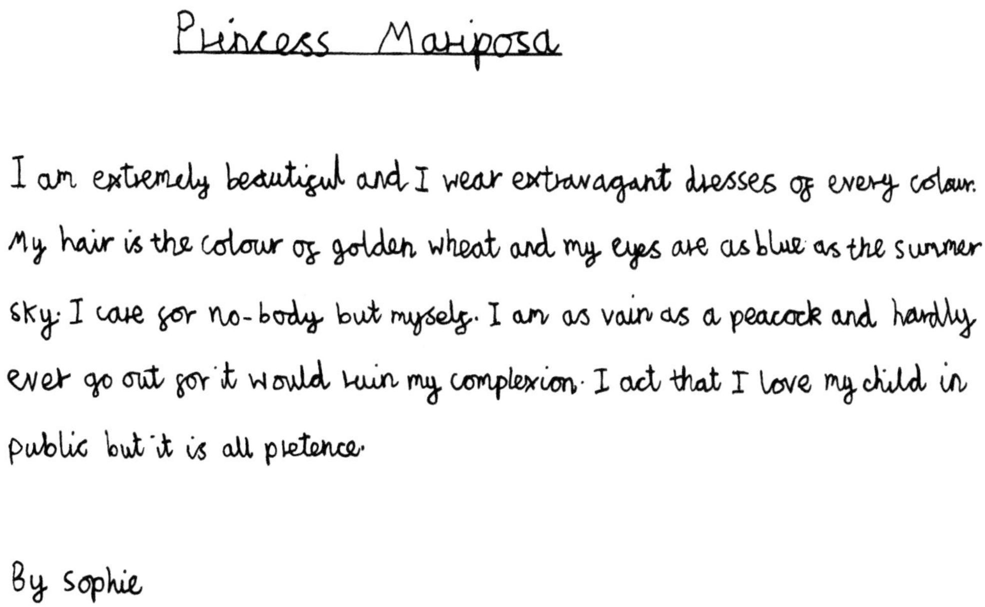

Princess Mariposa

I am extremely beautiful and I wear extravagant dresses of every colour. My hair is the colour of golden wheat and my eyes are as blue as the summer sky. I care for no-body but myself. I am as vain as a peacock and hardly ever go out for it would ruin my complexion. I act that I love my child in public but it is all pretence.

By Sophie

Figure 3.5 Work by Sophie (Year 6).

Figure 3.6 Work by Isabelle (Year 6).

Gretl

All I ever do is work and I'm sick of it. My hands so much hurt from putting new logs on the fire, sweeping, serving drinks and lots more. I do not get paid I just work day after day. My cat Putzi is the only one who I can talk to, she is the only one who understands how I feel. I have got no friends just Putzi and my loving dad. Today I found a friend but I did not know his name because he could not speak (I think he had some kind of illness), that person made me feel happy and I felt like a big sister to him. I have no education not like the other kids.

By Laura

Figure 3.7 Work by Laura (Year 6).

Sir Ironsoul

I move by clockwork and am as stiff as rusty old metal.

I have shining iron armour and a sword which can pierce through your skin.

I wake up when I hear the word, 'devil' and destroy all who will say it.

I have a master who made me and he is the only one who can put me back into my death.

By Jordan

Figure 3.8 Work by Jordan (Year 6).

By
Jade. W.
29. 3. 07

Baron
Stelgratz
(Friend of the royal family)

Figure 3.9 Work by Jade (Year 6).

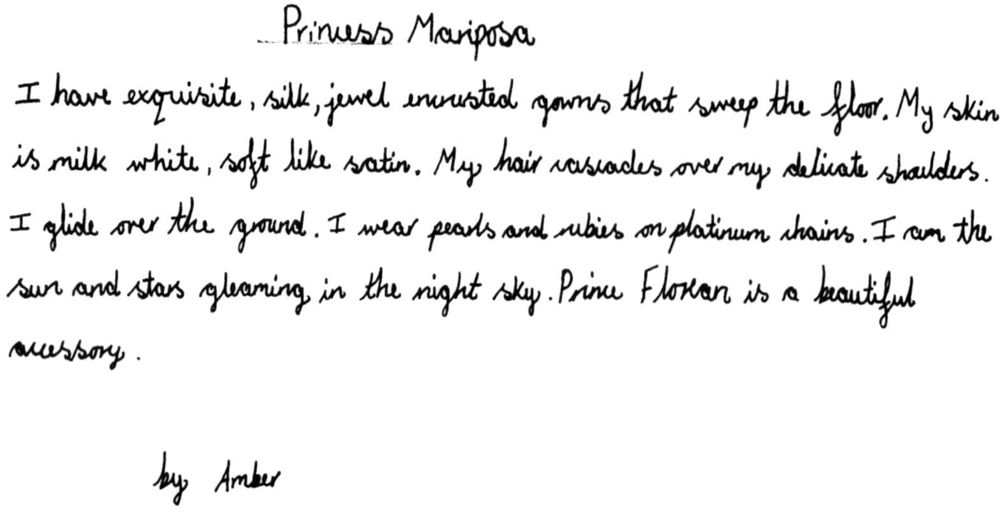

Princess Mariposa

I have exquisite, silk, jewel encrusted gowns that sweep the floor. My skin is milk white, soft like satin. My hair cascades over my delicate shoulders. I glide over the ground. I wear pearls and rubies on platinum chains. I am the sun and stars gleaming in the night sky. Prince Florian is a beautiful accessory.

by Amber

Figure 3.10 Work by Amber (Year 6).

Simple explanations of vocabulary and concepts arising from _Clockwork_

Artifice   A clever trick or device. It can also be a literary or dramatic tool that sets out to evoke a particular response from a reader, listener or viewer. Pullman's use of authorial captions to make particular moral points is a good example of literary artifice.

Apoplexy   A kind of stroke caused by severe bleeding in the brain.

Congenital   An illness or condition that is present at birth. It can also refer to an illness or personality characteristic and is ingrained in someone's character.

Illusion   Something that sets out to appear as one thing when it is really another. In literary terminology, it refers to the writer's creation of a convincing imagined world. _Clockwork_ is based entirely on illusion. For example, at the end of the story we are led to believe that Prince Florian is a living person and that Putzi, the cat, is somehow implicated in Karl's downfall.

Implacable   Impossible to pacify or reduce in strength. For example, a fierce blizzard or deadly enemy might be described as 'implacable'.

Inexorable   Impossible to stop, like ageing or time marching on.

Malign   Evil in nature, disposition or intent.

Teaching resources

- Copy of _Clockwork or All Wound Up_. The edition used for the whole-day workshop was P. Pullman (1997) _Clockwork or All Wound Up_, Corgi Yearling Books, London: Random House Children's Books. Two or three extra copies would be useful so that children can use them to refer to the text for help with the writing and drawing activities.
- Gothic Fire screensaver. This is a free screensaver that can be found on http://www. magentic.com/gallery/gallery. Click on the 'Fireplace' screensaver menu on the left. It is an

animated screensaver complete with the sound of crackling logs and ticking clock. If the screensaver is put on each time the story is read, it serves as a theatrical backdrop and intensifies the atmosphere.

- Chiming antique wall clock. Highly desirable but not essential. Few children may have seen, let alone heard, a chiming clock. If one can be borrowed from an educational resource centre, museum or local clockmaker which shows the pendulum and working parts, the story will have more meaning for the children. The one used for the workshop was borrowed from a local clockmaker for a returnable deposit fee only.
- An enlarged photocopy of the great clock of Glockenheim. Page 14 of the Corgi Yearling edition (1997).
- Photocopies or word documents (saved to a memory stick for use on an interactive whiteboard) of the description of Dr Kalmenius and extracts of speeches by Karl and Dr K.
- Historic pictures or paintings of men wearing long, hooded cloaks.

Useful websites and additional sources of information

For a very useful and comprehensive chapter on how to frame questions that enable children to develop their understanding of how books work, see:

Chambers, A. with Suter, I., Raven, B., Maxwell, J., Collins, A. and Bicknell, S. (1995) 'Tell me: are children critics?', in A. Chambers (1995) *Booktalk: Occasional writing on literature and children*, Stroud, UK: Thimble Press.

For a complete list of Philip Pullman's works, see:
http://www.randomhouse.com/features/pullman/books/books.html (accessed 17 October 2007).

Philip Pullman's own website contains a wealth of personal and authorial detail:
http://www.philip-pullman.com/about_the_author.asp (accessed 17 October 2007).

For details of the latest version of *Clockwork or All Wound Up* with illustrations by Leonid Gore:
http://www.arthuralevinebooks.com/book.asp?bookid=15 (accessed 17 October 2007).

Philip Pullman
Parallel worlds and penny dreadfuls

The writer and the man

Philip Pullman is a writer with an incandescent imagination and a prodigious talent for telling stories. Like Michael Morpurgo (see Chapter 1, Part 2), Pullman sees himself primarily as a storyteller. Both writers have been remarkable teachers and they know that children, regardless of age or generation, have always been in thrall to the power of stories if they are well told, have clearly developed characters, suspense, and moments of terror and relief. This belief in the centrality of stories to our lives is at the core of Pullman's intellectual and emotional being. He learned how to tell stories when he taught in Oxford middle schools for over twelve years. He fed his pupils with the sinewy and timeless tales from our vast and rich literary heritage, including those of one of history's greatest bards, Homer, retelling the epic myths of *The Iliad* and *The Odyssey* in his own words over several years. The opportunity to hone his storytelling skills in this way taught him an immense amount about the way narrative works to sustain interest, and it is likely that within these experiences the seeds of the nascent writer began to flourish. In an interview with Melvyn Bragg in 2003, he said that this was an invaluable experience which taught him a great deal about what he could do as a storyteller and about where to position the repetitive hooks so essential to the dramatic shape of the story and the flow of language.

Frustrated by the lack of suitable play texts for pupils aged between 9 and 13 years, he wrote his own play, a Victorian thriller called *The Ruby in the Smoke*, which was later published in book form as the first of the Sally Lockhart quartet. The same impulse produced *Count Karlstein* (1982) and *The Firework-Maker's Daughter* (1995). It was through the writing of these plays, which were written for dual audiences of parents and children, that Pullman began to experiment with 'various levels of narration and meaning in his texts' (Squires, 2006: 25). This was the beginning of a writing career that began in 1972 with a book called *The Haunted Storm*, with which Pullman was extremely dissatisfied. This was followed by a steady stream of stories that began to make his name in the children's book publishing world. However, it would be a further thirty-three years or so before his writing would attract serious public attention with the publication in 1995 of *Northern Lights*, the first of the *His Dark Materials* trilogy. This inventive and highly original work won the Carnegie Medal. This was followed by the second in the trilogy, *The Subtle Knife*, in 1997 and the third, *The Amber Spyglass*, in 2000. Pullman's success as a writer rocketed him to celebrity status when *The Amber Spyglass* won the Whitbread Children's Book of the Year award and the overall Whitbread Book of the Year Award, the first children's book ever to do so. Not only did this award significantly increase the status of children's literature as a serious literary genre but it also established a closer link between what is considered to be adult and what is considered to be children's literature. With Pullman's trilogy and J.K. Rowling's heptalogy, a new crossover cult began, with both adults and children following their books with intense interest. Pullman's spectacular epic quest of Lyra and Will's travels between parallel worlds to find a missing father and Lyra's best friend, Roger, sufficiently fired the imagination of director Nicholas Hytner at the National Theatre for him to mount a stage adaptation of the trilogy in 2003. It resulted in an astonishing feat of puppetry, theatrical effects and inspired direction. Demand to see the play was so overwhelming that it ran again in 2004 with a different cast. In December 2007, despite long-running internecine battles between various directors, and the objections of right-wing fundamentalist US religious groups and the Roman Catholic Church, the film, entitled *The Golden Compass*, went on general release on 5 December 2007 starring Nicole Kidman as Mrs Coulter, Daniel Craig as Lord Asriel and Dakota Blue Richards as Lyra Belacqua.

Philip Pullman was born in Norwich in 1946. Both his father and his stepfather were in the RAF, and their respective postings meant that the family lived for periods of time in Zimbabwe and Australia. It was in Australia that he met the wonders of comics; Superman and Batman were particular favourites, and it was through these and radio serials that he developed his love of storytelling and an ambition to write stories of his own. When the family returned from what was then called Southern Rhodesia, news came that Pullman's father had been killed in a plane crash. The news did not have much impact on him at the time because his father was frequently away and he scarcely knew him. However, he remembered feeling vividly that he was now 'half an orphan' (Ross, 2002), and he has written at some length about the effect that the death of his father had upon himself and his literary development. The events of his childhood would, according to Tucker (2003), eventually lead to a preoccupation in his writing with dead or missing fathers. This is certainly true of the *His Dark Materials* trilogy, in which both young protagonists are, in effect, orphaned (Duncan, 2007). Pullman also had an ambivalent relationship with his mother, who was both glamorous and distant. In fact, his mother was a bright but profoundly unhappy woman for whom life was a series of missed opportunities. Pullman's experience as her son was that she was very hard to please. 'She died before I had any success with my books. She thought I was a failure' (Rabinovitch, 2003b: 3). Notwithstanding, he describes the lives of both his parents as intensely alluring. It is likely that these sensual memories of his parents fuelled his imagination in the creation of Lord Asriel and Mrs Coulter in *His Dark Materials* (Squires, 2006). Of profound importance to the young Pullman was his love for his maternal grandfather, who was a vicar in a small Norfolk village. He was a formative influence in Pullman's life and, most importantly, had a talent for telling stories which became a source of inspiration throughout Pullman's life, as did the King James Bible and *Hymns Ancient and Modern*. It was the language and poetry of these latter sources that stayed with Pullman, not his belief in God or the established Church, which he later rejected in his adolescent years.

Why have his books, and this trilogy in particular, so ignited the imaginations of children? Pullman writes of strange, fantastical worlds that are spacious and wholly different from the domestic confines and digitally connected worlds in which many children live these days. Essentially, the story of Lyra and Will is about growing up in worlds where there are different rules, different boundaries, magical instruments whose powers are available only to those who have an intuitive knowledge of their potential. It is a vast and changing world, which is intellectually challenging and embedded in a moral and emotional integrity. His readers have to move fast to keep up with his 'suspenseful narrative' (Rustin and Rustin, 2003a: 425). The poetry of his language and the inventiveness of his multiple and believable worlds seldom lose sight of the fundamental human experience of what it is like to grow up knowing loyalty, love and trust in a relationship of true friendship when responsible adults have betrayed you.

His works

Pullman has written over twenty-one books, two plays and countless essays, articles, lectures and reviews. His lecture and essay narratives are as carefully constructed and consistently imaginative as his fictional works, perhaps because both are assiduously researched and grounded in the urgent contemporary issues of our times. His work falls into six main categories: *His Dark Materials*, contemporary novels, the Sally Lockhart quartet, The New Cut Gang, books with pictures and fairy tales, and published plays.

The first part of this chapter examined in detail the meta-fictive fairy story *Clockwork or All Wound Up*. His fairy stories are all 'suspenseful narratives' with a clear narrative authority. They are each set in different countries, are relatively short, read aloud extremely well and offer rich opportunities for discussion and drama. His latest book in this genre is *The Servant and His Scarecrow*, which is set in Italy and tells the story of a pea-brained scarecrow and his faithful servant, Jack, whose imaginative wit and storytelling prowess save them from serious trouble with the Buffaloni family. There are two realistic novels set in contemporary times, entitled *The Broken Bridge* and *The Butterfly Tattoo*. The New Cut Gang books concern a mixed bunch of vagabonds set in late Victorian London and their adventures among the crooks and market traders of the time. His two published plays are *Frankenstein* and *Sherlock Holmes and the Limehouse Horror*. The Sally Lockhart quartet comprises four novels set in Victorian England centred on the fearless, brave and feisty Sally Lockhart. Pullman calls them historical thrillers, and they include in order of publication *The Ruby in the Smoke*, *The Shadow in the North*, *The Tiger in the Well* and *The Tin Princess*. One of his most recent publications, written after the *His Dark Materials* trilogy, concerns Lyra two years later, when she has returned to Jordan College as a schoolchild. The book details Lyra's life in Oxford, and the story begins with a strange flock of birds rising in the sky above the Botanic Gardens. It is, as Pullman describes it, 'a sort of stepping stone' between the trilogy and the book he is currently writing, *The Book of Dust*. It is impossible to do justice to the range of genres in Pullman's works in one chapter, so the main discussion will focus on selected aspects of the Sally Lockhart quartet and *His Dark Materials*. The reasons for this are twofold: first, some of the precursors to *His Dark Materials* are to be found in the Sally Lockhart series, and the relationship between these two works is therefore worth exploring. Second, they represent very clearly some of Pullman's finest writing as well as the core philosophical and social themes within which his dazzling narratives are embedded.

The Sally Lockhart quartet

Philip Pullman describes the Sally Lockhart books as 'old-fashioned Victorian blood-and-thunder' (Pullman, n.d.). Drawing on his love of Sherlock Holmes's detective stories and the sensational melodramas of the Victorian 'penny dreadfuls' (a form of cheap and sensational literature prevalent in the 1880s), the books crackle with suspense and mystery. They were written initially to delight his 11- to 13-year-old pupils, and each has a 'cliché of melodrama' (Pullman, n.d.) at the heart of it. In the first, it is a cursed, blood-soaked ruby; in the second, a madman with a weapon that could destroy the world; in the third, Sally is trapped in a cellar with rising water; and in the fourth, the illiterate, abused Adelaide from the first book becomes the Crown Princess of Razkavia. The stories have tightly woven plots and richly drawn characters. The main characters are unusual and differently heroic, while the malevolence of the evildoers is so penetrating that it seeps through the pages and into the skin like a London smog. It is small wonder that the series was seen as highly suitable material for television adaptation. *The*

Ruby in the Smoke was televised on BBC1 in 2006 and *The Shadow in the North* was shown in December 2007, with the remaining two scheduled for 2008.

The title of the first, *The Ruby in the Smoke*, is in itself intriguing, and the reader has to travel some distance into the story before the link between a cursed ruby, the opium trade and its British colonial connection is revealed. The story is set in 1872 amid the riverside docks and warehouses of Victorian London. On the first page, we are introduced to 16-year-old Sally Lockhart, who is blonde, in mourning dress and 'uncommonly pretty' (Pullman, 1985: 1). Pullman typically grips his readers from the start with the stark revelation that 'within fifteen minutes, she was going to kill a man' (ibid.: 1). Sally is indeed the indirect cause of Mr Higgs's death when she mentions the words 'The Seven Blessings', but his death does not stem from any conscious action on her part. We also learn that Sally is twice an orphan, her father having been killed in an unexplained drowning at sea and her mother shot in the Indian Mutiny when she was only a few months old. Orphaned women heroines who have to make their way in the world using their wits, inner resources and the knowledge acquired from their unconventional upbringing are the intriguing heroines in Pullman's books. Sally Lockhart and Lyra Belacqua in *His Dark Materials* have much in common, and throughout the quartet we witness in the older Sally the same attractive qualities of strength and fortitude in the face of immense danger shown by the younger and more immature Lyra. Sally attracts danger wherever she goes (Tucker, 2003), but she will not be trapped into submission by her self-seeking and vindictive distant aunt, Caroline Rees, who has grudgingly provided her with accommodation. She decides to leave, makes herself homeless and seeks solace in the friendship of Frederick Garland, a talented photographic artist who is hopeless at managing his business. Sally has no formal education, but she can use a gun with formidable accuracy, has a close acquaintance with the affairs of the stock market and possesses a canny sense of what will ensure that Garland's business makes money. Frederick and his vibrant actor sister, Rosa, happily agree to her moving into their bohemian home. Here she meets Jim Taylor, a scruffy cockney office boy with a shrewd and quick intelligence, along with Trembler Malloy, an ex-pickpocket who is now a partner in Garland's business. Together, these loyal friends help Sally solve the mystery of her father's death. She discovers for herself what it is that is so odd but so life-enhancing about her new friends, namely their unquestioning domestic democracy and refusal to countenance the social hierarchies so deeply entrenched in Victorian value systems: 'They don't think of Trembler as a servant. And they don't think of me as a girl. We're all equal. That's what's so odd' (Pullman, 1985: 75). It is not enough to grip his readers by the pull and sweep of his racing plots; Pullman also makes them think about the social and emotional contexts in which his characters are placed. The brutalising effects of poverty among the Victorian unemployed are vividly portrayed when Sally and Frederick set out to find out more about the opium den managed by the surprisingly dignified and wise Madame Chang. Their journey takes them into the depths of the West India Docks:

> Barefoot children, ragged and filthy, played among the rubbish and the streams of stinking water that trickled thickly over the cobbles. Women standing in their doorways fell silent as they passed, and stared with hostile eyes, arms folded, until they had gone by. They look so old, thought Sally; even the children had pinched, old-men's faces, with wrinkled brows and tight-drawn lips. . . . Their clothes were torn and clotted with dirt, their eyes were full of hatred.
>
> (ibid.: 87–8)

The streetwise Frederick points out to Sally the stark choices for those who fall on the wrong side of employment: 'It's either the street corner or the workhouse, and who'd choose the workhouse?' (ibid.: 88).

There are moments in the story when the plot's credibility is stretched (Tucker, 2003), but Pullman's accurate internal geography of the bridges and streets of Wapping and Hangman's Wharf makes the cut-and-thrust chase to rescue the kidnapped Adelaide from the villainous clutches of Mrs Holland entirely believable. Pullman's assiduous research of the network of bridges and alleyways of these grimy docklands, where 'the masts of ships and the jibs of cranes pointed to the grey skies like skeletal fingers' (Pullman, 1985: 87), foregrounds the intricately described worlds of Lyra's Oxford, Bolvangar and Cittàgazze of *His Dark Materials*.

The third book, *The Tiger in the Well*, perhaps the most thrilling of the series, sees Sally at 25 as the mother of a beloved 2-year-old daughter, Harriet. Not only is she unmarried but she has successfully set up her own financial business, both of which were condemned by Victorian society as improper behaviour for a woman. Sally manages to ride out her uncomfortable position in this prurient society, but her life almost unravels when a man claiming to be her husband seizes her money and property and, with the law on his side, sets out on a determined course of action to abduct Harriet. The indomitable Sally manages to thwart his plans, but not before she has fallen into the path of the Tzaddik, the opium pirate who we were led to believe had been killed off by Sally's pistol at the end of *The Ruby in the Smoke*. The now paralysed Tzaddik has an evil dybbuk servant in the form of a demon monkey who is a 'prototype for the dæmons in *His Dark Materials*' (Squires, 2006: 179). He is nothing like the constant, loving companion of Lyra's Pantalaimon but bears a striking resemblance to Marisa Coulter's dangerous and viciously protective golden monkey dæmon.

Having highlighted some of the narrative sources for *His Dark Materials*, I now turn to an analysis of some the characters, themes and universes of Pullman's most original and inventive work.

His Dark Materials

The idea for the *His Dark Materials* trilogy began with Pullman's long-held ambition to write the story of Milton's epic poem *Paradise Lost* for teenagers. What resulted is a deeply textured narrative of cosmic power and force. It is, in every sense of the word, a 'big read'. Its 1,300 pages traverse strange and shifting landscapes peopled with daemons, witches, spectres, armoured bears, angels and anthropomorphised dragonflies.[1] Despite the intellectual complexity of its themes and its rich intertextuality, the heart of the story concerns two young protagonists who grow up and fall in love in pursuit of their destiny to save others. Pullman states simply and eloquently what he wanted to achieve in this imaginative enterprise: 'I'm trying to write a book about what it means to be human, to grow up, to suffer and learn' (*The South Bank Show*, 2003).

Genre

The trilogy embraces more than one genre, crossing between fantasy, science fiction, the adventure story and the crime thriller. Having experimented for many years with a range of narrative styles and writing genres, Pullman succeeds in moving from one to another with seemingly effortless flair. According to Squires (2006), his genre-traversing tendency both heightens his writing and displays his virtuosity. Pullman has often strenuously distanced himself from being perceived as a writer of fantasy. He claims not to like or to have read fantasy himself and vehemently disassociates his work from the fantasy writings of J.R.R. Tolkien and C.S. Lewis. What he is interested in is human beings and their social and psychological reality. However, the *His Dark Materials* trilogy unquestionably draws on a phenomenal range of fantasy devices, including instruments that have the power to measure truth and cut windows into other worlds. The distinguishing feature in Pullman's fantasy is that it has something interesting to say about what it means to be a human being in the face of indescribable fear and to find love when it is least expected. Most importantly, for Pullman, truth and knowledge make up a rich seam that runs to the core of the story.

The main characters

The main characters are Lyra, Will, Lord Asriel, Marisa Coulter and Mary Malone.

Lyra Belacqua

Lyra is the first and last word of the trilogy and she is, as Lenz (2001) observes, one of the most believable characters since Alice. She is disobedient, wilful and 'a barbarian', and spends much of her time with her best friend, Roger, a kitchen boy, scrambling around on the roof of Jordan College. She has the most endearing dæmon of all Pullman's dæmons, Pantalaimon, who, like all children's dæmons, changes, but he frequently takes the form of an agile, wide-eyed pine marten. Her upbringing is left to the sporadic care of the servants and masters of Jordan College on the assumption that both her parents have been killed in an accident. In fact, neither is dead; Lord Asriel is her ambivalent and distant father and she was conceived in a relationship with his lover, Marisa Coulter. Neither of them has been sufficiently committed to their child to love or protect her. When Asriel makes the occasional appearance in her life, he is not interested in her well-being and almost breaks her arm at the beginning of *Northern Lights*. Her mother's appalling experiments in Bolvangar with kidnapped children nearly cause the severing of Lyra's beloved companion, Pantalaimon. Mrs Coulter arrives just in time to halt the intercision.

Lyra is the trilogy's most important character and the key to its central theme: a young, uneducated girl who is orphaned in the sense that she has no constancy of parental presence and yet succeeds in growing up and rising consistently to challenges of unspeakable danger and terror. Freed from responsible parentage of any palpable and meaningful kind, she is available for adventure and the forging of relationships with responsible others. Her name has been carefully chosen by Pullman with its play on the words 'lyre', the musical instrument, and 'liar', which is associated with her ability to spin stories at whim. When, for example, she tricks Iofur Rakinson, Iorek commends her skills of verbal mastery (Squires, 2006) and artful deceit by calling her 'Lyra Silvertongue'. Her storytelling talent mostly gets her out of trouble and wins her favour until she is finally and terrifyingly confronted by the harpies in the Suburbs of the Dead, who utterly reject and scorn her mendacious fantasy. It is only at this point that she realises that truth and responsibility in storytelling really matter. The morality of storytelling is a central theme in Pullman's trilogy. Lyra is an irresistible heroine who is wholly believable, mostly because she proves to be eminently capable of change and growth.

Will Parry

In another play on words, Will has strong will-power. Like Lyra, but different in certain respects, he is doubly abandoned (Rustin and Rustin, 2003b). He has lost his father in an exploration expedition and his mother to mental illness. For some years, Will has had to take on a parenting role for his mother. Will and Lyra have much in common in their quests to find a father and a close friend. Will first meets Lyra in Cittàgazze, where they quickly develop a mutually trusting relationship.

Lord Asriel

Strong, and radiating a fierce energetic physicality, Lord Asriel is revealed as a mysterious and ruthlessly focused scientist and explorer. His investigation of Dust is intensely beguiling and dangerous. He is both sexually attractive and malevolent, using his immense power chiefly to further his own political interests. Lyra becomes worthy of his attention only when he discovers she has access to the Subtle Knife and to Roger, whose death can further his exploration into the potential of Dust to open gateways into other worlds. He has no scruples in using both his wife and Lyra for his own ends, but he does, finally, sacrifice his life for Lyra.

Marisa Coulter

One of Pullman's most interesting and complex characters, Mrs Coulter is cold, beautiful and manipulative to the point of almost killing her own daughter. She seeks power in whatever form it takes, the Church *for* Authority and the Church *against* it. Pullman is deeply fascinated by her 'because she's so completely free of any moral constraint' (*The South Bank Show*, 2003). However, she is additionally fascinating because she too changes. Her initial interest in Lyra is not in her but in the alethiometer, which she is determined to steal. Indeed, she will use almost anyone and anything to advantage her power position in the General Oblation Board. However, when she holds Lyra captive in the cave, she is taken unawares by an overwhelming maternal love for her, which she tells Asriel stole upon her 'like a thief in the night' (Pullman, 2000: 426–7). She regrets her lying and deceit and, like Asriel, sacrifices her life for her.

Mary Malone

In Pullman's inverted story of the fall of Adam and Eve, Mary Malone is the serpent temptress. She was once a nun and is now a physicist experimenting in the field of dark matter. She is intelligent and wise and cares deeply for the ecologically threatened mulefa. She provides a stark contrast to the calculating and self-interested Mrs Coulter (Duncan, 2007). She gives Lyra an important source of mental and emotional comfort that sustains and inspires her. She also opens the door of love and sexual awakening to Lyra through her own experience of her first kiss. Mary is the source of Lyra's temptation into love and wisdom.

Synopsis of the trilogy

Northern Lights

The story of *Northern Lights* begins with Lyra, an orphaned 11-year-old secretly entering the forbidden retiring room of Jordan's College, where she lives. She hides behind a chair and witnesses the Master of the College pouring poison into a decanter of Tokay. Lord Asriel arrives sooner than expected, and Lyra prevents him from drinking the poisoned wine. She then sees Lord Asriel showing the scholars the existence of Dust on a series of slides. This is a strange elementary particle believed by the Church to be evidence for Original Sin. Connected with this view of Dust are some appalling experiments being conducted by Church-controlled scientists involving the severing of dæmons from kidnapped children in Bolvangar, leaving them lifeless. Lyra's best friend, Roger, has been captured by the ruthless Marisa Coulter, who is instrumental in this work and who, we later learn, is Lyra's mother. With the help of the alethiometer, the Gyptians (a nomadic group of canal-water farers) and an armoured bear, Lyra sets out to find and rescue Roger. They succeed in finding him, but not before his dæmon has been severed. In the midst of their plans to rescue all the kidnapped children, Lord Asriel, now revealed as Lyra's father, captures Roger and uses the power caused by the separation of his dæmon to open a gateway to a new world. Roger dies in the process.

The Subtle Knife

It is in *The Subtle Knife* that we meet Will, a 12-year-old boy whose father is a scientific explorer and who has mysteriously disappeared somewhere in Alaska. Will has killed a man who had broken into his home. In search of his lost father, he stumbles into Cittàgazze, where he meets Lyra and the terrifying soul-eating spectres. In the Tower of the Angels he meets Giacomo Paradisi, the bearer of the Subtle Knife, which has the power to cut windows into other worlds. Will is told that he is now its new bearer and is shown how to use it. Lyra and Will journey on to find Will's father, who has the assumed name of Stanislaus Grumman. With the help of Lee Scoresby, Will finds his father, but they do not recognise each other until moments before Grumman is shot dead with an arrow from the bow of Juta Kamainen, a witch he once scorned. Lyra is then kidnapped by her mother, an agent of the Magisterium, who has learned that Lyra is prophesied to be the next Eve.

The Amber Spyglass

With the help of a local girl called Ama, Iorek Byrnison, the armoured bear and Lord Asriel's Gallivespian spies, Will rescues Lyra from the caves, where she has lain drugged for several weeks. In a quest to find Roger, Lyra and Will reach the most terrifying and searing part of their journey when they travel into the Suburbs of the Dead to find his ghost. Here Lyra is confronted by the hideous harpies, who scorn her duplicitous stories and scream at her for telling them lies. Forced to tell them stories that are real and nourishing, she strikes a bargain with them to release the ghosts from their captivity so that their Dust can be part of the living world. Lyra meets Mary Malone, an ex-nun and scientist who is interested in Dust. In a beautiful but ecologically fragile country, she meets the elephantine mulefa – strange, intelligent creatures with two horns and a trunk, who propel themselves round the countryside by means of large, circular seed pods. Through the special powers of Mary Malone's amber spyglass, Lyra learns of the true nature of Dust. Meanwhile, Lord Asriel and a reformed Mrs Coulter team up to destroy the Authority's regent, Metatron, but are killed in the process. The Authority dies and Will and Lyra, having been awakened to the love between them, have to face an ethical and moral decision of unbearable weight.

Language

This is a story of such complexity with respect to multiplicity of characters and philosophical, scientific, political and religious ideas, to say nothing of parallel worlds, that it is surprising that the narrative does not collapse under its own weight. It succeeds in not doing so because of the elegant simplicity and beauty of Pullman's writing. His long apprenticeship in writing across genres has honed his craft so finely that some of his best work ever is strikingly apparent in *His Dark Materials*. His own maxim, written in the acknowledgement pages at the end of *The Amber Spyglass*, is to 'Read like a butterfly, write like a bee' (Pullman, 2000). He has been a strict observer of his own advice, and his 'nectar' has come from an uncountable number of sources, including Milton, Blake, Shelley, Coleridge, comic books and von Kleist (1982), to name but a few. In his writing he always aims for clarity, and in the trilogy, even if some of the concepts, ideas and terminology are not immediately comprehensible, his energetic, direct and lucid prose impels the reader to continue turning the pages.

This is not to imply that his work is an easy read; it most certainly is not. His readers are expected to work hard, think, ponder, wonder and puzzle as they try to keep up with the fast-moving twists and turns of his plot and narrative drive. In a lecture delivered in New York in April 2002, using the metaphor of water, whereby he eschews murkiness and obscurity, Pullman states:

> It is much better to write in such a way that the readers can see all the way down; but that's not the end of it, because you then have to provide interesting things down there for them to look at.
>
> (Cited in Tucker, 2003: 185)

As Tucker (2003) rightly observes, he is 'Equally at home both with everyday dialogue and with those moments when his imagination soars to meet the challenge of describing scenes of great, sometimes unearthly, beauty' (ibid.: 186).

An example of the first occurs at the beginning of *The Subtle Knife*, when Will is first introduced as the carer of his mother, who is suffering from confusion and mental illness brought on by distress and grief for her lost husband. It is an example of 'everyday dialogue' with several very short sentences that powerfully convey the poignancy and desperation of their plight (Pullman, 1997a: 2). An example of the second can be found in *Northern Lights* and shows Pullman's deft handling of a description of unearthly beauty when Lyra sees her first aurora and is moved to tears by its evanescent beauty. In this extract there is something of the grace and strength of Milton's poetry, as well as elegantly crafted prose:

> The sight filled the northern sky; the immensity of it was scarcely conceivable. As if from Heaven itself, great curtains of delicate light hung and trembled. Pale green and rose-pink, and as transparent as the most fragile fabric, and at the bottom edge a profound and fiery crimson like the fires of Hell, they swung and shimmered loosely with more grace than the most skilful dancer.
>
> (Pullman, 1995a: 183)

Now that I have given an outline of the plot, the main characters and Pullman's mastery of the written language, the three remaining sections will examine one of Pullman's central concepts, the dæmon, his main themes and the problematic ending of the story.

Dæmons

In simple terms, a dæmon is an externalised soul in animal form. Dæmons are always of the opposite sex to their human counterpart. In childhood, they constantly change shape, but in adolescence they settle permanently into one animal form. As Vincent puts it, 'it is the creature of your deepest essence; it is your guardian angel, your confidante, your conscience, your representative' (2001: 2). It is an original and extraordinarily rich concept without which the trilogy would lose much of its internal coherence and humanity. It is, according to Pullman, 'the best idea I've had in my life' (*The South Bank Show*, 2003). He had been struggling with the beginning of *Northern Lights*, which did not seem to be working even after fourteen drafts. Suddenly, the idea of a dæmon for Lyra 'appeared at the end of my pen' (ibid.). In an interview with Melvyn Bragg, he tells him how this original idea not only started to make the book come alive but also resolved a narrative problem in so far as it was much easier to tell the story when there were two characters having a dialogue with each other.

Pullman may not have been conscious of it at the time, but, as stated previously, Pullman's dæmon has a direct lineage with the servant monkey in an earlier book, *The Tiger and the Well*. The idea of a 'daimon' appeared long ago in Greek history as a kind of inner voice, guardian angel and conscience. Socrates possessed a personal daimon which was so important to him that he never took an important decision without consulting it. The idea of an inner voice and guiding conscience is also akin to Freud's concept of the super-ego and Jung's alter ego. Pullman considers that previously unrecognised dæmons have appeared in portraits throughout the ages, for example in Leonardo da Vinci's painting *Lady with an Ermine* and Hans Holbein's *Lady with a Squirrel*.

Pantalaimon is a crucial source of love, friendship and loyalty to Lyra. Given Lyra's deprived childhood, parental neglect and lack of any constant source of loving attention and care, it would be difficult to understand how, without the constancy of Pantalaimon's loyal companionship, she could have found the immense strength and psychological resources needed to cope with the grave dangers and responsibilities she has to confront. The dæmon not only lends psychological credibility to Lyra's ability to survive the many emotional and physical challenges she faces on her quest to find Roger, but also serves as a metaphor for the essential differences between childhood and adulthood.

Themes and beliefs

The chapter began with a discussion on Pullman's mastery as a storyteller, because this is the fulcrum on which both his narrative and his plot turn. Storytelling is taken to new heights in *His Dark Materials*, where it is the driving force that propels the narrative and the plot to the point when Lyra, in the midst of her greatest fear and anguish, is called to account by the harpies, who will not accept her fantasy of lies. For the first time, she realises that storytelling must have morality at its heart, or it is of no value. Telling real stories in the end liberates the dead from their anguished limbo.

Pullman's trilogy is essentially 'a story about stories: a meta-story' (Squires, 2006: 93). The same theme underpins *Clockwork or All Wound Up*, but in *His Dark Materials* it is a much more complex, intertextual and multi-layered meta-narrative. The morality of storytelling is connected to the subjects of consciousness and knowledge, and the concept of Dust is an integral part of the changing state of self-consciousness and growing up. It has its roots in the Old Testament when Adam has eaten the forbidden fruit and is cursed by God, who tells him of the consequence of his disobedience: 'For dust thou art, and unto dust shalt thou return' (Tucker, 2003: 134). However, Dust is seldom clearly defined by Pullman and seems to possess several meanings:

as original sin, the form of thoughts not yet born, dark matter, shadow-particles, particles of consciousness and even as rebel angels. . . . Death is described as a joyful process of re-integration with Dust rather than with any Christian idea of God.

(ibid.: 134–5)

It is, in Pullman's words, 'all the wisdom, literature, books, stories, traditions – all the things it's possible to know and understand – that's Dust' (*The South Bank Show*, 2003).

His inversion of the fall of Adam and Eve when Eve decides to eat the forbidden fruit is, in Pullman's account, the best thing she could have done, because it gave her wisdom. This is another key theme in the story, that of growth from innocence to wisdom. Part of the deep attraction of Lyra over the course of the trilogy is that she changes from a barbaric, wilful child to a responsible human being. Her learning is gained from raw experience and the loving guidance of others who consistently demonstrate strength, dignity and humane intelligence. During the course of her quest, she discovers that she is capable of rising to acts of selflessness, which alter the way in which she sees the world and how she relates to others. Part of her growth towards maturity is the acquisition of new levels of consciousness and understanding. She and Will care deeply about the plight of those in the Suburbs of the Dead, the outcome of the war in heaven and the fragility of the ecological disaster that is threatening the life of the peace-loving mulefa. Environmentalism and a moral concern about the current precariousness of our planet powerfully inform Pullman's belief system. Mary Malone's ethical approach to her scientific investigations is revealed in her humane interest and respect for the intelligent, trunk-twitching mulefa. They are faced with extinction because Dust is flowing out to the sea and causing the inexorable disintegration of the trees that provide the seedpods so vital to their life. This is a compelling allegory of our time, and speaks potently to both children and adults.

Much more provocative are Pullman's views on organised religion and, in particular, the Anglican and Catholic Churches. He has raised the ire of religious fundamentalists and spokespeople for the Catholic Church. Several critics have condemned his books for being blasphemous and anti-God. The sentence that seems to have stirred up much of this anger is the ex-nun Mary Malone's stark comment to Lyra that 'The Christian religion is a very powerful and convincing mistake, that's all' (Pullman, 2000: 464). Hitchens (2002) went so far as to comment that Pullman's condemnation of both C.S. Lewis and the Church made him 'the most dangerous author in Britain'. However, the stage version of *His Dark Materials* received a warm and positive reception from Archbishop Rowan Williams (2004), who believed that the controversy provoked by Pullman's reworking of the creation story provided an intellectual challenge to the Church and one which drama should highlight and portray. Pullman does, however, believe that we need a heaven, not the Kingdom of Heaven but a *republic* of heaven, here on earth, in which 'we're connected to other people by love and joy and delight in the universe and the physical world' (Pullman, cited in Barger, 2002: 4). This is not the heaven of the afterlife espoused by the Christian Church, but it is nonetheless a compelling and radical idea which asks us to believe that 'we can build a new, highly moral world without the precepts of religion' (Walter, 2002).

The ending: some problems and contradictions

Another central motif, which occurs throughout the trilogy, is the juxtaposition of love and loss. Indeed, in Pullman's universes one cannot exist without the other. Lyra and Will find emotional sustenance and love in the characters of Mary Malone, Lee Scoresby and Iorek Byrnison, and they also find it with each other. Towards the end of the trilogy they have a brief moment when they can forget the terrors and exhaustion of the wars; in a lush and beautiful setting they abandon themselves to a tender adolescent love. However, no sooner have they tasted this intense moment of delight than they have to agree to go their separate ways back to their different worlds (Duncan, 2007: 280). This is a deeply problematic ending to the story. It suggests that the acquisition of wisdom, maturity and growth through their many agonies of suffering and loss has resulted not in reward but in immense loss. Will returns to his world to begin the difficult process of caring for his mother, having lost his father, Lyra, his dæmon and two fingers. Lyra still has Pantalaimon, but she has lost Will, her parents and all the significant others who guided and helped her through moments of unspeakable anguish and pain. While a romantic ending would have seriously weakened the story, it is, as several writers have pointed out (Squires, 2006; Moruzi, 2005; Spanner, 2000), a chilling and disturbingly unsatisfactory ending. Moruzi criticises the contradiction that Pullman's ending creates by emphasising, on the one hand, the importance of independent choices while, on the other, leaving only one viable option for the two lovers: to return to their respective worlds in which they 'are still forced to work within the adult institutions for their survival' (2005: 62). Squires locates the problem in Pullman's omniscient storytelling authority, which she maintains 'is as dictatorial in its didacticism as he claims the Church to be' (2006: 108).

Rustin and Rustin offer a somewhat different view. Their psychological interpretation of his trilogy holds that the separation of Lyra and Will is consistent with Pullman's belief in himself as a social realist rather than a writer of fantasy:

> The separation of the two adolescents is rooted in [an] understanding of the separateness of selves, and of the psychic and philosophical importance of acceptance of the limits of each individual. . . . The omnipotence and omniscience of childhood – sustained and protected as it is by the delight of loving adults in children's growing powers – has to be surrendered as adolescence looms.
>
> (2003a: 425–6)

Perhaps some of these paradoxes and contradictions will be resolved in Pullman's eagerly awaited forthcoming book *The Book of Dust*.

Chapter 4

Teaching comics

Tim Stafford

If you have not read, or even picked up, a comic since childhood, where do you begin when teaching comics? This chapter provides teachers and other adults working in education with some suggestions and guidelines for using comics in the classroom. Activities can be taught as an ongoing programme of study or as individual, discrete sessions according to the teacher's choice.

Selecting suitable texts

Before we begin to discuss *how* to use comic book literature with pupils, it is vital to consider *which* comics to use with children. The thought of visiting a specialist comic book shop, to be faced with a multitude of titles and characters that you may never have heard of, is potentially bewildering, but this need not be the case.

Several issues need to be considered when selecting comic books for children, but the most important factor must be suitability of content. The majority of mainstream American comics published by Marvel and DC, such as *Batman*, *Spider-Man* and the *X-Men*, are not targeted at children of primary school age, and are more likely to be aimed at teenagers and adults. While most of the well-known monthly superhero titles are aimed at a general audience, it is important to be aware that they may occasionally contain artwork or language that might not be suitable for younger children.

Some comics publishers provide guidance in selecting material for children. DC Comics has a dedicated range of children's comics (including such publications as *Justice League Unlimited* and *The Batman Strikes!*) identifiable by the colourful character Johnny DC, who can usually be spotted near to the DC logo at the top of the front cover. The vast majority of these titles, often tied in with television companies such as Cartoon Network and Kids' WB!, will be suitable for even very young children. Marvel Comics takes a self-regulatory approach to its own publications, which is extremely helpful. If you examine the front or back cover of a Marvel comic, you will be able to find an age rating (usually located above, or adjacent to, the barcode on the comic). This rating, similar in concept to the classification system used for films, will help you to locate suitable texts more quickly and effectively. The Marvel website (www.marvel.com) lists the current ratings, displayed on comics published after June 2005, as follows: 'ALL AGES – appropriate for readers of all ages, A – appropriate for ages 9 and up, T+TEENS & UP – Appropriate for most readers 13 and up, parents are advised that they may want to read before or with younger children' (Marvel, 2005). The two older categories, Parental

Advisory and Marvel Max, will generally not be suitable for any children under 15 and so will not be relevant here. While these ratings are only guidelines (you will need to check content yourself), they do provide a clear indication of general suitability of content, and when working with young children it is best to use the All Ages and A titles.

In places, comic books do depict acts of violence (as of course do children's novels, such as J.K. Rowling's Harry Potter series and Philip Pullman's *His Dark Materials* trilogy), and the rule here is simple: if you are not comfortable showing certain parts of a comic to pupils, then do not. No one will be a better judge of what is suitable for your class than you, so, as when selecting any materials to use with children, be your own judge. It is important to stress here that having to check content of comic books does not mean that you will need to spend hours of your precious time poring over these texts in order to edit material. An average twenty-four-page comic book can be checked through in a matter of minutes, and if there are parts that you feel are not entirely suitable, then simply do not use these pages. Looking at selected pages as opposed to the whole comic is worthwhile. Indeed, most of the activities in this chapter will involve looking at parts of comic books, sometimes only a page and sometimes a few more. Therefore, consider material by individual page rather than by complete issue.

When you are selecting comic books for use with children, it is also important to ensure that they are not presented with superhero titles only. Part 2 of this chapter will discuss the misconception that the only type of comic is the superhero comic, which is far from accurate. While superhero stories can form a thrilling and interesting part of comics education, you need to ensure that children's initial experiences of the medium go beyond the superhero genre so that they realise that *any* story can be told in this format. Recommended titles to use here include publications such as *The Beano*. It is possible and, indeed, likely that many of the children in the class will already be familiar with these titles and with many of their iconic characters such as Dennis the Menace and Minnie the Minx. Some children might be regular readers of these comics and can therefore be encouraged to tell their peers about them. *The Beano* is particularly effective for use with younger children, not only because the content is relatively suitable but also because the artwork is often more traditional in its layout and serves as an accessible introduction to the medium.

Wonderland: Children of the future age

The text around which most of the activities in this chapter will be based is *Wonderland: Children of the future age*, written by Derek Watson and illustrated by Kit Wallis. The story (which is a complete narrative in itself, published in one volume) is set in a dystopian future in which a plague has swept through London and transformed its victims into murderous creatures called Slinks. The story centres around three teenagers, Sarah, Edison and their adopted older brother, Poncho, who live in an abandoned department store with their robot, Mike-9, their elephant, Lulu, and their cat, Tab-Tab. The plot becomes a quest narrative as Sarah and Poncho set out to find their missing father, who has not been seen for some time. Presenting traditional elements of children's literature, such as the absence of the parental figure, the epic quest and battles with nightmarish monsters, in an innovative way, *Wonderland* is driven by a thrilling, sometimes frightening but emotionally powerful narrative that stands as an excellent example of the medium's storytelling potential. Perhaps its greatest strength is Derek Watson's characterisation, which encourages us to share in the adventure of the protagonists and to care deeply about their fate. Of course, no comic can tell a story without visuals, and Kit Wallis's distinctive and highly stylised watercolour artwork conveys both the strange beauty and the sinister threat of a world robbed of humanity. The layout of the comic is also consistently visually stimulating and provides an excellent opportunity to teach formal aspects of the medium such as panel composition and use of dialogue.

In addition to the points listed above, there are several reasons why I have selected this comic for use with pupils. First, in relation to the point made earlier, *Wonderland* is an excellent example of a non-superhero comic book. While it sits comfortably in the science fiction and fantasy genres, it offers a refreshing alternative from the superhero stereotypes and allows children to see that comics are not all about men who fly. Another particularly pleasing aspect of the text is its young female protagonist, Sarah. For too long, the world of comics has been associated with males in terms of both readership and content, and the inclusion of a strong, heroic female character who is not merely a passive love interest is an excellent way to demonstrate to students and teachers that comics need not exclude females.

Derek Watson interviewed

I interviewed Derek Watson in order to find out more about the text.

TS   Where did the idea for *Wonderland* originally come from?

DW   Kit [Wallis] and I originally had a discussion – just some characters that he wanted to do a story about. He said he wanted to do a story set in a post-apocalyptic world with children, and it was as simple as that. We just came up with a story based around the characters he wanted to draw. He wanted the protagonist to be female and for her to have a brother and a friend, and I just built the story around that.

TS   Did you then take responsibility for the writing of the story?

DW   Yes. After that initial discussion, we had very little discussion about the direction of the story. It was pretty much me writing it and Kit drawing what I wrote.

TS   Why tell this story as a comic book and not a novel?

DW   The reason was because Kit's an artist and he wanted to draw those characters – it was never going to be anything else. The genesis of the story didn't begin with me, it began with him, so I was really just contributing a story to some characters that he was thinking of. In terms of character designs, the girl and the brother and Poncho were pretty much already in his mind. The cat and the elephant were creations from myself, as were the bad guys. They were additional characters for him to play around with and stretch him a little bit, artistically. But it was never going to be anything other than a comic book because that's what he does!

TS   You use some of the traditional staples of children's literature, such as the orphaned children and the quest narrative. Was this deliberate on your part?

DW   Yes, totally deliberate. A lot of these elements allude to other children's stories, which I did on purpose. I just wanted to play around with those traditional sorts of ideas and see if I could set them in a post-apocalyptic future. So when Kit first wanted to do it, I immediately thought about famous children's books – *The Wizard of Oz*, *Alice in Wonderland*, obviously – and other quest-based stories. I've always liked that idea of children banding together to

TS   overcome some sort of adversity, I think it's a fairly traditional thing. Certainly, when I was a child I identified with that idea. I think that's what makes an adventure interesting for children, to be able to identify with the characters – you feel you could do the same things. You don't have to have any super-powers or special abilities. By working hard and with people you can overcome things, being emotionally strong rather than physically strong.

TS   Like Philip Pullman and J.K. Rowling, you don't shy away from some of the scarier elements of the narrative. Is this something you believe needs to be done in children's stories?

DW   I don't know that it's something that needs to be done, I think it's just there – it's part and parcel. If you can have things that are funny, you can have things that are frightening, and I think children like to laugh and they like to be scared. You need certain boundaries – every writer self-disciplines to a certain degree in terms of how far you go. You're always aware of just how much you can show, or talk about, or what you can show graphically that you can't describe, or what you can describe that you can't show graphically. We've all been children so we've all got memories of what used to scare us and what was a little bit too much.

    Maybe things have changed over the years but I think generally, pretty much the same things scare children now that scared them fifty or a hundred years ago, in terms of monsters and those traditional kinds of scary things. I think the truth of the matter is that children can probably handle a lot more than most adults can because they don't think about things the same sort of way. But you don't want people to be overly scared, you just want them to have an enjoyable experience.

Teaching activities

I have chosen to focus the following teaching activities around a single text because it allows for a more specific discussion of how to teach comic books. However, most of these activities can be adapted relatively easily to fit any other comics you may wish to teach. I would suggest that *Wonderland* as a whole would generally be suitable for ages 10 and upwards, and while there is nothing highly unsuitable in the story, there are some moments of violence that may not be appropriate for younger children. The activities here are based around selected pages from the comic rather than the entire text, and were aimed at Year 6 children. If, however, you are working at Key Stage 1, or with the younger age groups of Key Stage 2 children, it may be appropriate to use comics aimed at a slightly younger audience. With some adjustments, the following activities can be adapted and used as a general framework for teaching any comic book.

Introducing children to comics

Before you start to study comics closely with a class, you may find it helpful to prepare the children in the days or weeks leading up to the sessions. This preparation may be as simple and as unobtrusive as including comics in the reading corner and displaying pages from them somewhere in the classroom, or as overt as reading a book to the class which either tells a story in comic book form or interweaves elements of a comic book with traditional prose, such as Raymond Briggs's *Ug* or Neil Gaiman and Dave McKean's *The Wolves in the Walls*. It might also be useful to have some initial discussions about comics, through which you can ascertain children's attitudes towards reading them.

Some initial questions are as follows:

◇   What are some of the comics you have heard of?
◇   What comics have you read or do you read regularly?
◇   Which comic book characters can you think of? Who are your favourites?
◇   How would you describe a comic book to someone who had never seen one?
◇   How is a comic different from a novel or storybook or picture book?

Initial discussions such as these are vital in transmitting to children the idea that comic books are credible literature and are to be treated as seriously as any other text in the classroom. It also helps children to realise that comics as a medium are storytelling vehicles which have their own unique methods of conveying information. During this unit of work you also have the opportunity to dispel any misconceptions about comic books (that they are for boys only, or that they are less complex than prose texts) and to suggest to children that you will be able to show them comic book material which proves that these initial impressions are not always true. If children perceive that this is a medium that you yourself treat with respect and approach seriously, it may encourage them to view comics in the same way. Of course, the aim here is not to make every child an avid fan of comics (just as you would not expect every child to love a book you might read to them), but rather to take time to dispel any inherent prejudices pupils may have here and to show children that the medium as a whole is too diverse for them to be able to make generalised statements about it.

Terms used in this chapter

Panels   The individual pictures on each page of a comic book. Panels may be any shape or size but they are usually rectangular or square. A page may be made up of any number of panels. Occasionally, comics have pages that are made up of one single panel.

Narrative boxes The small rectangular or square boxes which appear within panels. A narrative box contains written information regarding the story (for example, 'The next day' or 'Two weeks earlier'). It can also show a character's interior monologue or, sometimes, the words of other characters who are not shown in the panel.

Speech bubbles The spaces where the characters' dialogue is written.

Resources

These activities should require relatively minimal preparation. Ideally, when teaching these sessions you should be able to show the whole class enlarged pieces of colour artwork from comics, and with readily available interactive board technologies, there has never been a better time to teach comic books to children. This technology allows you to present scanned pages in an easily readable format and to zoom in on specific panels or enlarge parts of the comic for closer inspection, which you will need to do.

You will need:

•   an interactive whiteboard;

- individual pages from a range of comic books (I have used *Wonderland*) scanned into the computer and saved;
- A4 or A3 photocopies of some comic book pages for some of the sessions;
- A4 photocopies of a comic page with the dialogue removed from the speech bubbles so that the children can fill them with their own dialogue.

Introducing comics

Once you have had at least some discussion with children regarding comics and their views about them, a good starting point may be to select a page from a comic to analyse in more detail. Again, choice of material is important here. I have selected a page from *Wonderland* (Figure 4.1) because the children in the trial workshop responded to Kit Wallis's artwork positively and seemed to be intrigued by it. As stated earlier, however, you can use a page of any comic, provided it displays the range of features that you want the pupils to notice (for example, panels, narrative boxes, speech bubbles).

Put the full page (Figure 4.1) on the interactive whiteboard and ask the children (who ideally are in pairs) to discuss and write down anything and everything they notice about the page. It is essential to let children take time to simply *look* at the artwork and talk about it. The experience of teaching this material has taught me that even older children need time to absorb the page before them. You should not initially direct their attention to anything specific, just let them feed back with all the things they have noticed. When the children have discussed what they have observed with you, it is important to begin to ask more specific questions of the children so that they begin to consider some of the features of a comic book and/or how the page works as a narrative:

◇ What is going on here?
◇ Where is the story set? (The pupils may well pick up on Nelson's column in the bottom picture.)
◇ What are some of the things that make this different from a novel?
◇ Look at the circle coming out of the girl's mouth in the second picture ('Yep, they definitely went this way!'). What is it? What does it show us?
◇ Look at the little rectangles in each picture ('Edison was very angry with me' and others). What do these show? In this instance, the boxes show what Sarah is thinking, but this is not the case in all comics. Sometimes these boxes are used by comic book writers to provide story information or set the scene (for example, 'Two years later' or 'The forest, night time').

Of course, it doesn't matter if the children do not guess the exact nature of the story or the relationships between the characters; the activity is really designed to get them looking closely at the visual clues and to encourage them to link the information into some kind of story. The objective here is to introduce pupils to the main features of comic books, and it may help to put some of the terms on the board. You don't need to be too technical here, but you should introduce the following terms:

- **speech bubbles**;
- **narrative boxes** or **thought boxes** (for the small rectangular boxes);
- **panels** (for boxes which contain the pictures – for example, Figure 4.1 has three panels).

With older or more able children, the questioning needs to be more challenging:

Figure 4.1 Illustration from *Wonderland: Children of the future age*, written by Derek Watson and illustrated by Kit Wallis. The speech bubbles and narrative boxes have been blanked out.

◇ What do the pictures and the writing tell us about this girl? Ask children to list character descriptors and provide some evidence. They might pick up on the fact that Sarah is tough, strong and resourceful because she wears a flak helmet, or that she is intelligent because she follows tracks in the ground (panel 2).

◇ Describe the different views of Sarah in the three panels. How are they different? Why?

◇ Look at the first panel. Why do you think the artist has shown only Sarah's face? Why is only one eye visible? How does this panel differ from the third? Children's responses may vary here, but the idea is to get them to start thinking about the use of close-up (close-ups tend to make the reader think about what the character is thinking or feeling whereas wide shots, such as panel 3, usually depict action, landscape or movement).

◇ How would you describe the style of the artwork? Does it give us any clues as to what kind of story it might be (the genre)?

Reading images

Another activity that works well with children is to remove the dialogue from a page with speech on it and ask the children to work out what the characters could be saying. This activity can be surprisingly complex, so do not assume that children will find it easy. I used a page from *Wonderland* with Year 6 (Figure 4.2), which was appropriately challenging for most of the class, but you will need to use a less dialogue-heavy page with younger children (perhaps even something as simple as a three-panel comic strip from a newspaper). It is necessary, however, to use a comic that does not have easily recognisable figures such as superheroes or the *Beano* characters, purely because the children will have less scope to invent characters and narratives if they recognise the characters. Use correction fluid to delete the boxes on a comic page and photocopy this so each child has one (it also helps to scan the page so that the children can see it in colour on the whiteboard).

Here, it is important to reiterate two things to the children:

• that they need to take time to read all the way through the page initially and work out what they think the story is before starting to fill in the speech bubbles;

• that they are not supposed to be accurately guessing the missing words but that their dialogue does need to make sense in the context of the pictures. Children should be encouraged to read the pictures closely in order to decipher their meaning, and this activity, therefore, will take some time. It is also a good opportunity to talk through how speech is presented on the page.

Some questions you might wish to ask are:

◇ Which order do we read the speech bubbles in? Get the children to point to the correct order. Usually, the rule for working out the order of dialogue is that height decides precedence, so the highest speech bubble in the panel will be read first. For example, on the first panel in Figure 4.2 Edison speaks first (his bubble is highest), then Sarah replies (her bubble is slightly lower and to the right) and then Edison speaks again.

◇ In which order do we read the speech bubbles in the second panel?

◇ What does the line between the top two speech bubbles mean? Here, children can be encouraged to see that reading comics is an active and complex process in which conventions can often change as we read. Logic would dictate that if two bubbles are the same height, then we read them one after the other, the left bubble first. But if we examine the second

Figure 4.2 Illustration from *Wonderland: Children of the future age*, written by Derek Watson and illustrated by Kit Wallis. The speech bubbles have been blanked out.

Reproduced by permission of Derek Watson and Kit Wallis.

panel closely, we can see a bridge between Sarah's top two speech bubbles. Underneath this bridge is Edison's speech bubble ('You're what?!'). We need to read this bubble second and then return to Sarah's third bubble ('I said, I'm going to find father!') to complete the exchange. Children may correctly identify how to read this panel, but it is certainly worth taking some time to discuss how these features of the text work.

The learning objective of the filling speech bubbles activity is to help the children to develop their understanding of some of the features of comic books that they have learned about and to begin to use some of them themselves. It requires pupils to read the pictures extremely closely in order to see what narrative information might be conveyed and to see whether or not the emotions of the characters can be interpreted appropriately. The work that resulted from this activity in the trial workshop was generally of a good standard. Inevitably, the dialogue varied in terms of its creativity. Some children constructed simple arguments between the characters which did not drive a narrative, whereas the better work showed evidence of real imagination in terms of the relationships between the characters and the events which played out over the course of the artwork. What was clear from this activity was that the pupils had benefited from discussing and studying comic pages and that they had all read the images and facial expressions appropriately. This was demonstrated by the dialogue that the children had written, which reflected the fact that Sarah and Edison look as though they are arguing and that Sarah is clearly upset.

It is important here to resist the temptation to show the children the original dialogue at the end of the activity, as they may well feel they have succeeded or failed according to how closely it resembles their work. Again, this is not to suggest that the children should fill the vacant bubbles in a random way, because the more successful pieces of work will have dialogue that accompanies and accentuates the pictures. Indeed, what was especially exciting about the pieces of work produced was the myriad ways in which the children had interpreted the pictures. The original scene shows *Wonderland*'s three heroes, but some children had cast Sarah in the role of villain and many also believed Poncho to be posing a threat, interpreting the final close-up panel of his eyes as sinister.

This activity precedes work that will introduce children to the process of writing a comic book. Concentrating on dialogue alone in this activity ensures that children can begin to think about the ways in which a comic narrative is built without having to consider all the aspects of the writing process at once.

Moving towards writing comic books

As children become more confident working with comic book layouts and formats, they will most likely benefit from an insight into how comic books are written. Many children (and adults) are unaware that the majority of comic books start not with a page of drawings but with a written script, more akin to a film screenplay. Usually, comics are created by at least two people, a writer and an artist (although on the bigger mass-produced titles a whole team of people may be employed to break down the drawing process into pencilling, inking and lettering). The writer starts by writing a script which, for each panel, describes the visuals, and then sets out the dialogue like a play. This script is then given to the artist, who creates the artwork in their own style, but based on the writer's script. A particularly well-written example of this is shown in Figure 4.3, which is a page from Derek Watson's original *Wonderland* script. This provides a fascinating opportunity to witness the early stage of a comic's inception, especially when we compare it to its finished form (Figure 4.1).

WONDERLAND - PAGE 27

This page is simply a three-panel pullback of Sarah (and, in Panel 3, Sarah and Poncho). Both are fully equipped in their gear: ropes, water-skins, backpacks and weapons (Poncho has his pole and Sarah has her sword). See the following pages (28 & 29) for a fuller description of their surroundings.

Panel 1

Early morning, sunny - the ruins of a London street. Very tight close-up of Sarah's helmeted head (she has dusty goggles pulled back onto the helmet). She's looking downwards; she's looking thoughtful.

CAPTION (Sarah): Edison was very angry with me.

Panel 2

We pull back a little further to show that she's crouching on the ground whilst examining a Slink footprint in front of her. She's lightly touching the dusty area where the footprint is.

Depending on how you draw this scene, place either **one** clear footprint or a **series** of prints running down the road in the direction that Sarah and Poncho are going.

CAPTION (Sarah): Very angry and...very concerned.

SARAH: Yep, they definitely went this way!

CAPTION (Sarah): I know he's right to worry. About me. About us! 'This is a dangerous world!' he said. And of course it is!

Panel 3

Half-page panel. We pull back further to reveal both Sarah **and** Poncho. Poncho is slightly ahead of her, looking upwards to the sky and shading his eyes from the sun.

This panel forms the basis of the following 2-page spread. I'd like the spread to be a much more distant shot from this perspective which then takes in all of the scenery.

PONCHO: What the...?

CAPTION (Sarah): But what am I supposed to do? Stay at home all safe and secure while father may be out there in need of help?

Figure 4.3 A page from Derek Watson's original *Wonderland* script.

Reproduced by permission of Derek Watson.

If children are introduced to the scripting process, they can begin to see that a comic starts with writing, not drawing, and hopefully they will realise just how meticulous the planning for comics needs to be. Using comic scripts with pupils also leads to a wide range of activities which, ideally, not only will give them the opportunity to write in an exciting new format but also will develop their descriptive writing skills.

As a starting point, provide each child (or pair of children if you prefer) with a copy of the script page (Figure 4.3) and put an enlarged image of the finished page from *Wonderland* on the whiteboard. Spend some time talking through the script and comparing it to the final product:

◇ Look at the script. How is it organised?
◇ Why do the descriptions need to be so detailed?
◇ Who do you think this script is intended for? Who is the writer addressing?
◇ Why do you think the description of the panels and the dialogue are kept separate?
◇ Look at the instructions for the first panel and compare them with the finished picture. How has the artist managed to depict what is written?
◇ Look at the phrases 'pull back' and 'pull back further'. What do these mean? Here, you can make the connection with film and help the children to see that the two media are intrinsically linked.

After this discussion, put a different page from *Wonderland* up on the whiteboard and ask the children (working individually) to write a script for the page, modelled on Derek Watson's script. You can use any page from *Wonderland* but make sure that the page selected offers an appropriate level of challenge depending on how complex or simple you wish the scripts to be. In effect, the pupils are being asked to consider how a comic writer describes images. Even Year 6 children did not find this particularly easy, and in most cases this was because they were unfamiliar with the format of comic scripts, so instruct the children to ignore dialogue initially and focus on describing the artwork. An example of a panel description could be similar to the following: 'Poncho thunders towards us. He is furious. We can see his whole body from the knees upwards. He is crouched over in rage, his hand like a claw, ready for action. His teeth are bared, like an animal's.'

Progressing from this activity, the next session requires pupils to begin to write a full comic book script. Asking children to create characters and a storyline, to imagine the artwork and then to present all this in a written format that they have very little experience of will be too challenging for most primary school children, and you may wish to make the task more accessible by asking the children to continue an existing comic book story from a certain point. For instance, introduce the task by reading through some pages from *Wonderland* with them and then ask them to imagine what happens next and to write the script for the next page or two. This, of course, gives children the freedom to take the story where they want to, but also provides them with ready-made characters and settings so that the task is less daunting. You will need to remind the children that they have to set out the script as clearly as a comic writer would, in order to communicate their ideas to the artist. The children should follow the format of the script in Figure 4.3, clearly labelling the number of the panel, providing a description of the artwork and then including the dialogue. The children I worked with did find this challenging but were all able to produce work that followed the script format. The better pieces of work were extremely impressive and showed evidence of rich description and a consideration of how an interesting visual narrative might be structured.

There are several reasons why spending time on writing comic scripts with children is worthwhile. First, if the pupils are given good models of script writing such as Derek Watson's (or even examples which you yourself have written), the experience of describing panel layouts allows children to develop some very specific and accurate descriptive writing skills in a different medium. When they are required to observe panels in detail and then write down what they see, they will have to consider how to describe facial expressions, body language, setting and movement, and will need to use a wide range of verbs, adjectives and adverbs, not to mention similes and metaphors, to make their panel descriptions interesting. These are all skills that are required of children when they produce more familiar models of writing such as stories and poetry, and comic script writing can help children to find more effective ways to translate what they see in their imagination into their writing.

In addition, asking children to become comic writers and produce a script that they can imagine is going to be handed to an artist is an excellent way of helping them develop a sense of audience. We often ask children to consider who their writing might be intended for, and if they are made aware that the comic script's function is to clearly transmit the writer's ideas to the artist and inspire him or her to draw the story, then pupils will realise that their work needs to be written clearly and accurately. In fact, an effective follow-up activity to the script-writing session is to get the children to swap scripts in pairs and then ask each child to draw the comic pages to accompany their partner's script. This will allow the children to see just how effective their writing has been in transmitting their ideas and completes the comic-making process by establishing cross-curricular links with art. This is a particularly good way to conclude these activities because it brings the study of comics full circle, re-emphasising the importance of artwork in the narrative process. By telling children before they write that their peers will be using their scripts to work from, you will be providing them with a real purpose and a real audience for their writing.

Lesson objectives and learning outcomes

Lesson objectives

1   To introduce comic books to children in an educational context.
2   To clarify possible misconceptions about comic books and to show children that they are as worthy of study as any other form of literature.
3   To teach children about the unique conventions of comic books such as *panels*, *narrative boxes* and *speech bubbles*.
4   To think about the ways in which the words and the pictures in a comic book combine to transmit a narrative.
5   To consider the similarities and differences between comic books and other media such as film and written books.
6   To understand that a comic starts with a written script.
7   To write their own scripts, with a particular emphasis on detailed description.

Learning outcomes

By the end of the lesson/series of lessons/unit of work, the children will be able to:

1   make detailed observations about, and discuss pages from, comic books;
2   identify some of the ways in which comic books differ from other media and other narrative forms;

3   understand how comic books employ visual metaphor and symbolism;
4   make connections between film and comic books, in terms of how images are composed;
5   identify the main features of comics (*panels*, *narrative boxes* and *speech bubbles*) and begin to recognise the ways in which a comic book writer may use these to tell the story;
6   discuss the various techniques (*close-up*, *wide shots*, *body posture*) used by a comic book artist and consider how these techniques convey character and plot information and elicit an emotional response from the reader;
7   apply the above ideas when writing their own scripts for a comic page;
8   read comic books with greater understanding and critical insight.

Useful websites and additional sources of information

Both Marvel and DC have excellent digital versions of some of their comics online, and these are ideal for use on an interactive whiteboard. Their benefit is that they provide you with a vast array of colour images and pages from contemporary comic books which you can display easily to the class. Not all of the comics are aimed at children, so you will need to check them for suitability of content, but these are a great way to begin looking at comics with children. A wide range of Marvel titles are available at www.marvel.com (click on the heading 'Digital Comics'), and some titles specifically aimed at children can be viewed at www.dccomics.com/dckids. Both sites allow the reader to enlarge and reduce pages while reading them, but I prefer the Marvel site as it has a beautifully designed program that allows you to flip the digital pages, as if you were reading an actual comic.

In terms of comics currently available for children, in addition to *Wonderland* I would recommend a number of titles that are squarely aimed at a young audience. Marvel produce a range of stories under the banner *Marvel Adventures*, which tell simpler stories featuring characters such as Hulk and the Fantastic Four. Also, the titles *Power Pack, Franklin Richards: Son of a Genius* and *Spider-Man Loves Mary Jane* are enjoyable comics that have content suitable for children younger than Year 6. DC publishes a number of comics specifically aimed at children in the aforementioned Johnny DC range. These are particularly good to use with children because the range of titles include not only superhero comics such as *Legion of Superheroes in the 31st Century* and *Teen Titans Go!*, but also stories based on cartoons which children might already be familiar with such as *Scooby-Doo* and *Looney Tunes*. For teachers looking for more familiar stories to use with children, the *Marvel Illustrated* series is useful. In these titles, classic stories are retold in comic book form, some recent examples being James Fenimore Cooper's *The Last of the Mohicans*, Robert Louis Stevenson's *Treasure Island* and Alexandre Dumas's *The Man in the Iron Mask*. Suitable for most secondary school pupils, these comics would be particularly good resources to use when studying the process of adaptation (comparing a page from the original novel with a page from the comic version, for example, could lead to some particularly interesting work with older pupils). Of course, there are also many quality children's comics published by companies other than Marvel and DC. Hergé's iconic Tintin stories combine stunning artwork with thrilling tales of adventure and the humour of the Asterix books by René Goscinny and Albert Uderzo make them ideal for use with children. The ever-popular Simpsons also appear in their own regular title, *Simpsons Comics*, which might be an effective way to capture children's interest initially. Older children might also enjoy David Petersen's *Mouse Guard*, the story of a group of brave warrior mice fighting to protect their civilisation.

In terms of reference books that will aid your teaching of comics, I would recommend three titles. Scott McCloud's *Understanding Comics* is a useful guide to the medium and, interestingly, is itself written in comic book form, but the two best texts to use if you wish to deepen your understanding of how comics operate are Will Eisner's authoritative guides to the medium, *Comics and Sequential Art* and *Graphic Storytelling and Visual Narrative*. Eisner was a writer and artist who is considered a legend in the field of visual narratives, and these two detailed yet accessible books explore the range of narrative techniques evident in comic books and show how to read comic book panels and pages effectively.

PART 2

Powers and responsibilities

Comic books in education

Tim Stafford

I am often asked why I read comic books. For almost as long as they have existed as a medium, comic books have frequently been treated with disdain and are often considered to be simplistic, undemanding reading experiences and the poor relation of the 'literary' novel. In countries such as France, Japan and Italy, where the reading of comic books by adults is commonplace, visual narratives are accorded a higher cultural status, whereas in Britain and the United States they have been largely ignored and their artistic, literary and educational potential relatively squandered. As award-winning writer Neil Gaiman states,

> You can have a beautiful piece of artwork and have it considered fine art; you can have a beautiful piece of writing and have it considered fine literature; but if you put these two things together . . . it's considered something less.
>
> (Cited in Beale, 2003: 101)

While it would certainly be inaccurate to make universal claims as to the quality of all comic books, we must also be careful not to dismiss the medium as a whole. For example, if we read a novel or saw a film that we did not like, it would not be logical to claim that we do not like it simply *because* it was a novel or a film. Instead, we might perhaps try to identify which specific aspects of the work we did not like (for example, character, plot, authorial style, direction). Similarly, if we read a comic book that we did not engage with on any satisfying level as readers, it would be unfair to claim that we did not like it because it is a comic book. We must approach comic books as we would any piece of art: without prejudice. To do this, we need to treat each text individually, judging it on its own merits and not in terms of any negative generic assumptions, and as educators we have a responsibility to try to ensure that children take the same approach. As the teacher (played by Julia Roberts) in the film *Mona Lisa Smile* says to her students when she presents them with a piece of modern art, 'You're not required to write a paper, you're not even required to like it. You *are* required to consider it' (*Mona Lisa Smile*, 2003).

So, to return to the question I have been asked on numerous occasions: why *do* I read comic books? For me, the medium is arguably the one that best reflects the limitless realms of our imaginations, the finest examples marrying stunning artwork with surprisingly complex plots and characters. They present the act of storytelling in a way that no other form of art can, intertwining distinct visual and written narratives in a truly unique format. They can challenge and develop our reading skills even as literate adults, encouraging us to broaden our definitions of what literature is and develop our understanding of the myriad creative forms through which stories can be told.

Yet beyond my personal love of the medium, evidence suggests that comic books are becoming an increasingly relevant and visible part of our artistic culture. Despite the fact that the readership of comic books is selective and relatively small in Britain, many of the characters who populate the hundreds of titles produced by the industry every month enjoy a significant cultural presence. Superheroes such as Spider-Man, Superman, Hulk and the X-Men are instantly recognisable to children and adults alike, thanks in part to merchandising and cartoons, but mainly as a result of Hollywood's continuing love affair with the graphic novel. The demand (and box office takings) for comic book adaptations is currently stronger than ever, with films such as *Spider-Man*, *Batman* and *Hulk* attracting a wealth of highly regarded directors and actors, grossing millions of dollars worldwide and spawning numerous sequels.[1] Clearly, a vast audience of children, teenagers and adults (of both sexes) around the globe are engaging with these stories, and the demand for more films based on these characters is seemingly insatiable. Bryan Singer's *X-Men* (2000) showed superbly that, when approached with respect and taken seriously, comic books can yield exciting and emotionally sophisticated narratives that transcend their fantasy roots and confidently function on a metaphorical level (*X-Men* uses the story of Marvel Comics' outcast mutant heroes to comment on the highly relevant themes of prejudice, discrimination and basic human rights in contemporary society). Therefore, it is certainly true to say that many comic books and many of the characters who appear in their pages have a high level of cultural visibility and relevance.

Perhaps the main stumbling blocks on the path towards the wider acceptance of comic books are the numerous misconceptions about the medium, some of which will be addressed briefly here. First, many children and adults tend to view comic books and superhero comics as synonymous. It is important here to make a distinction between the two terms: *comic books* are the medium, whereas *superhero comics* are a genre within the medium. This point may appear obvious, but for many years comics such as *Superman*, *Batman* and *Spider-Man* have often been perceived as the sum total of the medium, meaning that, for many, interest in the comic book genre has gone only as far as their interest in the superhero. While there are some superb superhero titles on the market, to limit any study of comics purely to this genre and ignore others would be to miss out on some of the richest reading experiences the medium offers (the equivalent of limiting one's reading only to thriller novels for example). Delve beyond the assorted capes and sidekicks in any comic shop and you will find comics with a dizzying range of subject matters. Comics such as Derek Watson and Kit Wallis's *Wonderland* (discussed in Part 1 of this chapter), David Petersen's *Mouse Guard*, Hugo Pratt's Corto Maltese books and, of course, Hergé's Tintin adventures are all good examples of comic books that tell satisfying and often emotionally profound stories without a superhero in sight. This is an important area to clear up when teaching comic books because children can be as inherently prejudiced against the medium as any adult, and girls particularly tend initially to express lack of interest in the comic book format. A lack of enthusiasm from many female pupils is understandable if they equate the concept of a comic book narrative with the male-dominated world of the superhero genre. As teachers, we have a responsibility to ensure that pupils' initial exposure to the medium is as varied and atypical as possible (as was emphasised in Part 1 of the chapter).

The 'superhero' assumption is tied in to a further misconception about the medium: that it is an exclusively male genre or, to put it colloquially, 'just for the boys'. It is certainly undeniable that the comic book industry as a whole is male dominated in terms of its writers, artists and its subject matter. Historically speaking, female characters have more often than not played marginal roles in the more mainstream comic books, where well-written women were noticeable by their absence. In countries such as France and Japan, where the comic book is a more visible part of the national culture, this gender imbalance is often less marked, with many storylines spread over a range of genres frequently revolving around female protagonists. However, if we consider the average Marvel or DC superhero comic book, it is more than likely that it will be written and/or drawn by a man and that its protagonist and antagonist will be male. Norma Pecora accurately notes that the superhero narrative has historically depicted a world 'where the women are either young and buxom or old and frail – but never equals' (1992: 61). This masculine bias is also reflected in the audience, which is overwhelmingly male (the nickname for an avid comic book fan is, in fact, 'fanboy'). This is undoubtedly a frustrating imbalance, and there is no logical reason at all why females should be marginalised by the medium. When we consider these factors, it is understandable that the average American mainstream comic book may be perceived as being largely irrelevant, possessing little allure for many girls. There are, however, comic books that do have strong, intelligent female characters who are central parts of the narrative and whose inclusion is in no way tokenistic. In addition to *Wonderland*, notable examples of comics that contain positive female representations are *Exiles*, *X23*, *New X-Men* and *Runaways*. Introducing children to titles such as *X-Men*, where heroic women such as Jean Grey and Rogue constitute essential parts of the team,[2] provides a valuable opportunity for pupils of both genders to see powerful female characters occupying dominant space in a traditionally male context. Crucially, this can also help to challenge children's (possibly stereotypical) notions of gender, where models of physical heroism may all too often be male.

Both these misconceptions give rise to a third: that comic books are essentially violent, centring on pugilistic narratives which often glorify aggression and condone violence as a means of solving disputes. Again, as I have shown with the previous criticisms, there is some truth in these accusations. Characters such as Captain America and Superman who rose to prominence in America during the Second World War regularly engaged in violent altercations, seizing with relish the opportunity to beat up wrongdoers in an onomatopoeic frenzy. Superheroes such as these were undoubtedly the product of the openly jingoistic historical periods that spawned them, and their now dated early adventures seem comically quaint at best and distastefully aggressive at worst. While it is the case that fights and physical displays of strength are still intrinsic parts of the modern superhero narrative (it is fair to say that the majority of these comics will have at least one fight in every issue), it is also important to point out these comics do not all glorify violence, and many are equally likely to have pages filled with sophisticated dialogue and characterisation. Two good examples of this are Marvel's *Ultimate X-Men* and *Ultimate Spider-Man* (two of the most consistently well-written superhero comics), in which we are regularly presented with highly moral characters who take no joy in resorting to fighting and who do so only in self-defence.

As was stated earlier, it is important initially to give children access to comic books that do not contain any superheroes, yet this is not to suggest that the superhero genre should not be used in an educational context. Many titles, including those featuring Spider-Man and Superman, can in fact provide valuable learning opportunities for children. If we examine the conflict in these texts appropriately, it can be argued that some superhero stories, such as *X-Men*, actually encourage readers to reflect upon and discuss issues of violence and conflict resolution. The basic premise of the *X-Men* comics[3] is that there are 'mutants' among us, a relatively small minority who have strange powers and uncanny abilities. Some, like Scott Summers, can fire energy beams from their eyes, while others, like Jean Grey, have phenomenal telekinetic skills. What makes these people different from many other superheroes is that they have not been transformed into mutants through an accident or by magic, but rather they were born with these mutations (which normally manifest themselves at puberty). The comic shows how the often oppressed and politically marginalised mutants are received by the non-mutant majority, and the contrasting ways in which they organise resistance to this discrimination. The group of mutants known as the X-Men are led by the pacifist Professor Charles Xavier, who believes in educating those members of the public who are prejudiced against mutants and strives for peaceful integration. Opposing him is his nemesis Magneto, a powerful mutant with fascist tendencies who wishes to destroy 'normal' humans, fighting intolerance with terrorism. Here, the *X-Men* texts become more than just specialist science fiction for a select audience; like Singer's film adaptation, they can be read as a powerful analogy for civil rights struggles, exploring relevant political issues by focalising the stories through the oppressed group. Interestingly, Trushell (2004), in his study of the X-Men comics, develops this idea, arguing that Xavier's and Magneto's diametrically opposed approaches to mutant rights directly parallel Martin Luther King's and Malcolm X's differing methods of dealing with the issue of black civil rights.

From a moral standpoint, a character such as Charles Xavier, or 'Professor X' as he is more commonly known, is truly worthy of study. When we think of superheroes, we often tend to define them by their incredible powers. The pages of these comics are filled with impressive displays of powers: Superman flies and has X-ray vision, the Hulk is the strongest creature on earth, and Spider-Man climbs walls. However, many superhero comics also show that a true hero is defined not by the moments when they use their powers, but rather by those moments when they do not. In *X2*, the sequel to the film *X-Men*, Professor X focuses his psychic power in order to locate a rogue mutant, but admits he is having difficulty pinpointing his exact location. When Wolverine asks, 'Can't you just concentrate harder?', the Professor replies coolly, 'If I wanted to kill him, yes' (X2, 2003). Similarly, there are numerous storylines in which other mutants have requested that Professor X use his mental ability to forcibly override the free will of his opponents and claim victory, but he rarely agrees, using his power only when the alternative would be worse. When one is looking at these texts with children, these ideas cannot be emphasised enough. It would be easy for Professor X to invade his opponents' minds and force them to act the way he would like, or for Superman to kill anyone who stands in his way, but neither does so. Superheroes understand that power is not to be abused, that simply because they *can* do something, that does not mean they *should*, and this is precisely what separates them from the supervillains. Whereas Magneto and his team, the evil Brotherhood of Mutants, destroy opposition without hesitation, the X-Men dogmatically stick to the Professor's belief in peaceful conciliation and the use of power to protect, not subjugate. As the Professor himself puts it in an issue of *Ultimate X-Men*,

> 'Some people ask why we don't just wage war on The Brotherhood, but that's such an old-fashioned, imperialistic solution to the problem. . . . As we look around the world today, it's clear that violence breeds nothing but further violence. Ideas are the only way to change the world.'
>
> (Millar, Kubert and Miki 2005: 16)

This heroic determination to behave with integrity and compassion is perhaps best summed up by the famous quotation from the first ever issue of *Spider-Man*, 'With great power there must also come – great responsibility!' (Lee and Ditko, 2006: 15).

In addition to the moral aspect of comics, metaphorical readings of the characters are also a valuable part of any study of the medium. Although many of the situations and characters we encounter in the pages of comic books may seem outlandish and fantastical, they often offer worthwhile insights into the real world. Older pupils learning to read texts on a figurative level can be encouraged to read comics metaphorically, and the more well-written comics can easily sustain such analyses: *Wonderland*'s dystopian story of a gang of children battling against a plague that transforms people into monsters deals with the timeless issues of family, friendship, love and fear of abandonment, *Spider-Man* examines the often difficult process of becoming an adult, and *X-Men* articulates feelings of difference and of being an outsider. The fact that many of these characters are not, in a biological sense, human is the very thing that allows them to function so effectively as metaphors for the human condition. When characters such as these possess exaggerated powers that have repercussions for their whole lives, it is easier for children to read them more clearly as hyperbolic versions of everyday human flaws and strengths. In this way, the Hulk becomes a metaphor for the less desirable, repressed aspects of our personalities, Jean Grey's transformation into Dark Phoenix represents the struggle many face to use power responsibly, and the concept of mutants reflects the experience of feeling different from others which most children (and indeed most adults) have felt at one time or another. Ironically, it is characters such as these who help us understand what it is to be human.

Such readings as these are nothing new; many comic book characters (particularly Marvel's) were specifically designed to function in this way. I referred earlier to the militaristic American superhero comics of the 1930s and 1940s, which undoubtedly glamorised violence and male physicality. By the 1960s, cultural and social changes had rendered these types of narratives somewhat archaic and out of sync with many readers' tastes, the consequence of which was a slump in comic book sales. To combat this, Marvel employed writers and artists such as Stan Lee and Jack Kirby, who reinvigorated the medium by creating characters who did not conform to the tired model of the simplistic, flawless hero but instead presented readers with individuals who were often the unwilling recipients of strange powers, powers that frequently served only to complicate their lives and make them unhappy. Many of the famous characters seen today in comics and films were created in this era, such as Spider-Man, the X-Men, Hulk and the Fantastic Four. The common link between these diverse characters is that they are *human* first and *superhuman* second. This fresh spin on the hero archetype began a trend in superhero narratives that is still prevalent today. Many contemporary comic book writers, such as Mark Millar, Joss Whedon, Christopher Yost and Craig Kyle, consistently produce superhero comics that have complex plots, engaging characters and real emotional depth. It is important to show children that, like J.K. Rowling and Philip Pullman, the best comic writers refuse to compromise on characterisation simply because they are writing within the fantasy medium. The situations in which these heroines and heroes find themselves may well be incredible, but the characters themselves are completely credible and psychologically real. In other words, the power of a comic book as a storytelling vehicle is not to be underestimated. As we have seen in Part 1 of this chapter, what may appear initially to be a simple format that eschews the written text of the novel for a mixture of words and images often belies complex content.

Thus far, I have explored some of the moral and thematic aspects of comic book literature, yet in terms of classroom study it is also important to consider the specific ways in which comics function as texts and the demands that they make on their readers. I have argued that comic books can appear to be deceptively simple, and this is true not only in terms of their narrative content but also in terms of the ways in which they transmit those narratives. Research on comic books in educational contexts has shown that the skills which they help develop in young readers are varied and complex; they therefore deserve a place in the reading experiences of even the youngest pupils (Meek, 1991; Rosen, 1996). Frustratingly, the educational potential of this medium is often restricted in primary schools, where comics may function only as substitutes for story books, a medium to which children may 'transfer' (Smith, 1994: 113) before moving on to more text-heavy books. They may also be used with groups of children who have difficulties with literacy and struggle with more traditional prose texts, for example emergent readers or children for whom English is their second language. A survey conducted by Art & Society in 1991 and 1992 on the use of comics in education provides evidence of this frustratingly limited attitude towards comics. Among the groups surveyed were special educational needs organisations, some of which believed that 'The reading of comics *per se* was not considered a desirable goal. Comics should only be considered an intermediary stage towards the reading of conventional literature' (Selwood and Irving, 1993: 114). Limiting their classroom usage in this way not only fails to exploit the medium's full potential but also means that only a small section of pupils are given the opportunity to explore these texts. Furthermore, if comics are presented to children as simple, undemanding and semi-literate texts, those pupils who do read them will most likely not be encouraged to actively and critically decode the comic page, and therefore the reading experience will ultimately be a passive one. In educational terms, the teaching of comics is a self-fulfilling prophecy: if we present comics to children as offering relatively worthless reading experiences, they will become so for most pupils, yet if we show them to be important texts worthy of study in their own right, pupils may well learn to appreciate them as such.

Comics ideally need to be taught as an end in themselves, not as a stepping stone on the road towards 'proper' books, and there are a number of justifications for using them as part of literacy lessons. Curricula must now begin to show an understanding of what it means to be a Western citizen in the twenty-first century and reflect the fact that comics as a narrative model are becomingly increasingly relevant to children's lives. For some years now, the vast majority of schools have understood the need to widen definitions of the term 'text' beyond the printed page, and English lessons in which pupils are required to read both film and television programmes and consider the process of adaptation from page to screen are now commonplace in secondary schools. At GCSE level the examining bodies that determine syllabuses (such as OCR, Edexcel and AQA) are beginning to appreciate the significance of the visual image in contemporary society and recognising that areas of study such as advertising and the internet, formerly confined to the specialist subject of media studies, deserve a central place in the English curriculum (AQA, 2006; OCR, 2003; Edexcel, 2002). To those who have taught or studied the media, the notion that we are all surrounded, and indeed saturated, by images in daily life is nothing new. The point, however, bears repetition; it is imperative to keep in mind the degree to which the majority of children are exposed to visual information, whether it is in print, on television, on DVD or via a computer screen. We need to help children to become aware of the explicit and implicit messages which various forms of media transmit and not assume that they will be able to do this naturally. In short, we need to work towards what Bazalgette terms 'a new definition of what it may mean to be "literate" in a digital age' (1997: 110) if we want children to become more than just passive consumers. As Goodwin argues, 'The ability to be visually critical and discriminating in our image-rich society ensures that we are not vulnerable to any visually manipulative media' (2004: 126).

In addition to preparing children for life outside the classroom, comic books offer unique ways in which to study narrative. A wealth of research has shown time and time again that sharing picture books with children often leads to highly satisfying and educationally rich experiences for children and adults alike (Whitehead, 2004; Graham, 2004; Styles, 1996), and comic books have a similar potential to encourage 'sophisticated meaning making to take place' (Goodwin, 2004: 125). Indeed, Margaret Meek's famous claim that picture books 'make reading for all a distinctive kind of imaginative looking' (1991: 116) is also true of comics. However, comic books go beyond many picture books, in the sense that their stories are transmitted through a fusion of pictures and words, not one or the other.

To demonstrate this quite specific relationship between meaning, words and pictures, let us consider how other texts which incorporate pictures operate. In a traditional, illustrated storybook, pictures act merely as decoration for the written text, and were we to remove them altogether, no meaning would be lost; the narrative would remain complete (the key idea here is that images in books such as these are indeed only *illustrations*: they merely depict that which the printed text has already told the reader). An example of this is Michael Morpurgo's enchanting story *Wombat Goes Walkabout*. Here, Christian Birmingham's beautiful artwork acts as a visual retelling of Morpurgo's written text. The specific function of the pictures here is to illustrate, telling the story effectively in a visual form but not adding any additional narratives. A more complex variant of this model is the picture book. The picture book functions differently from the illustrated storybook because the pictures not only perform the basic task of illustrating what the written narrative has already told the reader but may often also develop beyond the confines of the print sentences and contain meanings of their own. A good example of this is Anthony Browne's *Gorilla*, where images and written text are generally in accord, but in addition the pictures frequently produce a dazzling multiplicity of meanings and narratives which are entirely, and deliberately, independent of Browne's written storyline. The simple tale of a young girl dreaming about a day out with a friendly gorilla is given extra depth and emotional intensity through Browne's gloriously surreal illustrations and use of motif. On one level the pictures are a straightforward representation of the events in the text, but on another level they imply ideas and themes that are entirely absent from the writing (for example, the images suggest a link between the fantasy gorilla and the girl's emotionally distant father). For an elaboration of this point, see the discussion of Anthony Browne in Chapter 2.

Books such as these are perhaps the model of storytelling closest to the style employed by comics. But comics are significantly different from both these narrative formats for the simple reason that they are entirely liberated from the basic rules of the written text. However complex or layered the pictures may be in storybooks and picture books, the reader can still rely on the written words to form the narrative core, whereas with comic books, sentences and paragraphs are eschewed for speech bubbles which show dialogue and thought bubbles or captions which show interior monologues. While the number of words on a comic page can vary greatly, the basic fact remains that the page will not employ many of the conventions of the written story, and therefore meaning must be relayed by other methods. The pictures, then, become active agents in the process of transmitting meaning; in effect, they *are* the prose and the sentences of the story, and we must therefore teach children to read these images with this in mind. For some pupils this may be a significant shift in the way they perceive the role of pictures in texts. The idea that a picture in a book is merely a passive decoration of the 'proper' story (the written part) needs to be challenged early on in literacy teaching, and comic-book-based activities are instrumental in helping children to develop the skills that will allow them to read images successfully.

But what exactly are these skills that comics can help children to develop? While they could certainly be described as 'reading' skills, they are of course different from those we aim to equip pupils with in order for them to successfully derive meaning from written texts. Visual reading skills include being able to read individual images metaphorically and to identify how abstract concepts such as tone and character might be transmitted by graphic cues. In addition, the ability to interpret the composition of images could also be developed through the study of comics. In this sense, comic panels, like shots from films, can be analysed in terms of the positioning of people and objects, and, with help, children can learn to see how these dynamics provide a deeper insight into characters and their relationships with one another. Similarly, by discussing the decisions that comic artists make, children can develop an awareness of how techniques such as close-up, shading and the use of background and foreground constantly supply implicit information to the reader. Moving beyond individual images, sequencing skills could also be taught through comics, as children learn how a successive series of pictures combine to tell a story and how, in line with the critical theory of structuralism, a single panel's meaning can alter greatly depending on the context it is placed in.

A good example of how comics might develop some of these skills can be seen in Craig Thompson's heartbreaking ode to friendship *Good-Bye Chunky Rice*, the story of a mouse named Dandel who is separated from her close friend Chunky when he leaves their small town to explore the wider world. In one series of panels, Thompson shows Dandel making her way over an outcrop of rocks to the water's edge, where she sits and looks out to sea and asks her absent friend, 'What does a breathtaking view of the ocean mean without you? Nothing' (Thompson, 2006: 46–47). In this segment of the text there are only five speech bubbles over two pages, but the thirteen panels that comprise this sequence combine to create a powerful emotional effect. The stark black-and-white artwork could be said to reflect Dandel's feelings of loneliness and unhappiness, and Thompson's inclusion of detritus bobbing by the rocks reminds us that the character sees nothing beautiful in her surroundings. The sequence is also enhanced by the varied composition of each picture. Some panels are wide shots, emphasising the fact that the mouse is a solitary figure, almost lost in a comfortless environment, whereas Thompson's close-up panels allow us to focus on Dandel's large eyes and huddled posture, which imply sadness. In addition, the series of pictures emphasises the importance of context as individual close-up panels of rocks become imbued with emotional significance when we consider them as parts of a larger sequence that deals with ideas of loneliness and separation.

The study of comic books can also help children develop their understanding of more sophisticated narrative concepts. Just as picture books can, in Jordan's words, 'exaggerate irony' (Jordan, 1996: 50), so too can comics. A recent issue of the comic *Marvel Team-Up* illustrates this point effectively. The narrative concerns a powerful alien named Titannus who tells his life story to a group of assembled superheroes in an attempt to persuade them that he is not a murderous villain but is, instead, an innocent victim who needs their help. While the written text states, 'I spread goodwill across my planet . . . I spread a message of peace throughout all the neighbouring star systems' (Kirkman, Medina and Vlasco, 2005: 14–15), the pictures show Titannus and his troops laying waste to towns, threatening innocent people and destroying spaceships. One particularly effective panel documents how Titannus became king. He claims that 'Eventually the [previous] King grew old, and passed on' (ibid.: 12), but the picture reveals that he has in fact murdered his predecessor by strangling him while he was in bed. The premise behind this text may seem quite simple. Titannus lies about his past, but it is, in fact, constructed in a relatively complex fashion. The comic simultaneously presents two conflicting narratives, one written (in this case, a lie) and one visual (clearly the true story), and juxtaposes them with one another, and in the process serves as a perfect illustration of the concept of irony. Jordan notes that, in picture books, 'A picture may extend the meaning of the words, but it may also contradict the feeling that is implied [or] counterpoint the text' (1996: 50) – and comics likewise are able to play with the narrative in similarly sophisticated ways. Using them in an educational context allows teachers to introduce children to relatively complex literary concepts that would arguably be harder to teach by using a text which consists purely of words.

Comic books, therefore, can be rich educational resources. The best examples of the medium not only tell stories in a unique and vibrant way but also provide an opportunity to examine narrative elements such as character and plot from a fresh perspective. As artist Paul Pope puts it,

> Comics, like all other arts, are elastic, open-ended and expansive. The medium has the power to contain and express all human thought, all feeling and experience, from the most sacred to the most profane, to heaven and hell and back again. There is absolutely nothing you can't express through the medium of comics. Nothing is beyond its scope.

(2007: 9)

Chapter 5

Teaching Jacqueline Wilson

The Suitcase Kid is a family fiction concerning the traumas experienced by a 10-year-old girl as a result of her parents' separation. The themes of marital breakdown, jealousy, anger and the dislocating experience of learning to live with two new families provide material that fits very well with the social and emotional aspects of learning (SEAL) framework. This unit of work will therefore focus on activities that can be interrelated with the SEAL framework and the English and art curriculum. The work suggested in this chapter is particularly applicable to themes 2, 6 and 7: *Getting on and falling out*, *Relationships* and *Changes*. The most important outcome of the work associated with this book is that children enjoy its gritty realism and engage with the central character's struggle to come to terms with her new life. Activities most suitable for a SEAL focus are identified by this icon: ☺ . The trial workshop took place with a mixed age group of Years 4, 5 and 6 pupils, and most of them demonstrated a strong identification and empathy with the issues raised in the book.

Synopsis of Jacqueline Wilson's *The Suitcase Kid*

Andy's parents no longer get on together, so they decide to separate. This means that 10-year-old Andy has to leave Mulberry Cottage and all that she loved about it. This is bad enough, but even worse is the reality of having to live with two new families in two different homes. Andy's life is suddenly turned upside down, and the weekly shuttle between her mother and father is tiring and destabilising. Andy clashes with 'little ratbag Katie', the indulged younger daughter of her mother's new partner, and she is deeply hostile to her dad's new partner, Carrie, and her hippy, peace-loving, wholefood lifestyle. Andy falls badly behind in her work at school, gets into trouble with both new families, and cannot ever be alone when the worst thing imaginable happens. She loses her beloved toy Radish, her only constant friend. Just when things could not get more unbearable, she finds kindness and affection in a new relationship and the beginnings of an acceptance of her new life, which holds some unexpected compensations.

Preparation

Some time spent on practising the different voices in advance of reading the story will enliven its reading. The most important ones are Andy, Katie, Graham (Katie's brother), Andy's mum and dad, Uncle Bill and Carrie.

Reading the story

As you read through the story, get the children, at the end of each chapter, to try to guess what subject the next letter in the alphabet will focus on and ask them to think about why Jacqueline Wilson has chosen to tell Andy's story using an alphabetical structure (leave any responses to this question until the discussion activities, after the story has been completed). While they are listening to the story, encourage them to put themselves in Andy's shoes and think about how they might have felt in her position. It would also be useful for the drama and discussion activities to prompt the children to step outside Andy's perspective occasionally and take *one* of the other characters in order to consider their side of the story and the difficulties *they* may be facing.

Responding to *The Suitcase Kid*

While the first-person narrative structure of *The Suitcase Kid* is straightforward and easy to follow, this does not mean that challenging and searching thinking cannot be demanded of the children. The discussion on questioning written texts in Chapter 3, Part 1 is equally applicable to this text and should be revisited before selecting questions for the discussion activity. Encouraging the children to move gradually from reporting story content to an analysis of the deeper meanings, patterns and connecting themes within the story is the key to ensuring that children gain greater insight and understanding about the book as well as its wider social and emotional issues. The model used in Chapter 3 is presented again, this time with some exemplifications from *The Suitcase Kid*. You are advised to make a selection for any one session which follows progressively from the *content – narrative – structure* framework.

A model for questioning written texts

1   Broad questions that focus on general impressions of the story as a whole. For example, Which parts of the story did you enjoy most? In which part of the story did you feel most sorry for Andy?

2   Questions about the characters and the parts they play. For example, Which character do you find most interesting? Who is the most important character? Which character do you like the most?

3   Search for puzzles in the story and those parts you did not like or understand. For example, Why is Graham so silent and why does he choose to spend so much time alone?

4   Question about narration and point of view. Who is telling the story? When the story is told in the first person through a particular character's viewpoint, does this make you more sympathetic to the character?

5   Identify patterns or links in the story. In *The Suitcase Kid*, for example, Wilson has deliberately chosen to use an alphabetical framing device as the structure or form for her book so that she can zoom in and out of Andy's experience of marital breakdown. Why has she chosen to tell the story in this way?

As has been suggested in previous chapters, seat the children next to someone they can work well with. In order to achieve maximum pupil involvement, use a paired discussion strategy for the first two or three activities at least. In the first few teacher-directed questions, I have indicated where paired and whole-class interactions might best take place. The remaining questions leave this to teachers' judgement and discretion. The following questions broadly follow the *content – narration – structure* framework detailed in the model on the previous page.

◇   Group discussion and interaction

◇   Why did you find the story interesting? Give at least two reasons. Discuss in pairs first. Share some responses with the whole class.

◇   Tell your partner why you enjoyed the story. Give three reasons. Share one or two different sets of reasons with the whole class.

◇   Which part of the story did you enjoy most and why? (Paired activity).

◇   Were there any parts of the story that puzzled or shocked you or which you did not understand?

◇   Divide the children into small groups and assign each of them one of the following characters: Andy, Graham, Andy's mum, Andy's dad, Katie, Paula, Carrie, Uncle Bill, Zen and Crystal. Each group is to contribute all they know from the story about their assigned characters. One person from each group should share their knowledge of the different characters with the rest of the class.

◇   Which character interested you most? Give reasons for your choice.

◇   Who do you think is the most important character in the story? Give reasons for your choice.

◇   Which character do you like or dislike most in the story? Refer to those parts of the story that make you react in this way about your chosen character so that you begin your answer like this: 'I like X because . . .' or 'I dislike X because . . .'

◇   Who is telling the story? When one particular character is telling the story, how does this affect the way you feel about the character narrator?

◇   Why do you think Jacqueline Wilson has chosen to tell her story from Andy's point of view?

◇   What part does Radish play in the telling of the story?

◇   What kinds of things do we learn about Andy that we would not know about without the inclusion of Radish in the story?

◇   Which character changes most in the book? Use examples from the story as evidence for your reasons.

◇   Why do you think the author has chosen letters of the alphabet to organise the way she tells her story?

◇   The author knew that she was writing this story for an audience of children, so what do you think were some of the reasons that led to her decision to use the alphabet device to structure her story?

☺   With a partner, make a list of at least three things that you learned from the story about what matters most when a child has to get used to living a new kind of life as a result of her or his parents splitting up.

Drama activities

The following activities do not depend on the use of the school hall. A space created in the classroom by moving the furniture safely to the sides of the room is perfectly adequate. The following sound effects are not essential, but they greatly enhanced the quality of dramatic involvement of the children who participated in the trial workshop.

Menu of activities

1   Individual character freeze-frame
2   Group sculpting activity
3   Hot-seating
4   Mime improvisation, warm-up
5   Mime improvisation, 'Andy tries to rescue Radish'
6   Group role play, 'Understanding Andy's feelings' ☺
7   Cool-down

Useful props

- Sound effect of footsteps crunching through leaves as though someone were walking through a forest. Available for a small fee at http://www.tradebit.com/tagworld.php/crunching+footsteps.
- Liquid suspense music. Sound Design Elements. Suspense music that can be used to add tension, suspense and fear. Available as above at http://www.tradebit.com/filedetail.php/838835.

Both of these sound effects can be downloaded on to a CD. Either or both would work well with the drama activity to be outlined later in this section.

Freeze-frame activity (ten minutes)

Before you begin this activity, it will be helpful to provide children with a list of the key characters and their role in the story, either in the form of a photocopied sheet or displayed on an interactive whiteboard. The idea of this activity is that children freeze in role on a given command.

> **The characters in *The Suitcase Kid***
>
> *Andy (Andrea) – central character, narrator and protagonist, 10 years old*
> *Andy's mum*
> *Andy's dad*
> *Radish (Andy's tiny spotted Sylvanian rabbit, her best friend)*
> *Katie (Andy's stepsister), 10 years old*
> *Graham (Andy's stepbrother), 12 years old*
> *Paula (Andy's stepsister), 14 years old*
> *Uncle Bill, Andy's mum's new partner*
> *Carrie, Andy's dad's new partner*
> *Crystal and Zen, Carrie's 5-year-old twins*

The children sit in a space on the floor and are asked to choose the character that they would like to be. Before beginning the activity, ask the children to:

 Think carefully about who you are and what you might be doing. You can either stand still and mime an action typical of the character you have chosen, or you can move around the room in role.

If you are moving in role, think about the differences in the way you would walk if you were, for instance, Graham, who has a jerky walk, or Paula, who thinks a lot about her appearance and loves make-up, cool clothes and pop stars.

On the instruction 'Go', the children move into role. On the command of '**Freeze**', the teacher and any other adults in the room have to guess which character a chosen child is playing. Repeat one more time, ensuring that the children hold their action absolutely still on the command of 'Freeze'.

Now split the class into two, one half watching while the other half mime a character different from the one they had chosen before. Tell the watching half of the class to concentrate on watching one or two children only.

 Go.
Freeze.

Selected members of the watching half try to guess which character(s) they were playing.

Praise the children for what they did well and change over so that the watching half become the acting half. Repeat as above.

Group sculpting activity (ten minutes)

 Get into groups of three. One of you is to be Andy, the other Andy's mum and the third, Andy's dad.

Make a group sculpture of Andy, her mum and her dad, showing the conflict and differences between the three as the parents are on the point of separating.

Share some of the group sculptures, asking selected groups to explain to the rest of the class the thinking behind their group sculpture.

Hot-seating activity (fifteen minutes)

Children choose which character they would like to be in 'the hot seat'. Limit the choice of characters to Andy, Katie, Andy's mum and Andy's dad. *(More characters can be added if you wish to extend this activity.)* You may need to remind the children of what was said in the discussion about the main characteristics of each of these before beginning the activity. Seat the children in a horseshoe shape with a chair in the gap of the crescent. Before beginning, ask the children to:

 Think carefully about the character you would like to play and the kind of person he or she is.

Close your eyes for a minute or so and think about the role their character plays in the story in relation to the other characters.

Begin the activity by choosing a child who is reasonably confident about performing in front of others and who will be able to sustain credibility in their chosen role. This will set the tone for the others. Children and teachers then ask questions of the character in the hot seat in turns. Keep the pace moving and give as many children as time allows a chance to be in the hot seat. If children choose to hot-seat the same character as one that has previously been 'hot-seated', it is important to encourage them to ask questions *different* from those asked before, otherwise the activity will become tedious and undemanding for the new child in the hot seat.

Mime improvisation: warm-up

Scenario: Andy cannot sleep without Radish, so she sneaks downstairs and out of the front door to try to find the house in Larkspur Lane where she lost her. She is very tired and frightened but she has to find Radish.

In order to raise children's awareness of how they might show their distress at losing something very precious to them, do the warm-up activity first, focusing on the movement and gestures made with the hands.

Find a space on the floor.

Imagine you have lost something very precious. You do not need to tell anyone what it is.

Watch while I mime something precious that I have lost and find again. Notice whether it is big or small, alive or not, by the way I use my hands and eyes.

Children then mime their own 'lost and found' scenario.

 Think about how big or small it is.

Is it an animal or a favourite toy or something very special which someone has given you?

Show by the movements of your hands and the way you pick it up what kind of 'thing' it is. Make sure you follow every movement of your hands with your eyes.

How do you show your distress when you realise you have lost it? What will you do to show your joy and relief when you have found it?

Think about where you lost your precious belonging. Is it outside in a garden, on a beach, in the woods or somewhere in your house?

Mime the sequence from the moment of loss to the moment of finding it again.

Share two or three examples of convincing and effective mime. Point out examples of the convincing use of hands and eyes.

Rescuing Radish

 Sit or lie down and think about Andy's desperate search in dangerous circumstances to find Radish. Shut your eyes and listen while I give you this sequence:

- Get out of bed.
- Creep carefully downstairs, trying not to make a sound.
- Put on your scarf.
- Slowly open the front door, trying not to make it creak.
- Start walking through the streets. All the time, you are scared that someone may be following you.
- Climb over the gate into the garden of the house in Larkspur Lane.
- Creep round the edge of the lake, treading very carefully in the dark.
- Find the tree where you dropped Radish.
- Try to reach for her inside the tree hole.
- While you are trying desperately to feel for her familiar shape . . . something startles you. Is it an animal? Something is making a rustling sound in the grass. Is it somebody's footsteps? What *is* it?
- Freeze into a position of fear and hold absolutely still.

Play the sound effects you have recorded while the children imagine the scenario you have given them.

Go into your first position (lying in bed, having made up your mind to find Radish, whatever danger it will involve).

Play the sound effect after they have crept downstairs, opened the door and started to walk away from the house. Ask the children to repeat the whole sequence at least once, saying clearly how it could be improved.

 Think about how you can increase the suspense in your mime. Perhaps one of the stairs creaks loudly as you go downstairs, and you have to stop, freeze and listen, fearing that you may have woken someone up. . . . Show this tension in your movements and in the expression in your face. . . .

No one seems to have stirred, and you go on towards the front door, grabbing your scarf as you go. Continue until the moment you freeze in terror as you hear a sound coming from somewhere in the Larkspur Road garden.

Share one or two individual mimes and get the children to say what worked well.

SEAL Theme 2: Getting on and falling out (twenty minutes)

Some of the children as well as adults in *The Suitcase Kid* do not always act in Andy's best interests and are sometimes thoughtless, unkind, selfish and hurtful. In this activity, the children are going to be asked to think about three different occasions when Andy is hurt very badly as a consequence of other people's selfishness and cruelty. The first of these incidents concerns Katie's, Paula's and Graham's grandparents, who deliberately exclude Andy from the presents they buy for their grandchildren, adding insult to injury with the words 'But Paula and Graham and Katie are our grandchildren. . . . Andrea's nothing to do with us.' Read from the third line on p. 96 beginning 'But the worst ones of all . . .' to the bottom of the page.

The second incident occurs when Andy's dad arrives to collect her for the weekly visit to his new family. Unfortunately, Andy is ill, but she is torn between staying with her mother until she gets better and leaving with her father, who is insisting that she get up and go with him as arranged. Read from the second line on page 56 of *The Suitcase Kid* beginning 'And then the others came home from school . . .' to the end of the first sentence on p. 57.

The third occasion happens when Andy is distraught because Radish has fallen down a hole in a tree in the garden at Larkspur Lane. Everyone else has gone to bed and only Andy and Katie are awake. Andy is desperately missing Radish; Katie knows it and plays on her distress. Read the last paragraph on p. 115 beginning 'Down a tree, is she, Andy Pandy?' When all three passages have been read, give the following instructions:

 Get into groups of three and four. Each group is given the 'grandparents', the 'Andy's dad' or the 'Katie' incident.

Find a space on the floor with your particular group. Discuss between you how Andy would have felt at the time of your assigned incident. When you have thought about how you would feel, think up a sentence you would like to say to the person responsible for your hurtful 'incident'.

Stand or sit in a way that shows how Andy is feeling.

Take it in turns to say one sentence each that expresses Andy's reaction to the incident.

Think carefully about the body posture she would adopt. What expression would be on your face? How will you show your feelings with your eyes and mouth? What will you be doing with your head, arms, hands and legs? Will you be lying, sitting or standing up?

Decide who is going to speak first, second, third, and so on.

Give the children one or two minutes to make this decision.

 On the count of three – Go!

Share one of each of the three different 'Andy' incidents and praise what was effective and convincing about each of them.

 Stay in the same 'incident' groups. Think of three or four things you could say and do to lessen the hurt and conflict they caused Andy.

Give children two or three minutes to discuss this in their groups.

 Sit or stand in their group and say one kind thing they could say to help Andy feel better.

Share one or two individual responses from each of the three group scenarios. Acknowledge each of the groups' responses, highlighting constructive and imaginative suggestions.

Cool-down activity (two to three minutes)

 Lie comfortably on the floor and close your eyes.

Either imagine you are Andy dreaming about Mulberry Cottage and all the things you used to do there or imagine the best place you have ever been to and what it was that made you so happy when you were there.

When you are ready, slowly get up and stand, breathing deeply in a relaxed position.

Writing, drawing and SEAL activities

Drawing and language work

Three or four extra copies of the text will be needed for this activity. The objective of this part of the unit of work is to draw two of the characters in *The Suitcase Kid* using Nick Sharratt's simple, bold black-and-white line drawings as a model, along with the descriptions of their appearance and personalities in the book. Begin by focusing the children's attention on one or two of Nick Sharratt's drawings, encouraging them to note, in particular, how he communicates the changing mood of his characters by very small alterations in the arch of their eyebrows, shape of the mouth, position of hands and arms, and so on. Enlarged paper photocopies or copies displayed on an interactive whiteboard will provide a fruitful focus for a whole-class discussion and analysis of why his illustrations fit so well with Jacqueline Wilson's stories.

Display an enlarged version of the following description of Andy and Katie on the interactive whiteboard from pp. 13–14.

> My name is Andrea West but I mostly get called Andy. My sly little stepsister Katie calls me Andy Pandy. Everyone just thinks she's being cute. Katie specializes in cute. We are exactly the same age – in actual fact she's five days older than me – and yet she barely comes up to my waist. I happen to be big. Katie is extremely small. People don't twig she's ten. They only think she's seven or eight and she plays up to this for all she's worth. She blinks her blue beady eyes and wrinkles her small pink nose and puts on this squeaky little sugar-mouse voice. People go all drooly and practically nibble her ears. Katie is not a sugar mouse. Katie is a King-Size Rat.

If the boys would prefer to draw two of the male characters, they could choose to do Uncle Bill, Graham or Andy's dad. There are descriptions of Uncle Bill (pp. 15–16) and Graham (p. 21). Encourage the children to find further information about Katie and Andy, or Uncle Bill and Graham, from copies of the text. When they have decided which two characters they are going to focus on, give each child an A4-sized piece of paper and ask them to fold it in half vertically. At the top of each side, write the names of each of your characters.

Questions to stimulate and direct the children's thinking

◇ Think about the kind of hair your character has and the expression he or she will wear.
◇ What kind of clothes and shoes will they be wearing? You can only use black colour or felt-tipped pens, so think carefully about pattern, design, shape, logo, etc.
◇ Think about an object that your character(s) would be most easily identified with. For example, Graham's would be a computer. This should be part of your drawing (see examples of work on pp. 155–156, 159–161).
◇ When you have found out all you can about your characters, list their characteristics in each of the columns on your piece of paper, including details of their clothes, design and shape of hair, and facial expression.
◇ When you are very clear about what the precise details you are going to put in your drawings, you are ready to begin your first drawing. Remember to make your character fill up most of a plain piece of A4 paper.
◇ You may wish to label parts of your drawings and/or draw a thought bubble coming out of your character's head saying what he or she is thinking at the time.

Writing and drawing activities

The following range of activities are designed to develop empathy and the ability to write and think from another point of view using *The Suitcase Kid* as the context. The development of this form of writing closely interrelates with empathy and the themes of *relationships and changes* in the SEAL curriculum. Teachers may wish to place a greater emphasis on one over the other, but the activities provide sufficient scope for development in *both* writing and social and emotional aspects of learning.

Radish's point of view

◇   Write two diary accounts of Radish's best and worst day. Start the first paragraph with the sentence 'My worst day was when . . .' and the second with 'My best day was when . . .' (see examples of work on pp. 157–158).

◇   It would help you to organise your thoughts better if you made two lists, under the headings of 'Worst Day' and 'Best Day', of all the things that happened, including who was there at the time when things happened, where you were at the time and what Andy was doing.

◇   Give very clear details about *why* it was your worst and your best day, describing your feelings as well as those of Andy.

◇   You will make your diary more interesting to read if you include what you thought about one or two of the other characters' behaviour and what they were doing on your best and worst days.

◇   Make your descriptions of where you were when good or bad things happened as clear and as detailed as possible – as though you were painting a picture with words instead of paint and brushes.

Acts of kindness – thinking, talking, writing and drawing

Acts of blatant self-interest, meanness and spite are balanced in the story by generosity, sensitivity and kindness. It is important that children see the latter as being as much a part of life as the former and that the balancing of these extremes of human behaviour in the plot and characterisation is a central ingredient in the power of any story to sustain its readers' interest and involvement. In the following activity, children are asked to consider what it was in Mr and Mrs Peters' behaviour that made such an impact on Andy and why their kindness mattered so much to her. Before starting the writing activity, get the children to think about the following in pairs or small groups:

◇   Help each other recall from the story everything you can remember about Mr and Mrs Peters and the kind things they did for Andy, sharing one or two contributions with the whole class.

Filling Larkspur Lake with kindness

◇   Work together in pairs with one large piece of paper between you. You are going to draw a large picture of a lake like the one in Larkspur Lane and fill it with kindness. You can make up your own shape for the lake and your own ideas for what you put in it. Nick Sharratt's drawing on p. 73 of *The Suitcase Kid* might give you some starting points. On another, smaller sheet of paper, make a list of all the kind things Mr and Mrs Peters did. You can do this on your own or together, taking it in turns to do the writing.

◇ Decide between you which you think are the most important things on the list which made Andy feel happier.

◇ You are going to write these in bold, clear writing on pieces of paper cut out in the shape of leaves, yacht sails or fishes, or any other shape that you think would fit well in a lake setting.

◇ You will need to make your shapes big enough to have enough space on each of them to write a sentence from your list of Mr and Mrs Peters' kind acts.

◇ Do not make your shapes too big or you will not be able to fit many of them on to your lake.

◇ When you have filled up your shapes with the most important 'kind acts' chosen from your list, stick them carefully on to your lake. Your lakes of kindness can then be part of a classroom display or the focus of an assembly.

If you wanted to place a greater emphasis on the SEAL aspect of this activity, you could involve the whole class in making a large frieze of the lake with everyone writing an 'act of kindness' sentence arising from the story, on an appropriate shape for sticking on to the lake. The display can be used as a visual reference point to remind children about the importance of kindness, especially when they are particularly unhappy. It can also be used in connection with other SEAL-related work on the theme of *relationships*.

 ### Writing activity: making changes

There are at least two other characters in the book who show kindness and sensitivity towards Andy and whose understanding behaviour slowly helps her begin to adjust to her new life. Towards the end of the story, Andy also makes some changes in *her* thinking and understanding about life.

◇ Organise the children into discussion groups of 4 to 6. Give them five minutes to come up with a response to the following:

1 Name two other characters in the book who display kindness and understanding towards Andy.

2 What do they do and say which makes them genuine acts of kindness (where they *do* something positive rather than just talking about what they *might* do)?

3 Suggest how these acts and words of kindness help Andy begin to make changes in her attitude to both her new families.

The last instruction is the most challenging because it makes demands upon the children to engage in some higher-order thinking about the way change can happen, even when it is unexpected and unanticipated. It may therefore need some teacher support and guidance.

Write a letter to your best friend

◇ Imagine you are Andy and you want to tell someone about some of the better things that are now happening in your life. Write a letter to your best friend telling her or him about the friendships you have made with Mr and Mrs Peters and Graham. Say how you met Mr and Mrs Peters and tell the friend about some of the kind things they have done for you.

◇ Explain how you did not think you would ever be friends with Graham because he shuts himself up in his bedroom all the time, but once you got to know him, he turned out to be a really good friend.

◇ Mention too how you are even beginning to like the irritating Carrie more than you did and tell your friend why.

◇ End your letter by telling your friend how these new friendships have helped you to change your attitude to both your new families and what new things you have learned as a result of the hard times you have had in recent months.

◇ You could conclude your letter with some face drawings of your new friends so that you best friend can see what they look like.

Writing in the style of Jacqueline Wilson

This is a demanding, extended writing task and is more appropriate for Year 5 and Year 6 children. It may take two or three sustained writing sessions to complete.

◇ Using the following five-part story structure, ask the children to write about Andy from the perspective of one of the other characters: Bill, Graham, Katie, Carrie, Paula, Zen, Crystal, her mum or her dad.

◇ Start by telling your readers what your name is. For example, you might begin like this: 'My name is Graham. I wear glasses and I'm a bit shorter than Andy even though I'm 12 years old. There's been a load of rows in the house since Andy and her mum came to live with us, especially between Katie and Andy. I can't stand shouting and bickering, so I keep out of the way and stay in my bedroom.'

1 Introduce yourself by giving your name, stating what you look like and what your first feelings are about Andy when you first meet her. Use the above example to help you.

2 Describe the first time Andy has breakfast in your house. What are your feelings towards her? Describe her from your point of view. What clothes is she wearing? What things do you like about her? What things irritate you? Invent a funny incident that occurs while you are all sitting round the table eating breakfast.

3 An incident occurs between you and Andy or another person in the family which really annoys you. Describe what led up to it, what happened and how it ended.

4 Andy loses Radish and is very upset about it. What are your feelings about this? Do you feel sorry for her? Do you think she is making a lot of fuss about a silly toy? What do you do?

5 Whatever happens, Andy is going to continue going back and forth between her mum and her dad's new homes. Something happens to make her new life less unhappy and

more bearable. Describe what it is. Do you have anything to do with it? How does it affect you and Andy? What happens can be different from the book; make up your own ending.

Things to think about as you write

◇ While Jacqueline Wilson writes about serious issues, she uses lots of humour to make things lighter and less serious. Bring some humour into your short story.
◇ Describe your characters in very clear detail which anyone reading your story would immediately be able to picture and imagine.
◇ Try to make the five parts of your story flow together so they become a whole story rather than five separate, disconnected parts.
◇ Enliven your short story by adding one or two illustrations in the style of Nick Sharratt.

Objectives and learning outcomes

Lesson/series of lessons/unit of work objectives

1   To deepen children's understanding, appreciation and enjoyment of *The Suitcase Kid*.
2   To help children develop a beginning understanding of how Jacqueline Wilson deals with the issues of marital separation and its effects on children and adults.
3   To provide writing, drawing, drama, and speaking and listening activities that will deepen and extend children's understanding of the characters in the story as well as how they change and develop.
4   To use parts of *The Suitcase Kid* to develop and increase children's social and emotional understanding of the effects of loss, unkindness and thoughtlessness, and how these can be countered with kindness, sensitivity, empathy and understanding.
5   To make explicit links with the themes of *Getting on and falling out*, *Relationships* and *Changes* in the SEAL curriculum.
6   To interrelate the SEAL framework with the English and art curriculum using *The Suitcase Kid* as the primary focus.
7   To extend children's knowledge and understanding of the first-person narration writing form and why it works so well for Jacqueline Wilson's family fictions.
8   To extend children's understanding of how Wilson's writing grips and sustains her readers' interest and engagement.
9   To sufficiently stimulate children's interest and understanding of *The Suitcase Kid* for them to want to read more books by Jacqueline Wilson and other writers of the family fiction genre.

Lesson/series of lessons/unit of work outcomes

By the end of the lesson/unit of work, the children will be able to:

1   apply the beginnings of a more critical and analytical understanding of *The Suitcase Kid*;
2   engage in writing, discussion, art and drama activities that deepen their understanding of characterisation and how characters change and develop in a fiction narrative;
3   see the connection between a fiction story and wider social and emotional learning with respect to empathy, managing feelings, relationships and changes;

4   write in a range of forms that show a developing ability to write at length using a first-person narration;

5   understand more about how and why Jacqueline Wilson's books sustain and engage such a large audience;

6   read a wider range of books by Jacqueline Wilson and other writers of the family fiction genre with interest, enjoyment and appreciation.

Diary

While most of the children in the trial workshop enjoyed the reading of *The Suitcase Kid*, it was evident that some of the older boys were less engaged. Given the girl protagonist and her close relationship with a toy girl rabbit, this was not too surprising. However, *all* the children were caught by the drama activities. The hot-seating activity revealed that the boys, in particular, were very interested in the issues of marital separation and its effects on both children and adults in the story. For example, a Year 6 boy chose to go in the hot seat as Andy's dad. One of the girls asked, 'Why did you leave Andy's mum? She is much better-looking than that skinny Carrie.' He quickly retorted, 'Looks aren't everything. I got sick of the nagging and shouting and I can talk to Carrie. She understands me and we can talk honestly with each other without the rows.' Another girl responded, 'You should have tried harder to understand Andy's mum and tried to work things out.' Again, the boy responded with remarkable poise: 'I like Carrie's personality and I can be happier with her than I ever could be with Andy's Mum. I wish we could have worked things out but we just didn't get on.'

The class teacher commented that all the drama activities helped the children to gain a deeper understanding and empathy with the key characters in the story. The mime activity based on a personal loss scenario followed by the 'Rescuing Radish' improvisation gripped the children's imagination, and the sound effects of crunching footsteps and spooky music certainly intensified their involvement. They were very keen to improve upon their first efforts, and by the end of the session their mime had reached a very high standard.

The key point of pedagogical interest here is the significance of the structured sequence to the children's commitment and engagement with the improvised mime. It gave them an internal narrative that they could replay as a kind of visual score in their minds. It also provided a clear and boundaried framework with a beginning, development and resolution, which also allowed scope for their own individual interpretation. All the children in this wide age range (Years 4 to 6) were able to experience success and enjoyment in this activity. The discussion beforehand had also served to sharpen their understanding of the characters' behaviour and their relationship within the story as a whole.

The writing and drawing activities were accessible to most of the children, and they especially liked drawing in the style of Nick Sharratt (see examples of work on pp. 155–161). The differentiated writing activities worked well for the younger age groups but those devised for the older children did not sufficiently draw upon their clear interest in the conflicts and relationship issues that arise between adults and children when parental separation occurs. They have therefore been redesigned to take greater account of their close interrelationship with the SEAL curriculum and to offer opportunities for more challenging and extended forms of writing.

Examples of children's work

Figure 5.1 Work by Flora (Year 5).

Figure 5.2 Work by Amy (Year 5).

Radish's View

My worst day was when I fell down a tree hole and I was stuck down their all night and all day. I couldn't see a thing and Andy dindnt come and save me straight away I was really scard because their was loads of spiders and slugs around me and loads of spider webs.

My best day was when I was sailing on the boat because the lake was really bumpy and their was lots of rocks to jump over. I liked it because I got wet alot and it was really funny.

Figure 5.3 Work by Rachel (Year 4).

Radish's View

My worst day was when I fell down a hole in a   and I banged my head on the side of the   and loads of slugs were surrounding me   and andi   was trying to reach me but her   arms uearnt long enough.

My best day was when I   was sailing on the lake on my new boat with andi pushing me along the water with the breeze wofting in my face.

Figure 5.4 Work by Holly (Year 4).

Rebecca

Katie.

Figure 5.5 Work by Rebecca (Year 5).

Figure 5.6 Work by Rachel (Year 4).

Figure 5.7 Work by Anna (Year 5).

Teaching resources

- Copy of *The Suitcase Kid*. The edition used for the trial workshop was J. Wilson (1993) *The Suitcase Kid*, Corgi Yearling Books, London: Random House Children's Books. Two or three extra copies would be useful so that children can use them to refer to the text for help with the writing and drawing activities.
- Sound effects of crunching footsteps and spooky music. Full details for these are given on p. 143.
- List of key characters (see p. 144). This can be displayed on an interactive whiteboard or large photocopied sheet.
- Enlarged photocopies of two of Nick Sharratt's illustrations.
- Good-quality black Berol Colourpens or felt pens.
- Sheets of plain white A3- and A4-sized paper.
- Paper for cutting into fish, yacht sails or leaf shapes.

Useful websites and additional sources of information

For an interesting and informative interview with Jacqueline Wilson in which she discusses her approach to writing including the source of her idea for the alphabetic framing device used in *The Suitcase Kid*, see:

Carter, J. (1999) 'Jacqueline Wilson', in *Talking Books: Children's authors talk about the craft, creativity and process of writing*, London: Routledge.

For a comprehensive biography and complete list of Jacqueline Wilson's books:
http://biography.jrank.org/pages/899/Wilson-Jacqueline-1945.html (accessed 25 October 2007).

For a profile on Jacqueline Wilson:
http://www.randomhouse.co.uk/childrens/ (accessed 25 October 2007).

For the official, interactive Jacqueline Wilson fan club website:
www.jacquelinewilson.co.uk (accessed 25 October 2007).

PART 2

Jacqueline Wilson

Girls behaving badly . . .

The writer, her life and her works

When you see Jacqueline Wilson speaking on stage or with a gathering of adoring fans in schools, she looks as though she has just stepped out from one of the many photographs featured on the inside covers of her books. She has short, cropped, silvery-grey hair, is dressed entirely in black brightened by sparkly tops and glittering handbags, her arms covered with dangling bracelets and every one of her fingers festooned with large opal, silver, purple and black rings that she buys from a particular shop which specialises in her quirky taste for 'witchy' jewellery. She has dubbed herself 'Granny Spice', and her iconic image is as marketable as the Tracy Beaker merchandise that has accompanied the book and television series. When Michael Morpurgo said in his Platform talk at the National Theatre (2007a) that 'children's literature has children at the heart of it', no statement could be a more accurate summation of Jacqueline Wilson's work. Children, mostly in the form of fiery, exuberant, resilient girls, are at the centre of many of her stories, and it is clear that Wilson's heart is wholly with her child narrators and the impact on them of the difficulties they are experiencing with friends or the tensions and fears that are a part of dysfunctional family life.

Wilson's writing falls within the genre of social realism. She has never been fond of fantasy, and even though she read Enid Blyton's books avidly as a child, she did not enjoy their escapist adventures and found the characters in the Famous Five and Secret Seven series anodyne and uninteresting. What she liked was stories about families – *real* families with real problems. Among her first most-loved books were Noel Streatfeild's *Ballet Shoes*, Louisa M. Alcott's *Little Women* and Frances Hodgson Burnett's *Secret Garden*. Wilson was drawn to girl characters who bucked the trend, who were quirky and full of life. As a child, she identified strongly with Jo March in *Little Women*, who was very different from her sisters, wildly reckless and a voracious reader with a fierce determination to be a writer. Like Jo, Jacqueline Wilson had a fervent ambition to write and publish. In her recently published autobiographical account of her childhood (Wilson, 2007), she can scarcely believe that she has now written not one but ninety-four books, with every hope of achieving her 'century'. Irritated by 'the smug, safe, middle-class world' so often depicted in children's books (2007a: 271–272), she wanted to write about the experience of poor families, and eventually found one of the first stories to portray the life of children from a working-class background in Eve Garnett's *The Family from One End Street*. This book inspired her at the age of 9 years to write her own story based on a large family. Encouraged by a kind and imaginative primary school teacher, she wrote her first twenty-one-page novel called 'The Maggots', the idea for the title coming from a popular radio serialisation of the time, *Meet the Huggetts* (ibid.). Wilson has kept this story, and frequently delights and inspires the many children she visits in schools by showing them a concrete example of her first tentative beginning as a writer, including drawings, spelling mistakes and blotchy, brown-inked writing.

Jacqueline Wilson's works

After a spell of work at D.C. Thompson's in Dundee, Wilson was given the chance to write her own problem page for teenagers, from which followed one of the first comics for girl teenagers. Called *Jackie*, it was named after her.

She began her writing career in 1973 with a series of crime novels for adults. Having written five of these, she decided that crime writing was not for her and that her interest lay much more in stories about children, especially those who, for some reason, were at odds with their peer group and who had problematic family lives. She had written some eighteen children's fiction books before she achieved national recognition in 1991 with the publication of *The Story of Tracy Beaker*, her breakthrough book, about a girl in care. This was later followed up with a sequel entitled *The Dare Game* (2000a), which centres on Tracy's life with her new foster mother, Cam, and the intensely damaging experience of being briefly reunited with her natural mother. The first of these was shortlisted for the 1991 Smarties Prize, which she won in 1995 with *Double Act*, the story of a contrasting pair of twins who deal with their mother's death by fantasising about stage acting (Karpf, 1999). *Double Act* also won the Children's Book Award of 1996, which, combined with the immensely popular television mini-series and stage adaptations (including a musical) based on Tracy Beaker, sealed Wilson's fame as one of the most prolific and popular children's writers of our time. Her books have sold over 20 million copies and have been translated into thirty different languages, and she is the most borrowed author from British libraries. Her range extends to a quartet of books for girl teenagers about love, boyfriends and the distressing conditions of anorexia and bulimia, which are particularly prevalent among teenage girls desperate to conform to a fashion cult in which a stick-thin size zero body image is obsessively celebrated by the mass media. She has also written a series of gritty crime fiction for teens in her Steve Day series. For much younger readers she has written a collection of stories designed to help them learn to read about an adventurous teddy in her Read-On series, and she has authored three radio plays. Besides television's interest in her Tracy Beaker books, there have also been adaptations of three of her other successful works, *Girls in Love*, *Best Friends* and *The Illustrated Mum*. Her commitment to work in schools to promote children's interest and confidence in reading and writing won her the OBE in 2002 for services to literacy, and she was appointed the Children's Laureate in 2005. Despite her fame and popularity in the world of children's literature, none of her books has won the prestigious Whitbread or Carnegie awards, although she was shortlisted for the 1999 Whitbread Children's Book Award for *The Illustrated Mum*, which, as Tucker and Gamble rightly argue, is 'Wilson's most impressive book to date' (2001: 83).

With the exception of the insightful and illuminating book on family fictions by Tucker and Gamble (2001), her work has rarely been the subject of serious critical discussion in either academic journals or books on children's literature. Given the increasing popularity of children's writing with both adults and children and the compellingly stark and uncomfortable issues that Wilson's books deal with from a child's perspective, it is surprising that her work has not attracted the critical attention of the many academics who have written articles and books that have engaged intellectually with the work, themes and ideas of her contemporaries, Philip Pullman and J.K. Rowling for example. There appears to be, as Benn observes, 'a sniffy reticence about Wilson's work in literary quarters' (2005: 2). Benn goes on to argue that it is her very accessibility and the 'deceptive simplicity of her books that has denied her full literary recognition' (ibid.: 2).

Are her books simply 'easy reads' or is there something else in her writing that resonates so powerfully with her immense following of readers? The next two sections will deal with this question by examining the connection with Wilson's childhood and the themes, style and form of her writing alongside the social and literary context from which her particular type of family stories have developed.

Childhood and the author

There is a veracity and immediacy in the kinds of stories Wilson writes which connect powerfully with children. The narration is almost entirely in the first person, so her books speak directly to her readers through a child's voice and from *their* point of view. Wilson is not interested in presenting a moral didacticism that comes *ex cathedra* from the perspective of the omniscient narrator. She confronts the problems that many children face today within their family lives, at school and in care through the narration of a child protagonist. Though not condoning cruel or malicious behaviour on the part of her child characters, she seldom judges them, preferring instead to imply reasons for their unacceptable and at times impossible behaviour.

Many of her stories deal with the pain and suffering that children experience in situations of death, abandonment, physical abuse, bullying, violence, alcoholism and manic depression. Few of these themes are new to children's literature or to children's experience. They have featured poignantly and memorably in the classical novels of Dickens, George Eliot, the Brontë sisters and Elizabeth Gaskell, among others. The tropes of childhood cruelty, orphaned poverty, and stepmother and stepsibling rivalry have long been the subjects of myths, legends and fairy stories. What is new in Jacqueline Wilson's treatment of these themes is her narration of the psychological effects of these intractable problems on children from their experience and perspective. Abandonment features in at least three of Wilson's books: *The Illustrated Mum*, *Tracy Beaker* and *Lola Rose*. Wilson uses child narrators in most of her books and presents them, even in the direst of dilemmas, as feisty, proactive children who think deeply and carefully about the possible solutions to their problems in ways that will not risk making matters worse or place them in the hands of social workers and care institutions. This is not to suggest that children who are young and without the benefit of experience or financial resources can do without adults; they cannot. While they may find support and comfort in siblings, friends, teachers and family relatives, what they need most of all is, as Tucker and Gamble rightly argue, 'to love and be loved. . . . But the person from whom they need it most is also the person from whom they should, all things being equal, most expect to receive it: their own mother' (2001: 84).

Jacqueline Wilson is in touch with children's experience of family and personal problems because she talks to them regularly during school visits, sometimes doing as many as three a week. She also receives approximately 300 letters a week from children. Some of these are fan mail, but others are heart-rending stories from children in distress who write to her to ask for help with a range of family and personal problems. Such is her commitment to the concerns of children that she replies to *all* of her correspondents, and some of her fans have developed such a strong relationship with her that they have written to her over a period of several years. This is a writer who is not only professional and disciplined in her writing but is also a committed and professional educationalist whose delight and intense interest in children shines through whenever she is seen or heard in company with them.

One of the striking features of Wilson's writing is the skill with which she gets the child's voice right. It is almost as though she is at one with the child and as much a part of their inner thoughts and desires as they are. This may be partly because she chooses to spend so much time with children, and partly because she draws upon a rich well of remembered experience while playing alone as a young child with her large collection of dolls and paper figurines. Like Beatrix

Potter, she created her own companions by cutting out figures from dressmaker's paper patterns and turning them into imaginary playmates. In her autobiography (2007a) she writes about giving each of her figures a name and a problem, and making up stories about them. Beatrix Potter's animal friends which came to life as she painted them and Wilson's paper dolls allowed both writers to escape into the inner worlds of their imaginations. Wilson rarely talked about this private world to her parents or friends. She had friends, longed for a baby sister, but essentially much preferred her own company, playing with paper models from fashion magazines until she was well into her teens (Carter, 1999).

Interestingly, neither Potter's nor Wilson's mother showed any interest in their writing, often disparaging their efforts with withering and dismissive comments; so it is small wonder that they kept their writing very much to themselves. Wilson's family life was often tense and claustrophobic, and this was one of the reasons why she liked writing about large families because there would be others to share problems with. Her mother seems to have been more interested in keeping her appearance in pristine condition than in showing any real interest in the things that mattered to Jacqueline. However, she was generous, and regularly bought her books and expensive toys when she could ill afford to do so. Her father was capable of kindness and affection, especially when she was ill, often reading her the stories she loved, including Dickens's *David Copperfield* (Wilson, 2007a). However, his mood could suddenly change from smiling kindness to vindictive spite and verbal cruelty, which he would direct at both his wife and Jacqueline. Family holidays had their moments of fun and laughter but there were frequent quarrels between her parents, which made a sensitive, only child fearful and distressed, often resulting in bouts of sickness that annoyed her parents still further. It is interesting to note that she refers to her parents throughout her autobiography as Biddy and Harry. Perhaps this can be understood as a way of distancing herself from their role as parents and from the pain of their very unhappy marriage. Years later, she discovered that both her father and her mother had love affairs while they were married and still living together.

Wilson's interest in the lives of dysfunctional families clearly has its roots very firmly in her own problematic childhood. And perhaps, as with many of the characters in her stories, the intensity of the tempestuous relationship between her mother and father drove her to find a way of coping with her fear and anxiety by displacing them on to the lives of the fictitious characters created from her imagination. Her vivid, highly imaginative inner life and increasing success in writing are likely to have given Jacqueline an inner strength and independence which she continues to draw upon.

Narrative form and style

Are Jacqueline Wilson's books simply 'easy reads'? Some teachers and parents regard them as insufficiently literary and do not encourage their children to read them. Others find the subject matter too uncomfortable and unsuitable for young children. It is certainly true to say that her first-person narratives do not contain descriptive passages where the language is densely eloquent with poetic and metaphoric imagery. Children will not learn much from her books about the power of language to convey intensely vivid pictures of landscapes or to heighten atmosphere. The mind-stretching mastery of language to be found in the books of Philip Pullman, Michael Morpurgo, David Almond or Kevin Crossley-Holland, for example, is not evident in Wilson's books. Whether this is because she cannot write in this way or does not choose to, is a matter for another debate. The point is that she has chosen to write books about the complexity of contemporary family life in a direct, simple and accessible manner. Her characters talk in the way one would expect children between the ages of 8 and 12 years to speak, so, of necessity, the language used is colloquial, unembellished and realistic.

When children read her books, they recognise themselves and their peers. This is a vital part of their appeal. However, they are not merely 'easy reads'; behind their easy-to-follow narrative and plot line there is a social, psychological and narrative complexity that reveals real sorrow, desperate hardship, moments of grief and unspeakable suffering that Wilson does not shrink from confronting. Yet while she tends to write about unhappy families, and some of her stories are certainly very sad, they are, as Tucker points out, 'never actually despairing' (2001: 70). This is a crucial point because Wilson is at pains not to make her readers feel that her characters are victims, unable to help themselves and without hope. Children actually like her books so much because, as one 12-year-old commented on ITV's *The South Bank Show*, 'They're not happily ever after books but about real life. You feel like you're that person in the book' (2005). The issues she deals with are part of the world in which we live, and many children will have had some experience, albeit different or vicarious, of the problems her characters face. The dramatic activities based on *The Suitcase Kid* in Part 1 of this chapter demonstrated very clearly that both boys and girls took very seriously the matter of parental separation, with its negative consequences for Andy. They understood clearly how hard it was for her to come to terms with the loss of what seemed to her to be a life of happy stability in Mulberry Cottage. Of course, this was far from the case because marital breakdown had already begun to take its inexorable course towards the finality of separation. Andy's dream of her parents' reconciliation was understandable but unrealistic. However, with the help of new relationships she eventually accepted that her new life was not entirely bad or without some compensations.

Wilson's characters invite compassion and understanding in ways that help her readers empathise with those both different from and similar to their own experiences. Her realistic, carefully constructed characters are entirely believable, and Wilson works very hard on the research for them, often drawing on the insights given to her by children and from people she has known from her childhood. She finds it easy to think her way into the mind of a 10-year-old by pretending to be the character while she is writing about her. She also has a capacity for vivid recall and a very efficient memory that enable her to retrieve an immense range of detail from her childhood. The essence of what Wilson set out to achieve in her books is best summed up in her own words:

> I wanted to write books . . . about realistic children who had difficult parents and all sorts of secrets and problems; easy-to-read books that still made you think hard; books with funny bits that made you laugh out loud, though sometimes the story was so sad it made you cry too.
>
> (2007a: 207)

Whether Wilson is writing about breast cancer, disability or the appalling cruelty of children to each other, she always does so with a light touch. Humour and jokes, some of them appalling, play a crucial part in the appeal of her books. She has an uncanny sense of what interests and fascinates today's children, including designer clothes, make-up, glittery nail varnish, jewellery, hair design and the kind of quirky taste in food that is featured in many of her books. Food seems to be a source of endless interest and importance to children, and few of her books are without drawings of iced cakes, sweets, chips and other kinds of junk food.

Another striking feature of her books is the much-loved bold black-and-white cartoon drawings created by Nick Sharratt. The distinctive cartoon style he has developed in the Wilson series appeals to both younger and older children, and his illustrations are closely matched and cleverly integrated with her writing. They have worked in a close and happy partnership for many years. Sharratt takes Wilson's work very seriously, carefully reading the text so that his illustrations convey the precise detail and emotion Wilson wishes to communicate. Like her writing, his drawings appear deceptively simple, but a closer look reveals just how accurately he 'reads' the differences between characters and their mood state. Sometimes a world of difference is created by the way in which he draws the line and angle of an eyebrow or the mouth, so that you can tell immediately whether the smile suggests insecurity and uncertainty, smugness or ecstatic glee. He points up small differences in clothing, even when it is school uniform, for example the way the hair falls around the head and face or the way in which a character is standing. There are dozens of examples of his remarkable ability to portray shade and nuance in emotion, personality type and fashion details, all of which say something revealing about the characters. One very good example of this is to be found on the first page of *Sleepovers* (2007b). The five girls in the 'alphabet club' are all standing in a line facing the reader showing their reaction to Amy's invitation to her sleepover party. Even though the children are all wearing school uniform tops, each of them shows slight differences in the way their top hangs, in their shoes, socks, hand gestures, hairstyle and body stance. Every one of these carefully constructed shades of pictorial meaning conveys something significant about the kind of girls they are and the emotion they are feeling at the time. The contrast between the smiles of four members of the gang and that of Daisy, who is unsure about whether or not she will be included in the invitation, is as interesting as the narrative itself. Sharratt and Wilson seem to be in complete synchrony with one another, so much so that Wilson commented to Melvyn Bragg (*South Bank Show*, 2005) that 'he can see inside my head'. This writer–illustrator symbiosis is another key reason for Wilson's phenomenal success and enthusiastic following. The vividly coloured cartoon pictures on the book covers are as much a part of the Wilson brand image as her black clothes and clacking, 'witchy' rings. She 'walks the walk', as does the distinctive branding of her books.

Wilson has been experimenting with different voices and styles in her writing over many years. In the past fifteen years or so, she seems to have hit upon a way of writing that shows all the skill of a very accomplished writer. She sets the plot moving at a brisk pace from the first page onwards. Her stories are sensitively and intelligently organised so that a fine balance is maintained between the frightening and distressing parts and those with humour and lighter scenes. One of her particular strengths is the way she varies the narrative form so that it differs from what she has referred to as 'boring old chapters' (*The South Bank Show*, 2005), as well as fitting appropriately with the subject matter.

Some of the devices she uses are not only ingeniously inventive but serve the purpose of enabling the reader to grapple with difficult issues in an appealing format that fits well with the characters and the subject matter. For example, in *The Suitcase Kid* she uses an alphabetical framing device that allows her to zoom in and out of the escalating rows between Andy's parents and stop before things became too ugly and upsetting. She is well aware that children who have been through the experience of divorce 'would be able to fill in the gaps' (Carter, 1999: 250). In *The Story of Tracy Beaker* she used an idea currently common in care institutions and foster homes in which children are encouraged to write a book all about themselves, which they take with them whenever they are moved on to another form of care. The book provides a kind of template that children can add to and individualise, including details of their personal appearance, what their favourite food is, pictures of their family, illustrations, best friends, people they don't like, and so on. 'My Book about Me' begins Tracy's story on the first page, and the device is used throughout the story to structure the plot. It also gives a great deal of insight into

Tracy's least and most appealing qualities as well as serving as a vivid account of her life and ongoing relationships. In *The Illustrated Mum*, every chapter begins with one of Marigold's many tattoos, each serving to provide a link with the next part of the story. It takes a great deal of flair and talent to make a device of this sort work so that it brings a cohering force to the story; it is revealing of Marigold's mental instability while also being visually compelling. In the hands of a less accomplished storyteller, narrative devices of this kind could serve as little more than gratuitous contrivance.

Girls behaving badly . . .

The title of this chapter serves to highlight a seldom explored aspect of Wilson's writing, which is her uncompromising portrayal of girls who are vindictive, cruel, manipulative and controlling. These young girls often make the lives of their friends intolerable and unbearably miserable. Their parents seem to be oblivious to their daughters' duplicitous behaviour and are apparently unaware that they are, in part, responsible for it. Wilson's girl protagonists are typically tough, full-blooded, quick on the draw verbally and 'no one's fool' (Tucker and Gamble, 2001: 70). They often find themselves placed in positions of premature maternal responsibility because of their mother's vulnerability, unreliability or immaturity of varying kinds. Rustin and Rustin define such children as the 'parentified child' (2003b: 234). In *The Illustrated Mum*, Dolphin and Star have to care for Marigold, their mother, when she is drunk or clinically depressed. Lola Rose, in the book of the same name, becomes the carer for her younger brother, Kendall, and her mother when she gets violently attacked by her husband, and seriously ill with breast cancer. In *The Lottie Project*, Charlie has a close and loving relationship with her single mother, Jo. They have each become dependent on one another's company, sleep in the same bed and are often regarded as two sisters rather than as a mother and 10-year-old daughter. While Charlie does not have to take on the role of a parental carer, Jo has allowed Charlie to develop an inappropriate and possessive adult relationship with her which eventually leads to disastrous consequences. Elsa, the ebullient lover of jokes and dreadful puns in *The Bed and Breakfast Star*, finds herself looking after her baby brother and younger sister when her despairing mother can no longer cope with the appalling conditions of a cramped hotel family room. A depressed mother and the fiery temper of her mother's new partner, Mack the Smack, often impose immense responsibilities upon Elsa. While these overburdened children occasionally become overwhelmed and frightened by the difficulties they are faced with, they somehow manage to find a way through with a gritty determination and resourcefulness way beyond their years. They engage our understanding, empathy and admiration as modern-day heroines who are often more than ready to forgive their parents' inadequacies and self-centred behaviour in the hope of better times and the restoration of love and closeness. In Wilson's dysfunctional and flawed families the potential for healing is always there, however intractable the problems.

Less sympathetically portrayed, and certainly not condoned, are the children who seek to find whatever means they can to hurt, belittle and control others in ways that cause immense pain and anxiety. Children who behave despicably towards others whom they consider to be in an inferior power relation are not uncommon and will be immediately recognised by children, teachers and parents. The combined issues of verbal bullying, controlling behaviour, family loyalty and disability are deftly handled in *Sleepovers*. This is one of Wilson's rare stories in which the protagonist's parents are consistently loving and caring. Apart from the understandable tensions created by the relentless needs of Lily, a severely disabled 11-year-old, Daisy has a stable and essentially happy home. She has just begun to make friends in a new school with four girls named Amy, Bella, Chloe and Emily, who dub themselves 'the Alphabet Girls'. Wilson dives straight into the plot with an announcement by Amy that she is allowed to invite her best friends to a sleepover birthday party. Daisy desperately hopes she will be invited, but knows she is still a relative outsider. To her ecstatic delight she is, and the story then proceeds at a fast pace as the birthdays of the others approach, with each one having to be better than, or different from, the one before.

The pressure mounts when it comes to Chloe's turn. She has consistently tried to control the activities of all her friends' parties, including the shape of the birthday cake and who will sleep where. Whenever she can, she insists they do the one 'cool' thing that does not come under her classification of 'boring', which is to watch seriously frightening videos. Daisy and Chloe have had a mutual dislike of each other from the start. Daisy is ambivalent about whether she really wants to go to Chloe's party, which the latter keeps telling the others will be the best ever. She revels in excluding Daisy from her party but pressure is exerted by her peers and Chloe grudgingly gives in and invites her.

She manipulates time, space and people so that she is rarely actually caught in the act by a parent. At Emily's party, Chloe deliberately pushes Daisy out of the car as they pull up at their picnic destination. At Chloe's party, she gives Daisy's dad a beaming smile as Daisy hands her a carefully chosen video present called *The Spooky Sleepover*, to which she replies:

> 'Ooh, what a super-sounding video! I hope it's not too frightening. Thank you ever so much, Daisy,' said Chloe.
>
> But the second Dad was gone Chloe stuck her tongue out at me and dropped the video on the floor.
>
> 'I saw this ages ago and it sucks. It isn't spooky at all. Trust you to pick a *baby* film, Daisy Diddums.'
>
> (Wilson, 2007b: 54)

It is not clear exactly what age the girls are in the story but textual inferences suggest they are aged somewhere between 8 and 9 years. Chloe has already learned with extraordinary sophistication exactly how to dupe her parents and which of Daisy's emotional buttons to press. One might expect the extent and degree of manipulation and emotional control that Chloe exerts to be more commonly found among teenage girls.

Even at her own elaborately sophisticated and showy birthday party, Chloe seems to be more interested in pushing Daisy to tearful despair than enjoying the 'best sleepover ever'. The children are allowed to make their own pizza, choosing their own decoration and toppings. Daisy makes a face on hers with pineapple, cheese and pepper slices, when Amy suggests using a couple of anchovies for the eyebrows. Daisy agrees that it's a good idea but states that she loathes anchovies. When the children are called in by the father to sit at the immaculately laid dining table, Chloe hangs behind and covers Daisy's pizza in anchovies. When Chloe's slimly elegant, designer-dressed mum arrives with the pizzas, she expresses surprise at Daisy's preference for so many anchovies. Daisy is devastated and cannot eat any of it. She knows this is Chloe's doing, and her bullying does not stop there.

The tension mounts as Daisy's birthday approaches. Not only is she fearful of how her friends will react to her disabled sister, who cannot speak and who screams loudly at anything unfamiliar or strange, but she does not know how they will manage to sleep together in a small house without waking Lily. She knows that Chloe's reaction will be cruel and insensitive, so decides not to invite her. Unfortunately, her mother has already done so, and Daisy is desperate. The day is saved by her father, who suggests putting up a tent in the garden where all her friends can sleep without disturbing Lily. Daisy's friends are disarmingly sensitive and kind to Lily, and Daisy is beginning to relax until Chloe turns up later. She looks like a miniature version of her mother in strappy pink shoes and expensive jewellery. In an act of vindictive spite, she gives Daisy a video present of *101 Dalmatians* which turns out to be a white, witchy ghost movie that frightens and upsets her friends. Even in someone else's house, Chloe manages to whip the video out the minute Daisy's father enters the room. He has begun to see through Daisy and has corrected her mean behaviour at least once. The children then play traditional party games, which they all love, except of course Chloe, who responds sulkily to every new activity with the retort, 'Boring!'

However, Chloe has overstepped the mark this time. Her friends are tiring of her controlling, bullying behaviour and discover to their glee the next morning that Chloe insisted on Daisy's dad taking her home in the middle of the night because she had wet her pyjamas. She had been frightened by the dark and Lily's piecing screams on her way to the bathroom. At school on Monday, Chloe relishes telling her friends about the worst sleepover ever, Daisy's 'poky' house and her 'totally batty, loopy, maniac baby sister who screams all the time' (2007b: 110). This is too much for Daisy's friends, and Emily calls Chloe a baby, with the clear implication that they all know she wet herself at Daisy's sleepover. The game is now up for Chloe, and in an act of peer solidarity they tell Chloe publicly that none of them wants to be her friend any longer.

This is an insightful study of the kind of unbridled cruelty that can occur when a child is selfishly over-indulged by parents who constantly tell her that she is the best girl in the world, allow her do what she likes and never present her with an alternative view of herself. She has not learned how to control her feelings in front of others and cares little about the implications of her malicious tongue and manipulative behaviour. There are interesting lessons to be learned here about the consequences of parenting that encourages an unchecked and distorted sense of power and self-importance in a child. Wilson does not condone Chloe's intentional and carefully contrived spite, but instead, true to her style and author belief system, leaves her censorship to Chloe's peers. It could be argued that both Chloe and her parents behave badly in this story. The parent's behaviour certainly provides a rich source for case-study discussion among both adults and children, especially in relation to Daisy's parents.

There are other children in Wilson' stories who, while not showing such gross egocentricity and mean-spiritedness, do have a damaging effect on others because of the control they have learned to exert over them. This is the case with Vicky in *Vicky Angel*, Charlie in *The Lottie Project* and Katie in *The Suitcase Kid*. There are also examples of girls behaving unkindly and dismissively when they are shown kind and sensitive behaviour by boys. In *The Lottie Project*, for example, the class swot, Jamie Edwards, invites Charlie to his three-story Victorian home, where he generously allows her to borrow books from the family library for her Victorian project. Jamie's parents are university lecturers and welcome her warmly into their home. These acts of genuine friendship make Charlie reassess her stereotypical judgement of James as aloof, snobbish and odd. He, too, is desperate for friendship. Two other characters, Fatboy Sam and Biscuits, are treated with similar disdain and rejection. Fatboy Sam in *Vicky Angel* tries to be friendly and understanding towards Jade, who is full of grief and guilt after her best friend, Vicky, has been killed in a car accident. She spurns his attempts to help her through her grief and refuses his offer to be her partner in a drama session. As Jade begins to come through her grief and anger, she apologises to Fatboy Sam for her unpleasantness and learns to respect the value of genuine friendship. Biscuits, in *Best Friends*, tries to befriend Alice, who is desperately missing her best friend, Gemma, after her move to Scotland. His humour, cooking talents and warm family home gradually connect with Alice and she learns something new about the meaning of friendship. It is interesting, too, that in each of these cases the boys are outsiders and come from warm, stable and loving family backgrounds.

Wilson is a writer of our time who knows and understands the complexity of the world in which children now live. Enormous numbers of children perceive her as a heroine writer. They are passionate about her books because she understands them. She has a streetwise and canny knowledge of their world, is in touch with what they both love and hate, and writes well-crafted and fast-moving stories. Her extraordinary accessibility is important because it means that large numbers of children read and reflect on some troubling contemporary social themes. She is a serious and highly professional writer with a genuine commitment to children. The fact that her work has not yet been a subject for serious academic debate in the world of children's literature is a matter for regret. A writer who sells two million books a year is a phenomenon that needs to be understood with greater critical insight than she currently is.

Chapter 6

Harry Potter and the magic of film

The story of seven years in the life of an orphaned wizard has attracted unprecedented media interest across the world. Many children have read the entire series, most have seen the films, while some have no interest in Harry Potter whatsoever. For this reason, the focus here will be on the comparison of written narratives with film. Children are part of a rapidly changing digital age and they are deeply interested in what it has to offer. However, the current literacy framework continues to give primacy of place to written texts. There has therefore been little, if any, space for the serious development of children's critical understanding of film. J.K. Rowling's Harry Potter series, in which the film releases have followed the book publications, provides an ideal opportunity to introduce children to a basic understanding of how film works to convey mood, atmosphere and characterisation. Even if the series has not captured *all* children's imaginations, most are likely to be caught by the quite different skills required for the 'reading' of moving images. The following unit of work is based on extracts from the books and DVDs of *Harry Potter and the Chamber of Secrets* and *Harry Potter and The Prisoner of Azkaban*. The trial workshop took place with a mixed age group of Years 3, 4, 5 and 6 children.

Preparation

Teachers are strongly advised to watch the DVDs of both the titles mentioned above beforehand, paying particular attention to the camera shots and angles listed on pp. 176–177. You will find it easier and quicker to access the film clips suggested if you 'bookmark' them on your laptop or desktop computer. The DVDs of the second and third in the series have been deliberately chosen because they have a film rating of 'Parental Guidance', which means they are suitable for general viewing. Those later on in the series are rated '12', signifying that they are fit for viewing by children aged 12 years or over. *If PG-rated DVDs or videos are used in school, you will need to seek parental permission to use them for educational purposes, even if the children have already seen them.*

The two key ideas to be understood in this media literacy approach to the Harry Potter series are:

1   That the medium of film communicates features of characterisation, mood and suspense in ways that are entirely *different* from those found in written texts. Films depend much more, for example, on the visual and emotional messages conveyed by specific camera angles,

atmospheric music, and lighting, and the images conveyed by costume, hairstyle, the 'colour' of vocal intonation and expression, body movements and scenic backdrop.

2   That there are similarities as well as differences between book and film texts, and a great deal can be learned about the way in which they both work to capture and sustain engagement.

Once you decide you are going to use the activities detailed in this chapter, the level of children's participation is likely to be greater if they are encouraged to read or reread at least *one* of the previously mentioned Harry Potter books and/or watch the DVDs if they have them at home. The activities will work without this preparation (as they did in the trial workshop), but children will have a richer context and more to contribute if they do at least some preparatory work

Group discussion and interaction

Before you begin the first film clip activity, a few general questions about the children's reactions to the Harry Potter series will give you some idea of how many children have followed the series faithfully and read all books, those who have seen the film versions only and those who have taken no interest in the series. *With the latter group of children – and there are likely to be some – it is important that you stress from the outset that it does not matter whether they are Harry Potter fans or not; the point of the activities is to teach them how to begin to 'read' films and to learn more about how they work.*

Arrange the seating so that children are next to a partner they work well with for the group discussion and interaction activities. If an expectation of maximum pupil involvement is set from the outset, it will help to use a paired discussion strategy for the first two or three activities at least.

General questions about the series

◇   Do you like the Harry Potter series? If so, tell your partner what you like most about it. Share some responses.

◇   If you have seen the films, tell each other what your favourite film is and why.

◇   Tell your partner which *part* you like best in your favourite book or film of the series.

If there are children who know nothing about the series, seat them with a pair of children who do. This will help prepare them for the forthcoming activities.

◇   Describe your favourite character in the series, telling your partner why you like her or him so much.

◇   Which character do you like least? Say what it is about him or her that you dislike.

◇   As a whole class or in groups of four, list all the qualities that make Harry Potter the justified hero of the series. (The teacher or group leader should scribe Harry's main qualities on a whiteboard or flip chart.)

◇   There are times in the series when Harry is not always calm, resourceful and in control of his emotions. Ask those children who know the series well to tell the others when these times occurred, giving as much detail about the context as possible. (The teacher should write up key points from the responses).

Comparing the book with extracts from the film 'Harry Potter and the Chamber of Secrets' using the 'Flying to Hogwarts' extract

Chapter 5 of *Harry Potter and the Chamber of Secrets* (book)
Scene 7 of *Harry Potter and the Chamber of Secrets* (DVD)

Chapter synopsis

All the Weasley family have made it through the barrier at Platform 9¾ except for Ron, together with Harry. For some reason they can't get through. They hear the Hogwarts Express steam out of the station without them. Ron hits on the idea of using his father's car, and they decide that this is their only option. The blue Ford Anglia soars up into the air but the invisibility booster stops working and they have to fly even higher to avoid being seen by Muggles (ordinary, non-magician people) while keeping their eyes on the Hogwarts Express. After hours in the sky, the novelty of flying to Hogwarts wears off and they are more than ready for a peaceful landing. No such luck! The engine starts to whine and splutter and they only just make Hogwarts before it cuts out completely. Unfortunately, they land not on the ground but in the Whomping Willow!

◇   Read the extract from the bottom of p. 55 of *Harry Potter and the Chamber of Secrets* beginning 'I think we'd better go and wait by the car' until the bottom of the penultimate paragraph on p. 57 ending with 'a great city alive with cars like multi-coloured ants.'

The scene to be shown from the film clip continues until the car lands in the Whomping Willow. In the book, the car's journey to Hogwarts continues until just over halfway down p. 60, which is too long an extract to read, so paraphrase the rest of the events, using your own words or the synopsis above. This will ensure that the children are able to make a fair comparison of the same scenario in both book and film.

●   Show the clip from the DVD of *Chamber of Secrets* (Scene 7). Start from the beginning of the scene and end it with the car landing in the Whomping Willow.
●   Watch the film clip, noticing the parts of the film that are the same as the story in the book and those that are different.

The children are going to watch the same clip again in their working pairs. They can use mini-whiteboards or photocopied sheets with two columns headed 'Similarities' and 'Differences'. Ask them to work in pairs, noting down what is the same as and what is different from the book.

◇   When they have seen the clip for the second time, ask them to share in their pairs what they have noticed. Share one or two responses.

Hopefully, the children will have noticed that in the film clip the Hogwarts Express comes *towards* them from behind in a close-up shot rather than travelling below them and in front of them as is the case in the book. There is also the added dramatic incident of Harry almost falling out of the car and holding on to the door handle while Ron desperately struggles to pull him back inside.

◇   Why do you think the film-makers chose to show a close-up shot of the Hogwarts Express travelling at speed *towards* Ron and Harry?

◇   Why do you think they decided to add the scene of Harry almost falling out of the car?

◇   How did the film make you feel as you watched Ron, Harry and Hedwig fly in their car towards Hogwarts? Did you feel you were with them on their dangerous journey? If so, *how* did the film make you feel that you were flying through the air with them?

◇   How did the film communicate a sense of fear and excitement? What part did music, facial expressions and camera shots play?

You are going to show the same clip for a third time. This time you will be focusing the children's attention on some basic camera shots. For this they need to be introduced to some basic film terminology. Seven terms are introduced and explained below.

Some basic film terms[1]

Establishing shot An opening shot or sequence. In the *Chamber of Secrets* film clip it is the blue Ford Anglia taking off against the background of St Pancras Station in London.

Close-up A picture that shows a fairly small part of the scene, such as the character's face and shoulders in detail, so that it fills the screen. There are several close-ups of Ron, Harry and Hedwig showing wide, startled eyes.

Cut A sudden change of shot from one viewpoint or location to another. It may be used deliberately to make a dramatic point. For example, the camera cuts many times from long-distance shots of the landscape below the car to the expressions on the faces of Ron, Harry and Hedwig. There are several cuts to Hedwig's face alone. In this clip, *cuts* and *close-ups* serve a strong dramatic purpose.

Wide shot A shot of a broad field of action taken with a wide-angle lens. There are several of these showing the Hogwarts Express, the car and an aerial landscape.

Zoom	When zooming in, the camera does not move. Instead, the lens is focused down from a long shot to close-up while the picture is still being shown. A good example of this is when the camera moves from the back window of the car and zooms in on the front of the train.
Tracking shot	In a tracking shot the camera moves forward with the action, as for example when the camera trails the movement of the train.
Panning	The camera swivels to follow a moving subject. The pan 'leads' rather than 'trails', as it does just before it follows the car's approach to Hogwarts.

◇   Children watch the clip for a third time while you point out some of the features above. (Until children are used to these terms, it is advisable to focus on the first four only.)

◇   Watch the clip for a fourth time, asking the children to discuss in pairs examples of the *establishing shot*, *cut*, *close-up* and *wide shot*.

◇   How do these different camera shots make you feel that you are part of the film and involved in Harry's, Ron's and Hedwig's experience of fear, suspense and excitement?

◇   Take each shot in turn, asking children what purpose they serve.

Comparing the book with 'The duelling club' extract from 'Harry Potter and the Chamber of Secrets'

FILM ACTIVITIES

Chapter 11, *Harry Potter and the Chamber of Secrets* (Book)
Scene 17 *Harry Potter and the Chamber of Secrets* (DVD)

Chapter synopsis

A buzz of excitement ripples round the Great Hall as the pupils gather towards a long stage and await their first duelling lesson with Gilderoy Lockhart, the new Defence against the Dark Arts teacher. Snape and Gilderoy confront each other in a demonstration of wand duelling. Snape is contemptuous of Lockhart, who clearly knows very little about the art. Potter and Malfoy are chosen to demonstrate their ability to block unfriendly spells, and that too goes wrong. A hissing black snake appears from the end of Malfoy's wand, and in an attempt to stop his fangs sinking into one of the nearby pupils, Harry speaks to it in Parseltongue (snake language). The snake recoils and becomes docile, but Snape has had enough. With an impatient sweep of his wand, the snake disappears in a cloud of black smoke. Snape gives Harry a knowing look, and his friends are horrified to learn that he is a Parselmouth.

◇   Read the passage at the top of p. 142 of *Chamber of Secrets* beginning with the words 'Gilderoy Lockhart was walking on the stage' until almost the bottom of p. 143, ending with the words '– we don't want any accidents. One . . . two . . . three . . .'.

◇   Now show the film clip of the duelling scene (Scene 17, *Chamber of Secrets*). Start the clip just after the Moaning Myrtle scene, which begins with the pupils gathering round a resplendent stage painted with moons and stars and finish with Professor Snape making the snake disappear. It involves the following characters:

> *Gilderoy Lockhart*
> *Professor Severus Snape*
> *Harry Potter*
> *Draco Malfoy*

Provide a photocopied sheet for each child with the names of the four characters and the camera terms shown on pp. 176–177. This will help children with the next activity.

◇   Show the scene through once, asking the children to see whether they can identify any of the four camera shots discussed in the previous clip.

◇   Show the clip again, this time asking them to talk together in their pairs in order to tell each other where they saw examples of any of the four shots they have been asked to identify.

◇   Play the clip again, checking that the children understand that the *establishing shot* is where the camera *zooms* in on the duelling table, with the pupils flocking towards it. There are several *close-ups* and *cuts* to the faces of Lockhart, Snape, Malfoy and Potter when they are duelling with their wands. There are also *cuts* from the duelling scene on the stage to the faces of Hermione, Ron and other pupils standing close by. The camera also *zooms* in on the snake's head and *tracks* its progress up and down the table as well as up towards the ceiling when Lockhart bungles the spell to make it disappear.

◇   What purpose does the first establishing shot serve? What information does it give you as the watcher?

◇   What impact do the camera shots of cuts and close-ups have on the way you feel about the characters and the atmosphere in the school hall?

◇   Do you experience the same feelings towards Lockhart as you do towards Snape? If not, why not? What are the main differences between the two characters and how does the film communicate the differences?

◇   What effect do you think the film makers want to create by the way they use the camera shots to zoom in and out of the stage and cutting to faces in the crowd?

Dramatic effects in film

The clip is going to be shown for a fourth time, with the focus turning away from camera shots to some dramatic effects features. For example, the differences between Snape and Lockhart are emphasised through costume. The showy, charlatan Lockhart is wearing immaculate, richly coloured robes and the sinister Snape is dressed entirely in black. Lockhart has short, blonde, wavy, bouncy hair while Snape's is long, lank and black. Their movements are different, and Snape's entry on the stage is accompanied by dark, sinister-sounding music. The list of dramatic effects below would be a useful aide-mémoire for children once they have volunteered their own list of the many dramatic devices used by film to make the narrative authentic, exciting and visually true to the characters' personalities.

Dramatic effects

Costume: colours, style, way they are worn
Hairstyle: texture, colour and style (curly, wavy, straight, lank, gelled, stiff, natural), etc.
Make-up
Facial expression: serious, stern, cocky, scared, proud
Props: wand, cloak
Music: light, dark, happy, sad, bouncy, sinister
The way the characters move
The way they speak: tone, accent, emotion in voice: harsh, soft, scared, angry, sarcastic, etc.

◇   Talk together in twos or groups of four and list all the things you noticed in the last film clip which added to the dramatic effect of the scene.

If the children have not picked up on the differences between the colour and style of Malfoy and Potter's hair, or the smooth, overconfident fluency of Lockhart's voice contrasted with the clipped, harsh and precise register of Snape's, then direct their attention to them before they watch the clip again.

◇ Watch the clip again and find as many examples of dramatic effects as you can. Share them with your partner as you watch.

Writing and drawing activities based on the 'Duelling Club' clip

Identifying the dramatic effects used in the film to highlight character differences

Give the children two sheets of paper each with two columns, one headed 'Snape and Lockhart' and the other, 'Potter and Malfoy'. Depending on the age and ability of the children, these can be prepared in advance, or children can prepare their own. The objective is for the children to list all the effects in the film that portray the differences in character of the two pairs. These should include sound, costume details, make-up, hairstyle, colour of hair, eyes, movement – especially the way they each move their bodies, facial expression and scenic atmosphere. The headings given on the 'Dramatic effects' sheet can be used to provide subheadings for the descriptions for each of the two pairs of characters so that their writing is organised into dramatic effect categories and not simply a random list recalled from memory.

Drawing activity

◇ Choose one of the pairs you have written about and draw pictures of each of your characters using the film clip as your source.

◇ Using your written descriptions of the contrasting differences between the two characters, label your drawings to highlight the various features.

◇ You will need to think about how you could represent the sound and scenic effects, perhaps by using appropriate symbols for them (*such as a stave of crotchets and quavers for music, for example*), so that your pictures could be used as a clear and detailed character guide for a film-maker to use. Your drawings will need to be uncluttered and easy for someone else to understand.

Drama activities

The following activities do *not* depend on the use of the school hall. A space created in the classroom by moving the furniture safely to the sides of the room is perfectly adequate.

Menu of activities

1   Individual freeze-frame. Immobilus!
2   Hot-seating
3   Group dramatisation. The duel
4   Cool-down

Freeze-frame: 'Immobilus'! (ten minutes)

The idea of this activity is that children freeze in role on a given command. Restrict their choice of character to those they have seen and heard from the book and film extracts: Harry, Ron, Hermione, Gilderoy Lockhart, Professor Snape and Draco Malfoy.

 Sit in a space on the floor and choose the character you would like to be.

Think carefully about who you are and what you might be doing. You can either stand still and mime an action typical of the character you have chosen, or move around the room in role.

If you are moving in role, think about the differences in the way you would walk if you were Lockhart or Harry, for example.

Think about the costume you would be wearing and the kind of hairstyle you have. Is it bouncy and wavy like Lockhart's or gelled and sleeked back like Malfoy's?

On the instruction 'Go', the children move into role. On the command of 'Freeze', the teacher and any other adults in the room have to guess which character a chosen child is playing. Stress the importance of what each of the characters might be doing at the time. Would they be using their wand, duelling, driving a flying car, falling out of it, watching the duelling scene, making a spell in a potions class or reading a book?

 Go.

Freeze.

Once the children have grasped the idea, tell them that instead of giving the command 'freeze', instead you will say, 'Immobilus!'

 Now choose a different character from the one before.

Think carefully about who you are going to be and how you will show their characteristics in mime.

This time instead of 'freeze' I will give the magic command, 'Immobilus!' so that you freeze into absolute stillness even better than you did last time.

Go.

Immobilus!

Praise the children for what they have done well. Repeat, with one half watching while the other half mime a character different from the one they chose previously. Tell the watching half of the class to focus on one or two children only.

Repeat, with the watching half becoming the actors and vice versa.

Hot-seating activity (fifteen minutes)

Children choose which character they would like to be in 'the hot seat'. You may need to remind the children of what was said in the discussion about the main points about each of the characters before beginning the activity. Seat the children in a horseshoe shape with a chair in the gap of the crescent. Before beginning the activity, ask the children to:

 Think carefully about the character you would like to play and the kind of person he or she is.

Close your eyes for a minute or so and think about the role the character played in the story in relation to the other characters.

Begin the activity by choosing a child who is reasonably confident about performing in front of others and who will be able to sustain credibility in their chosen role. This will set the tone for the others. Children and teachers then ask questions of the character in the hot seat in turn. Keep the pace moving and give as many children as time allows a chance to be in the hot seat. If children choose to hot-seat the same character as one that has previously been 'hot-seated', it is important to encourage them to ask questions *different* from the ones asked before (otherwise the activity will become tedious and undemanding for the new child in the hot seat).

Group improvisation: the duel

Building on the hot-seating, the freeze-frame activity and their memory of the duelling scene film clip, the children are going to work in groups of four. The children have to decide which role they will play: Lockhart, Snape, Potter or Malfoy. Give the following directions orally, having also written them out on a large sheet so that they can be displayed for everyone to see:

- Lockhart picks Harry to duel with Malfoy.
- Snape picks Malfoy to duel with Harry.
- Lockhart says, 'Good luck, Potter.'
- Snape nudges Malfoy forward to face Harry (*there needs to be a distance of several paces between them*).
- Harry and Malfoy walk slowly towards each other, carrying their wands at their sides. Neither takes his eyes off the other.
- Lockhart gives the command 'Wands at the ready!'
- Harry and Malfoy raise their wands sharply in front of their faces.
- Malfoy says menacingly, 'Scared, Potter?'
- Potter replies, 'You wish!'
- Snape says, 'Prepare to cast your charms to disarm.'
- Harry and Malfoy turn sharply and face the other way, each walking in the opposite direction for five steps.
- Harry and Malfoy turn to face each other and raise their wands high above their heads.
- Lockhart says, 'On the count of three . . . One, two, three.'
- Malfoy says, 'Expelliarmus!'
- Potter falls. (*Teachers need to coach a way of falling safely by getting the duellers to relax their knees and ankles and crumple to the floor. They should avoid leaping before falling.*)
- Potter gets up, points his wand at Malfoy and shouts in return, 'Expelliarmus!'
- Malfoy falls.
- Snape walks slowly towards both of them and tells them to get off the stage and go back to their places.

The children can decide on the words Snape might say to the pair of them as he dismisses them. The chosen words need to be sarcastic and sneering, and delivered in a commanding way.

  Decide in your groups what Snape will say to Malfoy and Potter.

Decide how they will react as they return to their places.

Once you have given the entire sequence to the children, you are advised to break it down into small steps that the children can manage, perhaps using only two or three of the sequences at any one time. Give the children time to practise and improvise ways of acting out the sequences before moving on to the next ones. It does not matter if the children depart from the 'script' and make up their own interpretations. The important thing is that they take their roles seriously. Their improvisation should include tension and suspense. The whole sequence is likely to need more than one session to work right through to the end. Depending on the level of the children's interest and involvement, the improvisation can be developed to include a music soundtrack that communicates suspense and a further sequence in which

Malfoy casts a dangerous charm on Potter. The children can decide how the action is resolved and ended.

Cool-down activity (two to three minutes)

 Lie down on the floor and imagine you have had a spell cast over you which makes you feel calm and happy, and that life could not be better. Think about what it is that makes you feel so happy. Give your mental picture colour and sound effects.

Let your body relax completely while you enjoy the peace your mental picture gives you.

Slowly stand up, relax and breathe deeply.

A comparison of two teachers: Gilderoy Lockhart and Professor Lupin

Scene 11 of *Harry Potter and the Chamber of Secrets* (DVD), 'Gilderoy Lockhart'
Scene 11 of *Harry Potter and the Prisoner of Azkaban* (DVD) 'Boggart in the wardrobe'

The objective in the reading of these film clips is twofold: to show the way in which the film portrays two Hogwarts teachers through dramatic effects; and to show the differences in the teaching management styles of Lockhart and Lupin and what is effective and ineffective about how they teach ways to repel two types of dangerous creatures: Cornish Pixies and Boggarts.

◇ Show the clip from *The Chamber of Secrets*, scene 11 entitled 'Gilderoy Lockhart'. Start the clip at the beginning of the scene and finish it as Lockhart leaves the classroom in confusion and chaos.
◇ Ask the children to watch the clip, noting the way in which Lockhart introduces himself, how he positions himself and what impression he communicates to the pupils. When they have watched the clip, begin the discussion.

◇ Tell your partner what you observed about Lockhart and what he conveyed about himself to the pupils. Share some responses.

◇ Watch the clip again, noting all the visual and dramatic features in the film that portray Lockhart as a self-obsessed show-off. This time, focus on his costume, manner of talking, behaviour and style.

◇ List on paper or mini-whiteboards everything you saw in the clip that emphasised Lockhart as wholly interested in *his* image, not the pupils' learning interests. *They may make connections here with the magazine* Hello *and similar 'glossies' with respect to their focus on celebrity style and image. Encourage them to draw upon their own contemporary knowledge of celebrity culture.*

◇ What did you notice about the pupils' expressions as Lockhart attempted to teach his pupils about controlling Cornish Pixies?

◇ What did this tell you about what the pupils thought about Lockhart?

◇ Were any of the pupils impressed by Lockhart? If so, who?

◇ Why do you think some of the pupils were fascinated and impressed by him?

◇ Is Lockhart a good teacher? If you think he is not, list with your working partner all the reasons why you think that. (Share some observations).

 ◇ Show the clip from *The Prisoner of Azkaban*. Start from Professor Lupin beginning his class and continue until he dismisses his pupils.

Scene synopsis

Professor Lupin has taken over from Lockhart as the new Defence against the Dark Arts teacher. In this lesson he is teaching the pupils how to deal with Boggarts. Boggarts are shape-shifters who can take the shape of whatever they think will frighten people most. The only way a Boggart can be defeated is for its victim to turn the object of image of fear into something funny so that everyone laughs. Boggarts do not like laughter because it destroys their power.

◇ While the children watch the clip, ask them to focus on everything Lupin does to teach his pupils about how to conquer their fears.
◇ From which part of the room does Lupin begin his lesson?
◇ Compare this with where Lockhart began his lesson.
◇ What does this tell them about Lupin as a person and as a teacher?
◇ What do they notice about *how* Professor Lupin gains the pupils' interest?
◇ Notice the pupils' expressions and behaviour. How does it differ from their reaction to Gilderoy Lockhart's lesson?
◇ What does Professor Lupin do to win the pupils' trust?
◇ Was Professor Lupin right to end the lesson when he did?
◇ If they think he was, encourage pupils to state why.

Writing and drawing/art activities

The objective here is to provide an opportunity for the children to write about the way in which the dramatic effects in the film succeed in presenting two different teachers who each have a different impact upon Hogwarts pupils.

◇ Imagine you are a Hogwarts pupil and you have just had a lesson given by Gilderoy Lockhart followed by another from Professor Lupin on how to destroy the power of harmful creatures. Write a letter to your best Muggle friend telling them all about Lupin and Lockhart.
◇ Describe everything that happened in Lockhart's and Lupin's lessons, including the details

of their dress, the way they spoke and where they stood in the classroom in relation to the pupils.
◇   Tell your friend what thoughts and feelings you had about both teachers as they were teaching you.

Drawing/painting activity

◇   You are a film artist and you have been asked to give visual guidance to a film director about how they should present either Lockhart or Lupin in film through clearly labelled drawings or paintings.
◇   You can make your costume, headwear, style of footwear, etc., different from that shown in the film clips.
◇   Draw or paint a picture at least as large as a sheet of A4 paper. Label the costume you have drawn or painted with arrows indicating colours, type of footwear, hairstyle, facial expression, colour of eyes, and so on.
◇   Indicate somewhere on your drawing the kind of personality your character has. It could be in a framed box, the use of arrowed labels – in fact, anywhere and in any form on your painting/drawing that will attract the film director's interest.
◇   On a separate piece of paper set out in writing, maybe with the odd sketch, the kind of classroom setting the teacher will be working in. Will it have steps with a kind of pulpit, as in the scene with Lockhart? What kind of design will you have for the Boggart's wardrobe in Lupin's classroom?
◇   What kind of lighting would you advise? Bright and sunny, dark and gloomy, fires burning in bowls or torches at the side of the classroom?
◇   What kind of music or sound effects will be played to open the scene? Present your writing and sketches in a way that will capture the film director's interest.

Lesson objectives and learning outcomes

Lesson/series of lessons/unit of work objectives

1   To deepen children's understanding, appreciation and enjoyment of film and text extracts from the Harry Potter series.
2   To teach children to appreciate some of the differences between paper and film versions of extracts from the Harry Potter series.
3   To teach children how to begin to 'read' film narratives by providing them with some basic film terminology.
4   To give children opportunities to apply the film-reading terminology by watching selected extracts from *The Chamber of Secrets* and *The Prisoner of Azkaban*.
5   To teach children to understand and apply what is meant by dramatic effects in selected film clips in relation to costume, make-up, hairstyle, ways of speaking, walking, props, music, etc.
6   To teach children to begin to understand how the use of dramatic effects helps to increase understanding of the differences between the characters the actors are playing, and how the audience is drawn into the film-maker's and author's interpretation of them.
7   To extend children's understanding and appreciation of the characters from the Harry Potter series through drama, discussion, drawing and writing activities.

Lesson/series of lessons/unit of work outcomes

By the end of the workshop, the children will:

1   be able to understand, know and apply the beginnings of critical reading of both film and print narratives;
2   know some of the differences and similarities between print and film narratives in relation to the Harry Potter series;
3   have acquired the beginnings of an understanding of film and camera technique terminology;
4   be able to apply the terms *cut*, *establishing shot*, *close-up*, *wide shot*, *zoom*, *tracking shot* and *panning* at a basic level of understanding;
5   have a deeper understanding of how the use of dramatic effects communicates difference in the characters as portrayed in Harry Potter film extracts;
6   be able to communicate in writing, drawing and/or art work the dramatic effects required for a chosen scene in the Harry Potter series.
7   have developed the beginnings of a critical appreciation of film texts;
8   appreciate, understand and enjoy the Harry Potter series through a range of drama, discussion and film-reading activities.

Diary

Reading film

Teaching the beginnings of reading film to an age range including Years 3, 4, 5 and 6 was a tough assignment, especially for the Year 3 group. The Year 3 pupils needed to be introduced to one or two film terms only to begin with and to learn to identify and apply these with a shorter film clip. The Year 4, 5 and 6 children quickly caught on to some of the basic film terms and enjoyed using this new (to them) way of reading narrative. Given further experience of reading film, I am confident that it would not take long for them to make progress and begin to apply what they had learned to other forms of moving images. The children who had no interest in the Harry Potter series were keen to begin to acquire a language for thinking and talking about film.

NB: The equipment I used for the workshop (laptop, DVD, interactive whiteboard) did not have a remote control for finding scenes or parts within scenes. I therefore bookmarked all the clips I needed to use. This should not be necessary if you have a good-quality remote control.

Discussion and group interaction

Most of the children were very forthcoming in their responses to the film, noticed more than I anticipated and were certainly able to compare the differences between written and film versions of the extracts chosen. The duelling scene followed on well from the previous clip with respect to the investigation of similarities and differences in the book and film extracts. The clear characterisation contrasts made it possible for them to begin to apply film reading concepts and to analyse dramatic effects. What was certainly strongly evident was that those children who both had read the books and seen the film had a much firmer grasp of plot, characterisation and contextual detail than those who had only seen the films.

> **Drama**
>
> All the children were highly involved in the drama activities, which focused entirely on the clips seen. Even those children who were a little hazy about the characters or who had no prior knowledge of the series were able to draw upon their recent experience of watching two clips several times. There is a great deal to be gained by concentrating on *one* clip only. Indeed, the class teacher commented in her workshop evaluation, 'I am particularly interested in drama and I was surprised by how much work can be generated by a single clip from a film.' Limiting the characters to those portrayed in the film and book extracts for the drama activities worked well, and even those children whose knowledge was based on the film clips alone presented robust defences of their characters when in the hot seat. However, those children who had a deeper knowledge to draw upon gave richer and more contextualised characterisations.

Examples of children's work

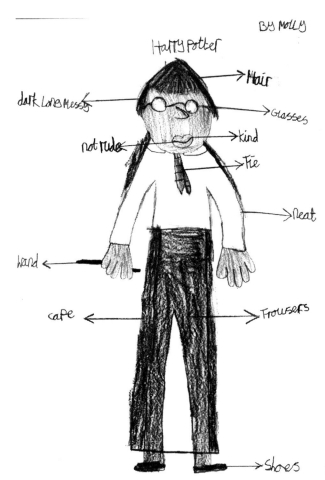

Figure 6.1 Work by Molly (Year 3).

Figure 6.2 Work by Alice (Year 4).

Figure 6.3 Work by Isabel (Year 4).

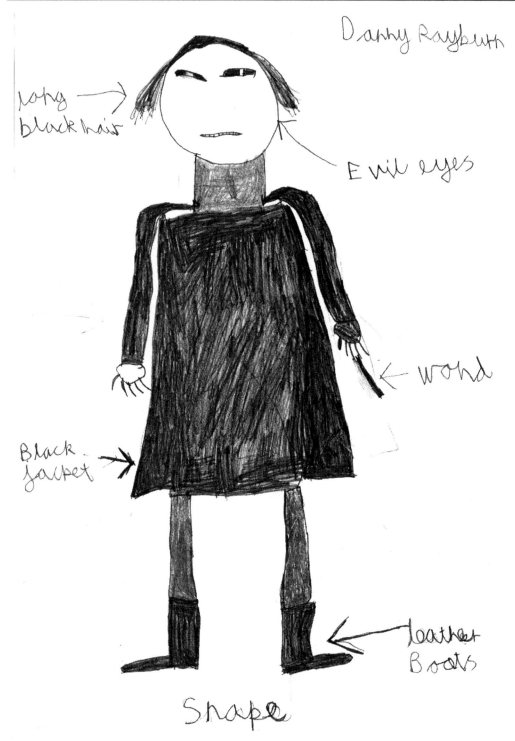

Danny Rayburn

long black hair

Evil eyes

Black Jacket

wand

leather Boots

Snape

Figure 6.4 Work by Danny (Year 4).

Teaching resources

- Copies of J.K. Rowling's *Harry Potter and the Chamber of Secrets* and *Harry Potter and the Prisoner of Azkaban*. The versions I used were: J.K. Rowling (1998) *Harry Potter and the Chamber of Secrets*, London: Bloomsbury Publishing. J.K. Rowling (1999) *Harry Potter and the Prisoner of Azkaban*, London: Bloomsbury Publishing.
- Copies of DVDs of *Harry Potter and the Chamber of Secrets* and *Harry Potter and the Prisoner of Azkaban*. The versions used in the workshop were:
  Warner Brothers Pictures (2002) *Harry Potter and the Chamber of Secrets* [DVD], New York: Warner Brothers. Warner Brothers Pictures (2004) *Harry Potter and the Prisoner of Azkaban* [DVD], New York: Warner Brothers.
- Photocopies and/or interactive whiteboard displays of the basic film terms, list of characters and list of dramatic effects.
- Enlarged version of the 'Duelling Scene' drama sequence.

Useful websites and additional sources of information

For a clear and very helpful introduction to television and film terminology, see the online source entitled *The 'Grammar' of Television and Film*, available at http://www.aber.ac.uk/media/Documents/short/gramtv.html.

For an excellent British Film Institute source on films and short stories (Key Stages 1 and 2) accompanied by comprehensive teacher guidance on how to use film, see the online materials at http://www.bfi.org/education/teaching/storyshorts2/films/film9.html.

For a comprehensive source for all you need to know about the books, characters, plot Hogwarts lexicon, themes, etc., see http://en.wikipedia.org/wiki.Harry_Potter.

If you have time, want to know more about J.K. Rowling and like virtual tours, consult her official website at http://www.jkrowling.com/.

NB: Please be aware that the next part of this chapter contains details of the plots of all the Harry Potter series, including the final book, *Harry Potter and the Deathly Hallows*. You are advised to read the books first if you do not want your enjoyment spoiled.

J.K. Rowling
Love, loss and magic[1]

The Harry Potter phenomenon

The seventh and final book of the series was released for sale at midnight on Saturday, 21 July 2007 to millions of excited children and adults standing somewhere in the world outside a supermarket or high street bookseller or, if they were very lucky, waiting outside the National History Museum in London to hear the first few pages of *Harry Potter and the Deathly Hallows* being read by the author herself. J.K. Rowling has achieved a unique feat. Not only has her audience stayed with her over a ten-year period but the interest in Harry and his epic adventures has actually spiralled and reader numbers have increased exponentially.

Of the many journalists and literary critics who debated the reasons for the success of the first four of the series (see, for example, Tucker, 1999; Mynott, 1999; Eccleshare, 2002; Zipes, 2002), several were sceptical of Rowling's ability to sustain the psychological reality needed to authenticate the troubled, mood-shifting years of growing adolescents. This was a daunting task, and the critics rightly highlighted the scale and nature of the challenge the author had set herself. Children throughout the world have grown up with Harry, his friends and enemies, all of whom have become part of their social and psychological reality. For a children's series to seize and hold an unprecedented number of readers' imaginations over ten years is a literary and global phenomenon.

Within twenty-four hours of the release of her final book, 11,000 copies had sold on both sides of the Atlantic. To date, the Harry Potter series has sold some 350 million copies in sixty-five different languages. Even though Rowling has now brought closure to the Harry Potter series after seventeen years of intensive writing, the fascination with Harry is set to continue until at least 2010, when the final film, *Harry Potter and the Deathly Hallows*, will be released. *Harry and the Half-Blood Prince* is scheduled for November 2008, and a musical adaptation is planned for the same year. The first five of the Warner Brothers films have been immensely successful, cleverly cast and consistently well directed despite changes in directors. The series has also generated video games, Potter-themed merchandise and highly popular interactive fan websites.[2] A 28-acre Harry Potter theme park to be built in Florida is currently being planned in collaboration with J.K. Rowling.

Rowling has won countless glittering prizes for her achievements, one of the most coveted being the inaugural Whitbread Children's Book of the Year Award for *Harry Potter and the Prisoner of Azkaban*. Its genre crosses over several narrative types: a fairy tale, with Harry as a kind of orphaned Cinderella figure who is loathed by his surrogate parents and their son; an alternative world of fantasy with Gothic thriller elements; an adventure story; and a school story. Harry's various quests, which include searches for the Horcruxes (a Horcrux is a place or thing in which parts of Voldemort's soul are hidden in order to ensure his immortality) and the Hallows (three sanctified legendary objects which, once united, are supposed to enable the finder to defeat death) draws upon Arthurian legends and the quest for the Holy Grail. The struggle against all-powerful forces of evil also, according to Rustin and Rustin (2001), calls to mind the science fiction worlds of Dr Who and his respective totalitarian enemies. All the books in the series have been designed with different book covers for children and adults so that, like Pullman's *His Dark Materials*, Rowling's Harry Potter series falls within a multifaceted cross-over genre.

Despite the global success of the series, Rowling's books have not received universal acclaim. Some commentaries on the first four books in the series, for example, have assessed them as having scant literary merit, being backward-looking by drawing on the old-fashioned school story genre populated by élite and privileged children, and showing an overdependence on stereotypical caricatures of malice with repellent physical features such as those portrayed by the Dursleys and Severus Snape (Tucker, 1999; Zipes, 2002). Her books have also been described as derivative and formulaic, and even by the end of the final book in the series some writers persist in their view that central characters like Harry and Hermione have not developed beyond the level of two-dimensional caricatures (Manthorpe, 2007; Zipes 2002). In parts of the United States her books have been banned in schools and libraries by Christian fundamentalists because of their alleged promotion of occult and magic practices.

Why, then, has this series caught the imagination and ardent admiration of so many millions of child and adult readers? Are they simply mesmerised by the pull of market demands and commodity consumption (Zipes, 2002) in a world where the genre of children's books has recently become big business, with enormous profits for major book publishing and marketing conglomerates? I have serious doubts about the latter view since I believe it unlikely that the millions of adolescents who have grown up with Harry would have allowed themselves to be hoodwinked by the media hype that has been such a persistent feature of the series' progress. Something deep and significant in the books has spoken to them about their own experiences and the psychological reality of what it means to grow up in a world where unsafe community life, ecological threat and terrorism are an inextricable part of their lives. Harry has had to learn to live with terror and death from an early point in his life. Indeed, death and loss are unifying themes in the whole series, and part of their power and intrigue is the compellingly convincing way in which they are presented and written about.

It is my contention that only an author who has had personal experience of the bleakness of loss and love through death could have written about Harry's experience with such conviction and certitude. I have written elsewhere (Duncan, 2007) about the ways in which the author's own biography of love and loss informs and drives the stories that Pullman and Morpurgo write. I suggest that the same applies to Rowling, who at 11 years of age knew that her mother had a particularly virulent form of multiple sclerosis. In 1990, just six months into the writing of the first book, her mother died. In a revealing recent television documentary entitled *J.K. Rowling: A Year in the Life* (2007), she stated that her mother's death had a profound and devastating impact on her life. She disclosed that while the plot for the series did not change, 'everything darkened and deepened, and my mother's death seeped into every part of the books'. She also had a very difficult relationship with her father, from whom she desperately sought approval. The distance between them became so fraught that for several years after her mother's death, she had no contact with him. This may account for the presence of idealised father figures in the form of Hagrid, Sirius Black and Dumbledore, all of whom knew and liked Harry's young parents, Lily and James. Having suffered the loss of her mother and the psychic loss of her father at the age of 25, Rowling has direct experience of what it is like to be an orphan. After a failed marriage during the same period, she succumbed to clinical depression in which she stated that a coldness and numbness drained the colour out of her life, the experience of which is likely to have given shape to the brilliantly conceived life-hating 'dementors' in the series, who have the power to suck the vitality and every happy memory out of their victims. Coincidently, the 'spectres' in Pullman's Dark Materials trilogy are strikingly similar and arise from the same personal experience of depression (Bridge, 2007). James Runcie the interlocutor in *J.K. Rowling: A year in the life* (2007), commented that while she had created an alternative fantasy world in her creation of Hogwarts, magic and wizardry, it is also a 'story filled with the pain and dilemmas of real life in which Harry Potter has to learn to be a force for good against the dark arts and Lord Voldemort'. In another incisive and perceptive comment, Runcie's view was that the whole of the Harry Potter series was 'one giant attempt to reclaim her childhood' (ibid.). Indeed, there are strong emotional links between Rowling and Harry. This candid and sensitively directed documentary lends support to my view that one of the central reasons for the popularity of, and intense interest in, the Harry Potter series is not that its readers have been spellbound into critical myopia but rather that they are compelled by the series because they trust its veracity, believe in Harry's increasing pain, anger and anxiety, and feel empowered by the way in which he and his loyal friends stand up to the forces of evil and terror. It is their own inner resources, tenacity, loyalty and responsibility as much as their knowledge of magic that enables them to confront the megalomaniacal nihilism of Voldemort.

Themes and values

There may some truth in Tucker's (1999) view that Rowling's school story is backward-looking and absolutist with respect to the somewhat tedious beginnings of each of the first six books set in the suburban sterility of the Dursley household and the Dursleys' despicable treatment of Harry. The escapist landscape of Hogwarts and its moving staircases and fire-lit common rooms, the camaraderie of school chums and the predictability of the headmaster's welcome speech at the beginning of term are all part of the familiar landscape of the boarding school story.

However, what Rowling has done with remarkable ingenuity is to reinvent and defamialiarise it (Mynott, 1999). Hogwarts is a school in which lessons are not about classics and the conjugation of Latin verbs but essentially practical lessons in the art of wizardry and magic, which include pupils' learning how to defend themselves against their worst fears. In *Harry Potter and the Prisoner of Azkaban*, the kind Professor Lupin, for example, shows patience and humour in demonstrating how his pupils can protect themselves against their most paralysing terrors by thinking of something positive and amusing whenever they are confronted with the objective form of their phobia, the Boggart. When the Boggart emerges from the wardrobe, the pupils have to focus on an image that makes them laugh, rather than succumb to paralysing panic. At the word 'Riddikulus', the Boggart will shape-shift into something comical, but only if the pupils truly believe in their image created in their minds. This is not simply a magical trick but a life-empowering strategy to overcome phobia and fear which Rowling has skilfully woven into her epic adventure. Lessons of this kind involve inner exploration on the part of the protagonists as well as their readers about the potential of mind-reordering strategies to overcome fear.

Knowledge of magic is hard-won, and there are very clear rules about how and when it is to be used. Rowling seldom condones its improper use, and throughout the series the importance of ethical and moral responsibility is emphasised, with severe penalties for those who test its long-established boundaries. Harry frequently disobeys these rules, and on one occasion risks expulsion. Hogwarts' teachers who abuse their powers are roundly condemned by both staff and pupils, as is the case when the fake Mad-Eye Moody turns Malfoy into a ferret and uses the forbidden curses in lessons. The gratuitous use of magic often backfires, for example when Ron, incensed by Malfoy's 'mudblood' slur on Hermione, directs his wand at Draco's face, with disastrous consequences. A jet of green light shoots out of the wrong end of his wand and sends Ron reeling. Even in a school of witchcraft and wizardry whose very purpose is to train its pupils to become wizards, the use of magic is governed by the principles of moral responsibility. This is an important theme in the book because the use of magic to serve the ends of power for perverse and evil ends, as is Voldemort's sole purpose, has horrific consequences, resulting in maimed lives and several deaths. Harry, on the other hand, though occasionally reckless and rule-breaking, when given the opportunity to see Pettigrew killed, the man who betrayed his parents to Voldemort, chooses to save him:

> 'Harry!' gasped Pettigrew, and he flung his arms around Harry's knees. . . .
> 'Get off me,' Harry spat, throwing Pettigrew's hands off him in disgust. 'I'm not doing this for you. I'm doing it because I don't reckon my dad would've wanted his best friends to become killers – just for you.'
>
> (*Prisoner of Azkaban*, Rowling, 1999: 275)

Despite the strong temptation to avenge his parents' deaths and the even stronger desire to do so on the part of Sirius and Lupin, Harry chooses not to kill Pettigrew because it would criminalise two of his father's best friends. This act of mercy could hardly be defined as altruistic, but it demonstrates Harry's ability at the age of 13 not to be swayed by others and to make a choice based upon the interests of others, especially those he values and loves. It is actions of this kind that make the damaged and petulant Harry an interesting and compassionate human being with an ability to make the right choice at the right time, and that elevate what might merely have been a ripping yarn into a moral fable about good and evil and life and death.

While much of the series is set in an ancient Gothic castle with a forbidden and dangerous forest populated by engorged spiders, giants, unicorns, centaurs and thestrals, among others, part of Rowling's skill lies in the way in which she makes this bygone world instantaneously modern to an age of children who live in an electronic multimedia world. For example, moving staircases, portraits of ancient Hogwartian dignitaries who talk and move, the Marauder's Map and flying dragons are familiar features of computer virtual reality games. The smiling faces of Harry's parents in the Mirror of Erised and the moving figures in the photographs of the *Daily Prophet* are not yet a part of the world in which readers live, but many will be familiar with the immediacy of photographs and video captured on mobile phones and digital cameras, and the moving images achieved by webcam recorders via the internet. The ingeniously conceived game of Quidditch, which is played on broomsticks with quaffles, bludgeons and the golden snitch, has all the thrill of a hockey game played at lightning speed in the air. The status attached to the type of broomsticks that Quidditch players own resonates strongly with the cachet attached to designer-label sportswear. Rowling has used the status of commodity consumerism in her series to good effect, enabling her readers to identify closely with Malfoy's smug superiority about the Slytherin team being provided with the latest, top-of-the-range Nimbus Two Thousand and One by his rich father. In an incisive analysis of the first four of the Potter series, Rustin and Rustin (2001) comment that 'This competition for the latest model of sporting broomstick puts Rowling right on the pulse of the consumer age – for broomsticks, imagine mountain bikes, trainers, or indeed computers' (2001: 266). The world of multimedia communication which many children inhabit and the imaginative use Rowling makes of it facilitates the ease with which her readers can code-switch between Harry's world and theirs. In this sense, the boundaries between Rowling's alternative world of fantasy and reality are more permeable than the fantasy worlds created, for example, by Nesbit and Tolkien.

While Rowling may be postmodern in her use of multi genres and the incorporation of multimedia forms, she is modernist when it comes to emotional and moral questions (Rustin and Rustin, 2001). A core theme that runs through the book is her non-relativist stance with respect to the racial conflict that exists between, on the one hand, the Malfoys, and others on the side of Lord Voldemort, for a pureblood wizard world and, on the other, the enlightened Dumbledore, who has actively encouraged a racially mixed school population. The loathing that Draco Malfoy has for what he calls 'half-bloods' or 'mudbloods' is expressed whenever he crosses the path of Hermione and Harry. However, his sniping prejudice does not stop at ethnicity but extends to poverty, status and to anyone who is not a pureblood, which Salazar Slytherin had long argued should be the chief criterion for entry into Hogwarts. The Weasley family are, for example, purebloods but they are frequently taunted by Malfoy, Crabbe and Goyle because they are poor and, even worse, close friends of the Muggle-born Harry and Hermione; they are therefore insultingly called 'blood traitors' by Malfoy and his followers. Hagrid and Professor Lupin are equally despised because they too are 'half-breeds' of a kind, Hagrid because he is half-wizard, half-giant, and Lupin because he is a werewolf. Dumbledore, by virtue of his support of all his staff and a mixed school population, is also a candidate for the Malfoys' contempt, and they stop at nothing to get him ousted from his position as headmaster. Their scheming and plotting does not succeed until the fifth book in the series, *The Order of the Phoenix*, when, with the collusion of the power-crazed Dolores Umbridge, Dumbledore is not only dismissed but also only narrowly avoids being sent to Azkaban by an act of spectacular disapparation. Prejudice extends too to the house elves, who are intelligent and possess feelings. Their servility to the purebloods condemns them to a life of domestic chores without pay or privilege of any kind, and their enslavement is symbolised by the wearing of a pillow-case, the only clothing allowed to them. This appalling injustice enrages Hermione, who spends much of her limited spare time knitting them hats, socks and scarves, the wearing of which gives them freedom and dignity.

Rowling is unequivocal in her disapproval of prejudice and injustice, which become increasingly sinister and on a larger scale in the last two books, invoking terrifying visions of the Ku Klux Klan, Stalinism and Nazi Germany in the rising numbers of attacks from dementors and the cowled Death Eaters in Voldemort's scheme for a master race. Dumbledore maintains his enlightened position until his death. At the end of the Triwizard Tournament he tells his assembled pupils the truth about the death of Cedric Diggory during the tournament – that it was a planned murder by Voldemort and not, as many would like to believe, the result of an accident. As he bids farewell to the tournament contenders from France and Durmstrang, he makes explicit his position about racial intolerance and disunity in the context of Voldemort's return:

> 'Every guest in this Hall,' said Dumbledore, and his eyes lingered upon the Durmstrang students, 'will be welcomed back here, at any time, should they wish to come. I say to you all, once again – in the light of Lord Voldemort's return, we are only as strong as we are united, as weak as we are divided. . . . We can fight it only by showing an equally strong bond of friendship and trust. Differences of habit and language are nothing at all if our aims are identical and our hearts are open.'
>
> (*Goblet of Fire*, Rowling, 2000: 627)

Equally important in the darkening themes and events that occur in the final two books is the primary significance given to the redemptive power of love. As Harry's emotional resources are stretched almost to breaking point, the one thing that sustains him through some moments of searing agony is the fact that love is the strongest power there is.

The themes of Rowling's books, along with her characterisations, give her readers a rich source for inner exploration about their own experience of the pains and pleasures that attend the process of growing up. Rustin and Rustin believe the series to be classics of their kind, arguing from a psychoanalytic perspective that 'We believe that the source of richness and emotional power of Rowling's stories lies in her empathy with and understanding of children's unconscious emotional life and that it is this that makes these books more than merely entertaining adventures' (2001: 273).

Plot and narrative

It is remarkable that Rowling conceived this intricate and complex story on a train journey from London to Manchester. The idea for this seven-year *Bildungsroman* apparently just strolled into her head almost fully formed. Rowling has always said that she is proud of Harry, and by the end of the series it is not difficult to see why. What is striking about him is that, despite his wizarding ability, he is a vulnerable and pained individual who can be reckless, mean-spirited, moody and angry, but as the pressures and responsibilities placed upon him mount, he rises to them, grows up, learns to see that things are rarely black or white and, in the final book, shows Herculean courage and an infallible ability to take the right path of action against unbelievable odds.

One of the tests of a good plot and the characters who stage its drama is the extent to which its audience cares about them. The speculation on the part of children and adults about what would happen to Harry in Book 7 in the weeks before it was released suggests strongly that they cared deeply about him, and several entries in the ever-spawning Harry Potter websites expressed a fervent hope that neither he nor his close friends would die.

One of the reasons for the success of the series lies not only in Rowling's immense powers of imagination but in the assiduous care that she took to plan the plot, characters' development and various back stories in dense, systematically organised detail, including finely worked sketches of the characters' appearance, Hogwarts and the game of Quidditch. She still retains boxes full of notes, drawings and the names given to each of her ever-multiplying characters, including their genealogy and subsequent lives beyond the end of the series ('J.K. Rowling goes beyond the epilogue', 2007). This epic narrative is not simply a series of exciting adventures but an immense project carved out with the painstaking research of a scholar in total control of her field of investigation. The clues to the denouement which have been let out on a slow but steady leash from Book 1 to Book 7 are not easy to keep track of. You need a phenomenally good memory to be able to recall all the minutiae of the parallel world of Hogwarts, the rules of magic and its many characters including the significance of Mr Ollivander's knowledge about wands and why Dumbledore is so distant with Harry in *The Order of the Phoenix*, and so on. Rowling makes her readers work hard to understand her dense and fast-moving narrative, so close attention has to be paid to the smallest of details or you risk losing the bigger picture. Having to puzzle out how one piece of action connects with another that occurred in an earlier book is an essential part of their intrigue and appeal.

The language she uses is clear and deliberately uncomplicated but not simplistic. Rowling drives the plot forward with unexpected detours and ever-surprising new turns. Things are seldom what they seem, and predicting what happens next taxes even mature adult readers. Her skill in inventing a new quest, an unexpected difficulty and a yet another twist is the key to the suspense which she has succeeded in maintaining throughout the series. There *are* some predictable parts to the series, especially at the beginning of the first four books, where what consistently happens with Harry at 4 Privet Drive risks tedium. It is a relief when the pattern is broken in Book 5 with the appearance of the dementors, one of whom would have killed Dudley had Harry not intervened by performing a Patronus charm to drive them away.

From *The Order of the Phoenix* onwards, the plot darkens, and sinister events occur in fast succession as the relative order and stability of Hogwarts begin to break down. In a brilliant move on Rowling's part, she places Cornelius Fudge's undersecretary, Delores Umbridge, in a political role on the school staff which gives her immense power over the staff and the curriculum. The intrusive and relentless inspections, which all Hogwarts' staff are subjected to, bear all the contemporary familiarity of the oppressive anxiety caused by Ofsted school inspections. Umbridge takes her role to intolerable excesses of surveillance and chilling acts of carefully rehearsed cruelty. She deserves her downfall at the end of Book 5, when she is unceremoniously dragged off into the forbidden forest by a herd of ferocious centaurs. Apart from Voldemort, her smiling indifference to the pain and suffering she causes to others, particularly the half-bloods, makes her one of Rowling's most malign characters. Umbridge's introduction into the book at this point is the catalyst for the formation of Dumbledore's Army, which unites a group of loyal supporters around Harry, who is elected their leader. After the depressive and angry mindset that has tormented Harry for much of *The Order of the Phoenix*, this gives Harry the spur to redirect his energy and a chance to show his immense leadership and teaching skills. This new turn in the plot enables Harry to emerge as a natural leader and empowers a group of pupils to feel that they can do something constructive about defending themselves against Voldemort and the repressive regime that Umbridge has imposed upon the school in Dumbledore's absence.

Examples of clichéd prose can be found in the earlier books, but as the series progresses, her writing became more assured, while the skill and mastery of her plot construction unquestionably reaches new heights in Book 7. Journalists on both sides of the Atlantic have confirmed this view. For example, Kakutani (2007: 2) commented that 'Ms Rowling has fitted together the jigsaw-puzzle pieces of this long undertaking with Dickensian ingenuity and ardor'. Commenting on the same book, Cottrell Boyce stated that 'nothing quite prepared me for that Orwellian image of the Ministry of Magic with its Stalinist statues and "Might is Magic" written on it. . . . Rowling touches on contemporary anxieties without drawing any obvious allegorical parallels' (2007: 1).

By the end of the series, Harry's prowess at Quidditch, the odd bit of serendipity and the companionship of Ron and Hermione are no longer enough to get him through the bone-chilling terrors and confrontations he now has to face increasingly on his own. Two pieces of Rowling's writing will serve to show, first, her adept use of language, and second, her ability to write prose in which action flashes across the brain at lightning speed. In the first extract, from Book 6, Harry accompanies Dumbledore to the cave which is the entrance to the black lake where one of Voldemort's horcruxes is hidden inside a stone basin:

> Harry could smell salt and hear rushing waves; a light, chilly breeze ruffled his hair as he looked out at moonlit sea and star-strewn sky. He was standing upon a high outcrop of dark rock, water foaming and churning below him. He glanced over his shoulder. A towering cliff stood behind, a sheer drop, black and faceless. A few large chunks of rock, such as the

one upon which Harry and Dumbledore were standing, looked as though they had broken away from the cliff face at some point in the past. It was a bleak, harsh view; the sea and the rock unrelieved by any tree or sweep of grass or sand.

(*Half Blood-Prince*, Rowling, 2005: 519)

In the second extract the action moves to a stone basin on a small island in which the Horcrux locket is hidden at the bottom of an emerald green, phosphorescent liquid which Dumbledore has commanded Harry to make him drink. Harry keeps his promise and watches in agony as Dumbledore suffers all the pain of having drunk neat poison. Dumbledore's breath is fading and Harry is terrified that he will die but Dumbledore insists he makes him empty the liquid in the basin. As Dumbledore's breathing fades, Harry fills the goblet with water in the hope of reviving him. When he tips the icy water over Dumbledore's face, he realises to his horror that they are both surrounded by inferi (animated corpses who do the bidding of the Dark Lord).

It was the best he could do, for the icy feeling on his arm not holding the cup was not the lingering chill of the water. A slimy white hand had gripped his wrist, and the creature to whom it belonged was pulling him, slowly, backwards across the rock. The surface of the lake was no longer mirror-smooth; it was churning, and everywhere Harry looked, white heads and hands were emerging from the dark water, men and women and children with sunken, sightless eyes were moving towards the rock: an army of the dead rising from the black water.

(ibid.: 537–538)

It is writing of this kind that keeps her readers turning the pages, in anticipation of the next surprise, the next quest and further revelations about characters whose real depths remain hidden until Book 7. Here, in her finest book of the series, the action moves away from the familiar routines of Hogwarts to makeshift campsites around the countryside as Ron, Hermione and Harry keep on the move in various guises in order to avoid Voldemort's Death Eaters. Harry realises that the search for the three Hallows and their crucial interconnection is more important than the Horcruxes. Rowling shows how substantial her characters are as they are increasingly forced to draw on their inner resources without the comfort of regular food and warm beds in the quest that will finally bring Harry face to face with Voldemort.

As in all the books of the series, Rowling balances the bleakest moments of loss, death and destruction with humour, warmth, love and generosity, mostly through the vibrant Weasley family. A brilliantly conceived plot is of little use without richly drawn characters to give it life, humanity and reality. The next section turns to a discussion of two of Rowling's richest characters.

Characterisation

Let us now examine the characters in an attempt to show how their unique differences and development over seven years serve to bring together many of the points made in the previous sections. By the time Book 7 was released, many of Rowling's readers were as keen to know whether Snape was actually a malign and twisted member of Voldemort's posse as they were concerned about the fate of Harry and his followers. It is, as Cotterell Boyce (2007) rightly argues, the 'emotional and moral ambiguity' of her central characters, including Dumbledore, that lies at the heart of Rowling's success as a writer. A key criterion for the success of any film, television, stage drama or written narrative rests on the issue of whether the audience seriously cares about the life and fate of its characters. Had Rowling's readers not done so, the brilliance of her suspenseful plot would not, in itself, have been sufficient to keep her readers fascinated and gripped by her books. The idea of emotional and moral ambiguity in Rowling's characterisation suggests uncertainty, indeterminacy and opacity. Rowling's gift for constructing characters who are seldom what they seem makes them more interesting and worthy of analysis than those who are simply no more than what you see.

One significant lesson which readers learn from Rowling's assured character development is that good people, like Dumbledore, can occasionally make the wrong decisions and that apparently malevolent people like Snape, are capable of protective and altruistic behaviour. Until the final book in the series, Dumbledore is shown to be a brilliant wizard and a tolerant, wise headmaster with strong principles and integrity. Not until the end of Book 7 do we learn that he is actually a deeply flawed person who has had to wrestle with immense guilt about his less than responsible behaviour towards his family in his youth. He cares deeply about Harry but sometimes, to Harry's intense fury, displays apparent indifference and a lack of concern about his well-being.

There are a number of characters who are worth exploring because of the way in which they change and develop over the course of the series, but the rest of this section will focus on Severus Snape and Harry Potter in relation to the concept of emotional and moral ambiguity and how it differentially manifests itself.

Severus Snape

Snape unquestionably abuses his power in the classroom with Harry and the muddle-headed Neville Longbottom, the chief targets of his scorn and ridicule. He seldom loses an opportunity to humiliate and belittle Harry for his lamentable skills in potions classes, and Harry, who in his early days at Hogwarts sees life, issues and people as either black or white, persists in perceiving Snape as despicable, cruel and malign until the last part of the final book. In fact, Snape is one of Rowling's finest characters; his complexity and ambiguity keep the reader in suspense until the end.

Snape is present in every book of her septology, so Rowling presents a vast canvas of detail from which to formulate hypotheses about who he really is and which side he is on: Dumbledore's or Voldemort's. Her skill lies in the constant dialectic she presents to her readers, who are presented with clues and facts that do not quite add up, along with Harry's perception of Snape as a vicious and vindictive teacher whom he strongly suspects of being in league with Voldemort. Rowling sustains a conflicting perspective on Snape through four narrative voices, all of which present contradictions and an ever-increasing ambiguity about his true nature. For example, Dumbledore consistently defends and trusts Snape without ever revealing why; Harry sees him as incapable of anything but spite and perverse behaviour; Snape consciously presents himself as enigmatic, cold and witheringly sarcastic while the author narrator herself sheds clues about his behaviour throughout the entire series all of which prompt further questions and speculation, but few answers.

The first clue comes in Book 1 when Professor Quirrell (who is secretly harbouring the disembodied Voldemort) utters a jinx that makes Harry's broomstick shake dangerously in his first Quidditch match. Snape is also seen muttering a jinx but is, in fact, countering the one sent by Quirrell. At an early point the discerning reader is led to question whether Snape is actually as bad as he seems. Later on we read that Snape is a superb occlumens (the art of magically defending the mind against external intrusion) and legilimens (the ability to extract emotions and memories from another's mind). This suggests that Snape was able to penetrate the mind of Quirrell in time to take action to protect Harry's safety. However, we also learn that Snape was a Death Eater with a deep interest in the dark arts, and had once been on Voldemort's side before the latter's downfall. He also appears to condone and connive at Draco Malfoy's insulting and racist behaviour towards Harry, and given that Draco's father, Lucius Malfoy, works for the Dark Lord, further doubts are thereby raised about Snape's loyalty to Dumbledore.

Even though Snape was once a Death Eater and still wears the Dark Mark on his arm, he is also a barely tolerated member of the Order of the Phoenix, a coterie formed by Dumbledore to fight against Voldemort's rumoured return to power. In Book 6 it is revealed that Snape has rejoined the Death Eaters in order to spy on Voldemort on Dumbledore's behalf. Meanwhile, Voldemort believes that Snape is working for him and spying on Dumbledore. Snape is thus working as a double agent.

It is, however, Snape's earlier life that is most revealing of a haunted and unhappy man who was neglected and brutalised by his father and teased mercilessly by Harry's father, James, when he and Snape were pupils together. James dubs him 'Snivellus' and on one occasion hexed him so that he ended up hanging upside down from a branch of a tree, thereby exposing his greying underwear. Even though James once rescued Snape from death, Snape deeply resented being in debt to James. We now have the beginnings of an understanding for Snape's intense dislike of Harry: Harry reminds Snape so much of Harry's dead father, who once taunted Snape as a boy. Harry's long-standing and deep distrust of Snape is confirmed when Snape kills Dumbledore with the Avada Kedavra curse after he has been seriously weakened by all that he had to endure in the black lake.

It is not until the end of Book 7 that the truth is revealed about Snape. He had tried to protect Harry and his parents from Voldemort's plan to kill Harry because of the prophecy that 'Neither can live whilst the other survives' (*Order of the Phoenix*, Rowling, 2003: 741). Snape unwisely entrusted Pettigrew with their protection, but Pettigrew, as Voldemort's servant, reneged on his agreement. Both Harry's parents were killed, but Harry survived. The reason for Snape's fervent wish to protect Harry's parents lay in his love for Lily, Harry's mother. He remained in love with her despite her marriage to James. Harry also finds out that Snape did not gratuitously kill Dumbledore but ended Dumbledore's life on the latter's instructions because he, Dumbledore was already dying as a result of a curse caused by one of Voldemort's Horcruxes. Snape was therefore loyal to Dumbledore to the last, but Harry only discovers this as Snape lies dying at the hands of Voldemort.

The reasons for Snape's dislike of Harry are now comprehensible. Harry can now see him as a steadfastly courageous man, and nineteen years later names one of his sons, Albus Severus, after two of the bravest men he knew.

While there were clear indications that there was far more to Snape than appeared on the surface, it is a mark of Rowling's cleverly crafted characterisation and plot construction that very few of her fans were able to guess what lay at the core of Snape's enigmatic personality.

Harry the reluctant hero

Much of the truth of Snape's character could only be gained from inference derived from several narrative voices, and then not fully, until his memories are collected in a flask by Harry as he lay dying from a fatal bite from the fangs of Voldemort's snake, Nagini. Harry's emotional and moral ambiguity lies within himself in the form of a psychic war that rages between his divided self, the outer sign of which is the lightning-shaped scar on his forehead that has connected him irretrievably to Voldemort. Harry's readers know he is truthful and loyal towards his friends and that he is a genuine Gryffindor, 'Where dwell the brave at heart'. They know too that the admiration and respect between Harry and Dumbledore is reciprocal. Despite Harry's deepest fears about being a 'bad' rather than a 'good' person, there is never any doubt about which side he is on. However, the source of Harry's complexity resides in his increasing fears and doubts about who he really is. Voldemort's presence invades his thoughts and dreams with increasing strength and vividness in Books 6 and 7. The intense pain that emanates from his scar is a further manifestation of Voldemort's controlling power. His parents were murdered by Voldemort, who had come to claim Harry's life because of the prophecy which decreed that:

> 'The one with the power to vanquish the Dark Lord approaches . . . and the Dark Lord will mark him as his equal, but he will have powers the Dark Lord knows not . . . and either must die at the hand of the other for neither can live while the other survives.'
>
> (*Order of the Phoenix*, Rowling, 2003: 741)

The prophecy is the fulcrum upon which the conflict between Voldemort and Harry pivots. It is central to the entire series because in 'marking him as his equal', Voldemort had unwittingly given Harry some of his power, which for Harry is both a blessing and a curse. Without some of Slytherin's traits and Voldemort's power within him, Harry would not have been able to succeed in rising so valiantly to the challenge of his many near impossible quests, which included vanquishing serpents, three-headed dogs, Horcruxes and Hallows along with several serious threats to his life and those of his friends.

Harry is connected to Voldemort in several ways. Both are orphans and half-bloods who have been brought up in unloving and deprived circumstances. Both have the rare ability to speak Parseltongue, a language that snakes can understand. They are also connected through their wands: both contain the phoenix feather, although the wood in Voldemort's case is yew while Harry's is holly. Mr Ollivander remembers every wand he sells to new students in Daigon Alley and he tells Harry that in wandlore, the wand finds its owner, not the other way round. The fact that Harry's scar hurts him every time he feels Voldemort in his mind makes him feel that he has the potential to become evil. Harry reveals to Dumbledore his intense anxiety that he really belongs to the House of Slytherin and not Gryffindor. Dumbledore reassures him:

> 'It [the Sorting Hat] only put me in Gryffindor', said Harry in a defeated voice, 'because I asked not to go in Slytherin . . .'
>
> '*Exactly*,' said Dumbledore, beaming once more. 'Which makes you very *different* from Tom Riddle [Voldemort's name as a pupil]. It is our choices, Harry, that show what we truly are, far more than our abilities.'
>
> (*Chamber of Secrets*, Rowling, 1998: 245)

The final sentence in this extract is the vital clue to the difference between Harry and Voldemort. He has an infallible ability to make the *right* choices, choices that are often based on the qualities of love, compassion and a strongly held set of values about loyalty, morality and friendship, the latter mattering deeply to a boy who has to endure more loss than most human beings could bear. The idealised father figures of Hagrid, Dumbledore and Sirius are therefore of immense importance to him. And, as Dumbledore points out to a bereft and enraged Harry just after the death of his godfather, Sirius Black, that the reason that Voldemort is unable to possess Harry is that 'he could not bear to reside in a body so full of the force he detests. In the end, it mattered not that you could not close your mind. It was your heart that saved you' (*Order of the Phoenix*, 2003: 743).

Despite the unremitting sense of loss and longing he has for his dead parents, he knows that they loved him enough to sacrifice their lives for him. Voldemort detests anything to do with love. Hate is the mainspring of his actions and he is largely consumed by it. Harry is sustained and nourished by the love of others. However, it is sufficient for Harry to learn to be a good wizard; he does not want to be a hero, or be different from the others. Nonetheless, he frequently finds himself faced with tasks demanding enormous courage, which he would prefer to shun. These challenges find Harry, not the other way round, but this is not how his friends perceive it. In Book 4, Harry is chosen by the Goblet of Fire to compete in the Triwizard Tournament, for which only those aged over 17 years are eligible. Harry is 14, and baffled and disconcerted that his name has risen on a piece of scorched parchment from the Goblet. He initially gets very little support from his housemates because most think that he has flouted the rules in some way. Harry does not want to compete in this dangerous tournament, and Ron is extremely jealous, believing that Harry's motivation was to gain attention and glory. Hermione tackles Harry about Ron's position, to which Harry heatedly retorts: 'Great. . . . Really great. Tell him from me I'll swap anytime he wants. Tell him from me he's welcome to it . . . people gawping at my forehead everywhere I go' (*Goblet of Fire*, Rowling, 2000: 254). However, despite the taunts from his peers and the mounting tension with his close friend Ron, Harry once more rises to the terrifying challenges of the tournament and shows yet again his sense of fair play and integrity. When both he and Cedric Diggory are within sight of the Triwizard Cup, Harry agrees that they should claim the victory together. As they are about to do so, the Triwizard Cup becomes a portkey which transports them to a graveyard where Wormtail appears in a cloak, and upon Voldemort's orders kills Cedric. Harry is overwhelmed with grief, and his sole concern is to get Cedric back to his father, but not before Wormtail cuts Harry with a knife to claim the blood he needs to enable Voldemort to realise his physical form in order to fight to claim victory and omnipotence. The death of his schoolmate Diggory, closely followed by the death of his godfather, Sirius, in the Department of Mysteries, is too much for Harry. After a year of Dumbledore's evasion and distance when he needed him most, his anger, depression and pain explodes:

> 'Harry, suffering like this proves that you are still a man! This pain is part of being human –'
>
> 'THEN – I – DON'T – WANT – TO – BE – HUMAN!' Harry roared, and he seized the delicate silver instrument from the spindle-legged table beside him and flung it across the room; it shattered into a hundred tiny pieces against the wall . . .
>
> 'I DON'T CARE!' Harry yelled at them, snatching up a lunascope, and throwing it into the fireplace. 'I'VE HAD ENOUGH, I'VE SEEN ENOUGH, I WANT OUT, I WANT IT TO END, I DON'T CARE ANY MORE –'
>
> (*Order of the Phoenix*, Rowling, 2003: 726)

Our reluctant hero has behaved in an entirely human way. Even the most fearless of heroes could not have been blamed for this outburst of grief-inflamed rage. The surprising thing is that Harry, given the immense loss, suffering, pain and humiliation he has endured, does not succumb to total psychological collapse. Remarkably, he goes on to form the rebel group, 'Dumbledore's

Army'. This moment of decisive action is, as Strimel (2004: 35) points out, both extraordinary and empowering because it allows the readers to 'confront and cope with the terrors and terrorism in their own lives'.

Towards the end of Book 7, after Dumbledore has appeared to Harry and revealed the truths about his own fallibility and flawed early years, Harry decides to face his own death by confronting Voldemort in the battle raging at Hogwarts. Feigning death while being carried into the Great Hall by a weeping Hagrid, Harry disappears under his invisibility cloak and watches the battle, which rapidly escalates as elves, giants and centaurs join the fray. He sees the courageous Neville Longbottom smite the head off Voldemort's snake, Nagini, with the Gryffindor sword, and at a chosen moment, Harry appears from under his invisibility cloak and confronts Voldemort coolly with all the command of an experienced leader. In a tour de force of climactic, driving action, Harry tells him the truth about Dumbledore's death and the rightful possessor of the Elder Wand, which Voldemort has mistakenly believed has granted him invincibility. In a brilliant, final twist, wandlore wins the day. It decrees that the true possessor of the wand is Draco Malfoy since he was the one who disarmed Dumbledore before his death, not Snape. Voldemort insists it is of no significance, not realising that Harry is now its true possessor, having previously disarmed Draco. Voldemort shrieks the killing curse in his high voice. Simultaneously, Harry disarms him, sending the elder wand spinning in the air towards him: 'And Harry, with the unerring skill of the Seeker, caught the wand in his free hand as Voldemort fell backwards, arms splayed, the slit pupils of the scarlet eyes rolling upwards' (*Deathly Hallows*, Rowling, 2007: 596). Like a symphonic coda, the end is as it was at the beginning. Voldemort's curse once more rebounded on him, this time killing him. He brings about his own nemesis by repeating the mistake he had made some sixteen years earlier.

Harry, reluctant or not, is now the true hero of the story, and it ends with the hope of a better world. Rowling has brought off a richly complex psychological drama in which love, courage and the right path of action win out over nihilism and the fanatical lust for power.

Notes

Chaper 2, Part 2 The art of Anthony Browne's picture books

1 Some of the biographical source material contained in this section has been taken from the following online source. Unfortunately, neither date of publication nor author is given, but it is a comprehensive overview of the author's background, career and writing achievements:

Other Free Encyclopedias: Brief Biographies: Famous Authors: Vol. 12, http://biography.jrank. org/pages/1779/Browne-Anthony-Edward-Tudor-1946.html (accessed 20 September 2007).

2 A comprehensive list of the various book prizes, awards and medals stating the purpose of each of them can be found in N. Gamble and S. Yates (2002) *Exploring Children's Literature: Teaching the language and reading of fiction*, London: Paul Chapman.

Chapter 3, Part 1 Teaching Philip Pullman

1 Some elements of this model have been drawn from the 'Tell Me' framework in A. Chambers (1995) *Booktalk: Occasional Writing on Literature and Children*, Stroud, UK: The Thimble Press.

Chapter 3, Part 2 Philip Pullman: Parallel words and penny dreadfuls

1 A glossary of all the terminology used in *His Dark Materials* trilogy can be found in the Wikipedia, the free encyclopedia, at http://en.wikipedia.org/wiki/His_Dark_Materials_terminology and in the online source at http://www.hisdarkmaterials.org/information/his-dark-materials-book. An excellent recently published encyclopedic guide to Philip Pullman's trilogy is L. Frost, (2007) *The Elements of 'His Dark Materials': A Guide to Philip Pullman's Trilogy*, Buffalo Grove, IL: Fell Press. Its meticulous coverage of all the aspects of the trilogy has been highly praised by Philip Pullman.

Chapter 4, Part 2 Powers and responsibilities: Comic books in education

1 *X-Men: The Last Stand* grossed over $234 million at the US box office and £19 million in the United Kingdom. At the time of writing, *Spider-Man 3* has recently opened, taking $151 million in the United States in its opening weekend alone, making it the film with the biggest single opening weekend of all time (IMDb, May 2007).

2 Bradford W. Wright identifies the X-Men comics written by Chris Claremont, who began writing the title in the late 1970s, as having particularly well-realised female characters 'who played more than the token supporting role traditionally allotted to women in comic books' (Wright 2003: 263)

3 *X-Men*, still one of Marvel's most popular comics even today, was created by Stan Lee and Jack Kirby in the early 1960s during a period known as the Silver Age, which saw a resurgence in comic book popularity in America.

Chapter 6, Part 1 Harry Potter and the magic of film

1   Some of the definitions given for these terms have been drawn from *The 'Grammar' of Television and Film*, available online from http://www.aber.ac.uk/media/Documents/short/gramtv.html (accessed 12 June 2007).

Chapter 6, Part 2 J.K. Rowling: Love, loss and magic

1   Part of the title for this chapter is borrowed from an article entitled 'Love, loss and magic: connecting author and story', in D. Duncan (2007) *Changing English*, vol. 14(3): 271–84. Also online. Available http://www.informaworld.com.

2   For details of some of these websites, please refer to the 'Harry Potter fan websites' listing at the end of the bibliography.

Children's literature journals and magazines

Books for Keeps, 6 Brightfield Road, Lee, London SE12 8FQ

Carousel, 7 Carrs Lane, Birmingham B4 7TG

Changing English: Studies in Culture and Education, Institute of Education, University of London, Routledge, Taylor & Francis Group

Children's Literature Association Quarterly (USA) – Children's Literature Association, PO Box 138, Battle Creek, MI 49016

Children's Literature in Education, Geoff Fox, University of Exeter, School of Education, St Luke's, Exeter, Devon EX1 2UU

The Lion and the Unicorn (USA), Johns Hopkins University Press, Journals Division, 2715 North Charles Street, Baltimore MD, 21218–4319

New Review of Children's Literature and Librarianship, Routledge, London

Reading: Journal of the United Kingdom Reading Association, Unit 6, First Floor, The Maltings, Green Drift, Royston, Hertfordshire SG8 5DB

School Librarian, School Library Association, Unit 2, Lotmead Business Village, Lotmead Farm, Wanborough, Swindon, Wiltshire SN4 0UY

Signal: Approaches to Children's Books, Thimble Press, Lockwood, Station Road, South Woodchester, Stroud, Gloustershire GL15 5EQ

National Association for the Teaching of English journals and magazines:

Classroom: The Magazine of the National Association for the Teaching of English, NATE

English Drama Media, NATE

English in Education: The Future of English Teaching, NATE, 50, Broadfield Road, Broadfield Business Centre, Sheffield S8 0XJ

A new resource

The Story Museum, Town Hall, Blue Boar Street, Oxford OX1 4EY

This is a new venture set up in 2003 to create a museum for children's books and stories. Its long-term aim is to build a magical museum in the centre of Oxford. At the moment, it is a virtual museum: www.storymuseum.org.uk. Its patrons are Philip Pullman and Jacqueline Wilson.

Bibliography

Agro, S. (writer), Carzon, W. (penciller) and Torreiro, R. (inker) (2007) *Looney Tunes No. 143*, New York: DC Comics.

Alcott, L.M. (1994) *Little Women*, London: Penguin. First published 1868.

AQA (2006) *General Certificate of Secondary Education English 3701, English (Mature) 3703 – Specification B 2008*. Online. Available HTTP: http://www.aqa.org.uk/qual/pdf/AQA-3701-W-SP-08.PDF (accessed 27 November 2007).

Arizpe, E. and Styles, M. (2003) *Children Reading Pictures: Interpreting visual texts*, London: RoutledgeFalmer.

Bader, B. (1976) *American Picturebooks from Noah's Ark to the Beast Within*, New York: Macmillan.

Barger, J. (2002) 'Philip Pullman resources on the Web'. Online. Available http://www.robotwisdom. com/jorn/pullman.html (accessed 28 November 2007).

Bazalgette, C. (1997) 'Literacy and the moving image', in N. McClelland (ed.) *Building a Literate Nation*, Stoke-on-Trent: Trentham Books.

Beale, S. (2003) 'Power brokers', *Arena*, 137: 94–101.

Benn, M. (2005) 'Bad girl for laureate', *Guardian*, 11 February 2005. Online. Available http://books. guardian.co.uk/departments/childrenandteens/story/0,,1410705,00.html (accessed 7 December 2007).

Boothby, I. (writer), Ortiz, P. (penciller) and DeCarlo, M. (inker) (2007) *Simpsons Comics Number 134*, Santa Monica, CA: Bongo Entertainment.

Bridge, M. (2007) 'Philip Pullman in conversation with Marie Bridge', in Bridge, M. (ed.) *On the Way Home: Conversations between writers and psychoanalysts*, London: Karnac Books.

Briggs, R. (2002) *Ug: Boy genius of the Stone Age*, London: Red Fox.

Browne, A. (1976) *Through the Magic Mirror*, London: Hamish Hamilton Children's Books.

—— (1981) *Hansel and Gretel*, London: Julia MacRae Books.

—— (1983) *Gorilla*, London: Julia MacRae/Walker Books.

—— (1985) *Willy the Wimp*, London: Julia MacRae/Walker Books.

—— (1988) *Alice's Adventures in Wonderland*, written by Lewis Carroll, London: Puffin Books.

—— (1994) *Anthony Browne's King Kong*. From the story conceived by Edgar Wallace and Merian C. Cooper, London: Julia MacRae Books.

—— (1998) *Voices in the Park*, London: Doubleday.

—— (2001) *My Dad*, London: Picture Corgi.

—— (2002) *Gorilla*, London: Walker Books.

—— (2005) *My Mum*, London: Doubleday.

—— (2007) *My Brother*, London: Doubleday.

Burnett, F.H. (1994) *The Secret Garden*, London: Puffin Books. First published 1911.

Burningham, J. (1984) *Granpa*, London: Jonathan Cape.

Busch, R. (writer), Pope, R. (penciller) and McRae, S. (inker) (2007) *Scooby-Doo No. 119*, New York: DC Comics.

Carter, J. (1999) *Talking Books: Children's authors talk about the craft, creativity and process of writing*, London: RoutledgeFalmer.

Chambers, A. (1993) *Tell Me: Children, reading and talk*, Stroud: Thimble Press.

—— (1995) *Booktalk: Occasional writing on literature and children*, Stroud: Thimble Press.

Cottrell Boyce, F. (2007) '*Harry Potter and the Deathly Hallows*, by JK Rowling', *Independent*, 27 July 2007. Online. Available http://arts.independent.co.uk/books/reviews/article2806620.ece (accessed 12 December 2007).

Department for Education and Skills (DfES) (2005a) *Every Child Matters: Change for children*, London: DfES.

—— (2005b) *The Social and Emotional Aspects of Learning* (SEAL), London: DfES.

DfES (2005c) *Primary National Strategy. Excellence and Enjoyment: Social and emotional aspects of learning. Guidance*, London: The Stationery Office.

Doonan, J. (1983) 'Talking pictures: a new look at "Hansel and Gretel"', *Signal*, 42: 123–31.

—— (1986) 'The object lesson: picturebooks of Anthony Browne', *Word and Image*, 2(2): 159–72.

—— (1999) 'Drawing out ideas: a second decade of the work of Anthony Browne', *The Lion and the Unicorn*, 23(1): 30–56.

Duncan, D. (2007) 'Love, loss and magic: connecting author and story', *Changing English*, 14(3): 271–84. Available http://www.informaworld.com.

Eccleshare, J. (2000) 'Portrait of the artist as a gorilla', *Guardian Unlimited Books*, Online. Available http://books.guardian.co.uk/departments/childrenandteens/story/0,6000,348137,00.html (accessed 22 January 2007).

—— (2002) *A Guide to the Harry Potter Novels: Contemporary classics of children's literature*, London: Continuum.

Edexcel (2002) *Specification – Edexcel GCSE in English A*. Online. Available http://www.edexcel.org.uk/VirtualContent/66832.pdf (accessed 27 November 2007).

Eisner, W. (1985) *Comics and Sequential Art*, Tamarac, FL: Poorhouse Press.

—— (1996) *Graphic Storytelling and Visual Narrative*, Paramus, NJ: Poorhouse Press.

Fox, G. (1998) 'The silence of the critics: a symposium', *Children's Literature in Education*, 29(1): 1–18.

—— (2004) *Dear Mr Morpingo: Inside the World of Michael Morpurgo*, Cambridge: Wizard Books.

Gaiman, N. and McKean, D. (2004) *The Wolves in the Walls*, London: Bloomsbury.

Gamble, N. (2001) 'Introduction', in N. Tucker and N. Gamble, *Family Fictions*, Contemporary Classics of Children's Literature Series, London: Continuum.

Gamble, N. and Yates, S. (2002) *Exploring Children's Literature: Teaching the language and reading of fiction*, London: Paul Chapman Publishing.

Garnet, E. (1994) *The Family from One End Street*, Harmondsworth: Puffin Classics. First published 1937.

Goodwin, P. (2004) 'Looking to be literate', in P. Goodwin (ed.) *Literacy through Creativity*, London: David Fulton.

Goscinny, R. and Uderzo, A. (2004) *Asterix and Cleopatra*, translated by A. Bell and D. Hockridge, London: Orion.

Graham, J. (2004) 'Creativity and picture books', in P. Goodwin (ed.) *Literacy through Creativity*, London: David Fulton.

—— (2005) 'Reading contemporary picturebooks', in K. Reynolds (ed.) *Modern Children's Literature: An introduction*, Basingstoke: Palgrave Macmillan.

'Grammar' of Television and Film, The (n.d.) Online. Available http://www.aber.ac.uk/media/Documents/short/gramtv.html (accessed 12 June 2007).

Harrison, L. (2006) 'Giving the framework a fettle', *Primary English Magazine*, 11(5): 5–6.

Hergé (2005) *The Adventures of Tintin: Cigars of the Pharaoh*, London: Egmont.

Hitchens, P. (2002) 'The most dangerous author in Britain', *Mail on Sunday*, 27 January.

Hodgson, S. (2006) 'The storyteller', excerpt from *The Environmentalist*, issue 34, February, Consilience Media for the Institute of Environmental Management and Assessment.

Hunt, P. (ed.) (1999) *Understanding Children's Literature*, London: Routledge.

—— (2001) *Children's Literature*, Oxford: Blackwell.

IMDb (2007) *Trivia for Spider-Man 3*. Online. Available: http://www.imdb.com/title/tt0413300/trivia (accessed 22 May 2007).

J.K. Rowling: A year in the life, television documentary produced and directed by James Runcie, ITV1, broadcast 7 p.m., 30 December.

'J.K. Rowling goes beyond the epilogue' (2007) *Today Show*, broadcast 26 July NBC TV. Online. Available http://www.beyondhogwarts.com/harry-potter/articles/jk-rowling-goes-beyond-the-ep (accessed 3 January 2008).

Jordan, B. (1996) 'Tricks and treats: picture books and forms of comedy', in V. Watson and M. Styles (eds) *Talking Pictures*, London: Hodder & Stoughton.

Kakutani, M. (2007) 'An epic showdown as Harry Potter is initiated into adulthood', *New York Times*, 19 July. Online. Available http://www.nytimes.com/2007/07/19/books/19potter.html?ex=12009 74400&en=7cf00c9e (accessed 12 December 2007).

Karpf, A. (1999) 'Granny Spice's secret', *Guardian*, 6 November. Online. Available http://books.guardian.co.uk/specialreports/whitbread/story/0,,101799,00.html (accessed 7 December 2007).

Kellaway, K. (2002) 'Sword's lore', *Guardian Unlimited Books*, 24 March. Online. Available http://books.guardian.co.uk/departments/childrenandteens/story/0,6000,672804,00.html (accessed 7 April 2007).

Kirkman, R. (writer), Medina, P. (penciller) and Vlasco, J. (inker) (2005) *Marvel Team-Up Number 12*, New York: Marvel Comics.

Kyle, C., Yost, C. (writers), Tan, B. (penciller) and Sibal, J. (inker) (2005) *X-23 Number 1*, New York: Marvel Comics.

Lee, S. (writer) and Ditko, S. (artist) (2006) 'Amazing Fantasy 15', in *Essential Spider-Man Vol. 1*, New York: Marvel Comics.

Lenz, M. (2001) 'Philip Pullman', in P. Hunt and M. Lenz (eds) *Alternative Worlds in Fantasy Fiction*, London: Continuum.

Lewis, D. (1990) 'The constructedness of texts: picture books and the metafictive', *Signal*, 62: 131–46.

—— (2001) *Reading Contemporary Picture Books*, London: RoutledgeFalmer.

McAfee, A. and Browne, A. (1984) *The Visitors Who Came to Stay*, New York: Viking Kestrel.

McCloud, S. (1994) *Understanding Comics*, New York: Kitchen Sink, for HarperCollins.

Manning, M.K. (writer) and Archer, A. (artist) (2007) *The Batman Strikes! No. 40*, New York: DC.

Manthorpe, R. (2007) 'A farewell to charms', *Observer*, 29 July. Online. Available http://books.guardian.co.uk/departments/childrenandteens/story/0,,2136869,00.html (accessed 12 December 2007).

Marvel (2005) *Marvel Rating System*. Online. Available http://www.marvel.com/catalog/ratings.htm (accessed 2 October 2007).

Meek, M. (1991) *On Being Literate*, London: The Bodley Head.

Millar, M. (writer), Kubert, A. (penciller) and Miki, D. (inker) (2005) 'Ultimate X-Men Number 13', in *Ultimate X-Men Volume 3: World Tour*, New York: Marvel Comics.

Mona Lisa Smile (2003) directed by Mike Newell, screenplay by Lawrence Konner and Mark Rosenthal, 120 minutes, released by Columbia Pictures and Revolution Studios.

Morpurgo, M. (1974) *It Never Rained: Five Stories*, London: Macmillan.

—— (1982; reissued 2002) *War Horse*, London: Egmont Books.

—— (1985) *Why the Whales Came*, London: Heinemann.

—— (1990) *Waiting for Anya*, London: Heinemann.

—— (1993a) 'The making of Anya, or a tale of two villages', *Children's Literature in Education*, 24(4): 235–9.

—— (1993b) *The War of Jenkins' Ear*, London: Heinemann Ltd.

—— (1995; reissued 2003) *The Wreck of the Zanzibar*, London: Egmont Books.

—— (1996) *The Butterfly Lion*, London: HarperCollins Children's Books.

—— (1999) *Kensuke's Kingdom*, London: Egmont Books.

—— (2000a) *Dear Olly*, London: Collins.

—— (2000b) 'Special guest – Michael Morpurgo', *Achuka Interview Archive*. Online. Available http://www.achuka.co.uk/archive/interviews/mmint.php (accessed 22 September 2007).

—— (2002) *The Last Wolf*, London: Doubleday.

—— (2003) *Private Peaceful*, London: HarperCollins Children's Books.

—— (2004) 'Spread the word', *Guardian*, 29 June. Online. Available http:education.guardian.co.uk/egweekly/story/0,,1248987,700.html (accessed 15 November 2007).

—— (2006a) 'I believe in unicorns', in *Singing for Mrs Pettigrew: A story-maker's journey*, London: Walker Books.

—— (2006b) *Alone on a Wide Wide Sea*, London: HarperCollins Children's Books.

—— (2006c; reissued 2007) 'The Mozart Question', in *Singing for Mrs Pettigrew: A story-maker's journey*, London: Walker Books.

—— (2007a) 'The former Children's Laureate discusses his work and *War Horse*'s journey to the stage', Platform talk, National Theatre, 26 October, London.

—— (2007b) *Born to Run*, London: HarperCollins Children's Books.

—— (2007c), 'The Mozart question', in *Singing for Mrs Pettigrew: A story-maker's journey*, London: Walker Books (reissue).

Morpugo, M. (writer) and Birmingham, C. (artist) (2000) *Wombat Goes Walkabout*, London: HarperCollins.

Moruzi, K. (2005) 'Missed opportunities: the subordination of children in Philip Pullman's "His Dark Materials"', *Children's Literature in Education*, 36(1): 55–68.

Mynott, G. (1999) 'The Harry Potter phenomenon', *New Review of Children's Literature and Librarianship*, 1999: 13–27.

Nodelman, P. (1988) *Words about Pictures: The narrative art of children's picture books*, Athens, GA: University of Georgia Press.

OCR (2003) *Complete Specification*, second edition – *OCR GCSE in English (Opening Minds)*. Online. Available http://www.ocr.org.uk/Data/publications/key_documents/cquartetOCRTempFilesnwHy0Md6o.pdf (accessed 27 November 2007).

Pecora, N. (1992) 'Superman/superboys/supermen: the comic book hero as socializing agent', in S. Craig (ed.) *Men, Masculinity and the Media*, London: Sage.

Petersen, D. (2007) *Mouse Guard: Fall 1152*, Fort Lee: ASP Comics.

Pope, P. (2007) *PulpHope: The Art of Paul Pope*, Richmond, VA: AdHouse Books.

Primary Review, Children, Their World, Their Education (2007) Interim Reports, Research Survey 3/4 'The Quality of Learning: Assessment Alternatives for Primary Education, Esmée Fairbairn Foundation, University of Cambridge, Faculty of Education.

Pullman, P. (n.d.) Achuka interview. Online. Available http://www.achuka.co.uk/ppint.htm (accessed 21 May 2002).

—— (n.d.) *The Sally Lockhart Quartet*. Online. Available http://www.philip-pullman.com (accessed 27 November 2007).

—— (n.d.) *About the Writing*. Online. Available http://www.philip-pullman.com/about_the_writing.asp (accessed 25 November 2007).

—— (1972) *The Haunted Storm*, London: New English Library.

—— (1982) *Count Karlstein*, London: Chatto & Windus.

—— (1985; reissued 2006) *Ruby in the Smoke*, London: Scholastic.

—— (1986; reissued 2004) *The Shadow in the Plate*, Oxford: Oxford University Press. (Later published as *The Shadow in the North*, London: Scholastic Point.)

—— (1990a) *Frankenstein* (adaptation), Oxford: Oxford University Press.

—— (1990b) *The Broken Bridge*, London: Macmillan.

—— (1991) *The Tiger in the Well*, London: Penguin.

—— (1992) *Sherlock Holmes and the Limehouse Horror*, Walton-on-Thames: Thomas Nelson.

—— (1994a) *The New Cut Gang: Thunderbolt's Waxwork*, London: Viking.

—— (1994b) *The Tin Princess*, London: Penguin.

—— (1995a) *Northern Lights*, London: Scholastic.

—— (1995b) *The Firework-Maker's Daughter*, London: Doubleday.

—— (1995c) *The New Cut Gang: The Gas-Fitter's Ball*, London: Viking.

—— (1996) 'Carnegie Medal Acceptance Speech', Online. Available http://www.randomhouse.com/features/pullman/author/carnegie/speech.html (accessed 24 May 2007).

—— (1997a) *The Subtle Knife*, London: Scholastic.

—— (1997b) *Clockwork or All Wound Up*, Corgi Yearling Books, London: Random House Children's Books.

—— (1998a) *The Butterfly Tattoo*, London: Macmillan's Children's Books.

—— (1998b) 'Let's write it in red: the Patrick Hardy lectures', *Signal*, 85: 44–62.

—— (2000) *The Amber Spyglass*, London: Scholastic Ltd.

—— (2003a) *Lyra's Oxford*, Oxford: David Fickling Books.

—— (2003b) 'Lost the plot', *Guardian*, 30 September 2003. Online. Available http://education.guardian.co.uk/schools/story/0,5500,1052077,00.html (accessed 28 November 2007).

—— (2003c) *Isis Lecture, 1 April 2003*. Online. Available http://www.philip-pullman.com/pages/content/index.asp?PageID=66 (accessed 14 January 2008).

—— (2004) *The Scarecrow and His Servant*, London: Doubleday.

Qualifications and Curriculum Authority (QCA) (2005) *English 21 Playback: A national conversation on the future of the subject English, pre-publication version*, 30 September, London: QCA.

Rabinovitch, D. (2003a) 'Author of the month: Anthony Browne', *Guardian Unlimited Books*, 27 August. Online. Available http://books.guardian.co.uk/departments/childrenandteens/story/0,,1030200,00.html (accessed 2 February 2007).

—— (2003b) 'His bright materials', *Guardian*, 10 December 2003.

Reynolds, K. (ed.) (2005) *Modern Children's Literature: An introduction*, Basingstoke: Palgrave Macmillan.

Rosen, M. (1996) 'Reading The Beano: a young boy's experience', in V. Watson and M. Styles (eds) *Talking Pictures*, London: Hodder & Stoughton.

Ross, D. (2002) 'Soap and the serious writer', *Independent*, 4 February.

Rowling, J.K. (1997) *Harry Potter and the Philosopher's Stone*, London: Bloomsbury.

—— (1998) *Harry Potter and the Chamber of Secrets*, London: Bloomsbury.

—— (1999) *The Prisoner of Azkaban*, London: Bloomsbury.

—— (2000) *Harry Potter and the Goblet of Fire*, London: Bloomsbury.

—— (2003) *Harry Potter and the Order of the Phoenix*, London: Bloomsbury.

—— (2005) *Harry Potter and the Half-Blood Prince*, London: Bloomsbury.

—— (2007) *Harry Potter and the Deathly Hallows*, London: Bloomsbury.

Rustin, M. and Rustin, M. (2001) *Narratives of Love and Loss: Studies in modern children's fiction*, London: Karnac Books (revised edition).

—— (2003a) 'Learning to say goodbye: an essay on Philip Pullman's "The Amber Spyglass", volume 3 of "His Dark Materials"', *Journal of Child Psychotherapy*, 29(3): 415–428.

—— (2003b) 'A new kind of friendship: an essay on Philip Pullman's "The Subtle Knife", volume 2 of "His Dark Materials"', *Journal of Child Psychotherapy*, 29(2): 2003: 227–41.

Selwood, S. and Irving, D. (1993) *Harmful Publications: Comics, education and disenfranchised young people*, London: Art & Society.

Smith, B. (1994) *Through Writing to Reading: Classroom strategies for supporting literacy*, London: Routledge.

South Bank Show, The (2003) Melvyn Bragg interviews Philip Pullman, ITV, February.

—— (2005) An interview with Melvyn Bragg and Jacqueline Smith, ITV, 5 March.

Spanner, H. (2000) Interview with Philip Pullman, *Third Way* website. Online. Available www.thirdway.org.uk/past/showpage.asp?page=3949 (accessed 26 November 2007).

Spiers, J. (2006) 'Retaining the inner child', *DevonLife*. Online. Available http://www.devonlife.co.uk/Editorial.aspx?page=1940.

Squires, C. (2006) *Philip Pullman, Master Storyteller: A guide to the worlds of 'His Dark Materials'*, London: Continuum.

Streatfeild, N. (1994) *Ballet Shoes*, London: Puffin Books. First published 1936.

Strimel, C.B. (2004) 'The politics of terror: rereading Harry Potter', *Children's Literature in Education*, 35(1): 35–52.

Styles, M. (1996) 'Inside the tunnel: a radical kind of reading – picture books, pupils and post-modernism', in V. Watson and M. Styles (eds) *Talking Pictures*, London: Hodder & Stoughton.

Thomas, R. (writer), Gully, M. (penciller) and Davidson, P. (inker) (2007) *Treasure Island No. 1*, New York: Marvel.

Thomas, R. (writer), Kurth, S. (penciller) and Smith, C. (inker) (2007) *The Last of the Mohicans No. 1*, New York: Marvel.

Thomas, R. (writer), Petrus, H. (penciller) and Palmer, T. (inker) (2007) *The Man in the Iron Mask No. 1*, New York: Marvel.

Thompson, C. (2006) *Good-Bye, Chunky Rice*, New York: Pantheon.

Torres, J. (writer) and Clugston, C. (artist) (2007) *Legion of Super-Heroes in the 31st Century No. 1*, New York: DC Comics.

Travis, M. (2006) 'Voyage of Discovery', *Booktrusted*. Online. Available http://www.booktrusted.co.uk/articles/documents (accessed 22 September 2007).

Trushell, J. M. (2004) 'American dreams of mutants: The X-Men – "pulp" fiction, science fiction, and superheroes', *Journal of Popular Culture*, 38(1): 149–68.

Tucker, N. (1999) 'The rise and rise of Harry Potter', *Children's Literature in Education*, 30(4): 221–34.

—— (2003) *Darkness Visible: Inside the world of Philip Pullman*, Cambridge: Wizard Books.

Tucker, N. and Gamble, N. (2001) *Family Fictions*, Contemporary Classics of Children's Literature Series, London: Continuum.

Tulk, S. (2005) 'Reading picture books is serious fun', *English Teaching: Practice and Critique*, 4(2): 89–95.

Vincent, S. (2001) 'Driven by dæmons', *Guardian*, 10 November. Online. Available http://books.guardian.co.uk/departments/childrenandteens/story/ (accessed 25 November 2007).

von Kleist, H. (1982) 'On the puppet theatre', in *An Abyss Deep Enough: Letters of Heinrich von Kleist with a selection of essays and anecdotes*, ed. and trans. P.B. Miller, New York: Dutton.

Walter, N. (2002) 'A moral vision for the modern age', *Independent*, 24 January.

Watson, D. (writer) and Wallis, K. (artist) (2004) *Wonderland: Children of the future age*, Orange, CA: Image Comics.

Watson, V. and Styles, M. (1996) *Talking Pictures: Pictorial texts and young readers*, London: Hodder & Stoughton.

Wayne, M. (writer) and Brizuela, D. (2007) *Justice League Unlimited No. 38*, New York: DC Comics.

Webb, J. (2005) *War, Heroism and Humanity in the Novels of Michael Morpurgo*. Online. Available http://www.michaelmorpurgo.org/jean_webb.html (accessed 7 April 2007).

Whedon, J. (writer) and Cassaday, J. (artist) (2004) *Astonishing X-Men Number 1*, New York: Marvel Comics.

Whitehead, M. (2004) *Language and Literacy in the Early Years*, third edition, London: Sage.

Williams, R. (2004) 'A near-miraculous triumph', *Guardian*, 3 March.

Wilson, J. (1991) *The Story of Tracy Beaker*, London: Doubleday.

—— (1995) *Double Act*, London: Doubleday.

—— (1997) *Girls in Love*, London: Doubleday.

—— (1999) *The Illustrated Mum*, London: Doubleday.

—— (2000a) *The Dare Game*, London: Doubleday.

—— (2000b) *Vicky Angel*, London: Doubleday.

—— (2003) *Lola Rose*, London: Doubleday.

—— (2004) *Best Friends*, London: Doubleday.

—— (2007a) *Jacky Daydream*, London: Doubleday.

—— (2007b) *Sleepovers*, London: Young Corgi Books. First published 2001.

Wright, B.W. (2003) *Comic Book Nation*, Baltimore: Johns Hopkins University Press.

X-Men (2000) Film directed by Bryan Singer, screenplay by David Hayter, 100 mins, released by Twentieth Century Fox Film Corporation.

X2 (2003) Film directed by Bryan Singer, screenplay by Michael Dougherty, Dan Harris and David Hayter, 128 minutes, released by Twentieth Century Fox Film Corporation.

Zipes, J. (2002) *Sticks and Stones: The troublesome success of children's literature from Slovenly Peter to Harry Potter*, London: Routledge.

Harry Potter fan websites

Accio Quote! http://www.accio-quote.org/.

Harry Potter Lexicon, proud member of The Floo Network, Online. Available http://www.hp-lexicon.org/.

Leaky Cauldron, Online. Available www.the-leaky-cauldron.org/.

J.K. Rowling's Official Website, Online. http://www.jkrowling.com/en.

Index

Lightning Source UK Ltd.
Milton Keynes UK
27 January 2011

166456UK00001B/43/P